This book has been published thanks to the support of **Swiss Bank Corporation,** Geneva

Boyce

SCOTT CHARLES

All
About
Geneva

georg
ÉDITEUR

© 1985 by Librairie de l'Université Georg et Cie S.A., Genève.
Droits de reproduction et d'adaptation réservés pour tous pays.
ISBN 2-8257-0122-X

IMPRIMÉ EN SUISSE

Contents

Part V If You Need To Know More...

Illustrations

Most grateful

acknowledgement is made of the work of the many who contributed to the third presentation of *All About Geneva*.

To prepare this expanded successor to the editions of 1957 and 1962, the fresh set of collaborators featured Diana Josselson on editing, Henri Weissenbach as master of coordination and publication, Gérard Deuber for the map work, José Suarez for drawings, Georges Schwizgébel for the cover design, Marc Vanappelghem for the photographs, and Pierre Bosson, the graphic artist responsible for the layout and typography.

For the refinements of the research and verification of the text, several of the foregoing served above and beyond the call of their primary responsibilities while the special talents of such as Roger de Candolle, Jean-Jacques Favre, Conrad-André Beerli, Louis Huber, Sven Welander, and Paul Fehlmann ranged alongside those of Mesdames Marie-José Aeschimann, Sylvia Baverstock, Patricia and Regan Charles, Josiane Favre, Heidi Friedlin, and Rosemary Novak-Kerr to produce a substantially documented result.

SCOTT CHARLES

The Preliminaries

Approaching Geneva

The prime purpose of any guidebook is to guide.

If you are in Geneva for a short visit and guidance is what you seek first, turn at once to page 25.

If you have more time and an interest in the origins of Geneva and its role in Switzerland and in the world, read on for a better appreciation of the town and the tour.

This guidebook is designed for all-in-one convenience. The format is by measurement suited to the average jacket pocket. The maps on the flyleaves aid navigation without the awkward juggle of text in one hand and multi-folded chart in the other. And the loose, tucked-in card serves first as a bookmark and finally as a report card — preaddressed and prestamped — to send the publisher your corrections, comments, or simply greetings.

For quick identification of major buildings, plaques, and monuments the large print in the tour text gives a brief description. For followup in more detail consult the smaller print intended for reading at greater leisure, en route in a park, café, or terrace or after the tour is over.

Regardless of any national accent in the style, the text is intended for any all Anglophones — the English-reading public including Scandinavians, Indians, Japanese and the many others who "travel in English". On the assumption that all Anglophones are not equally Francophone, certain French terms are translated into English. On the further assumption that not everyone's recollections of historical facts and figures is infallible, gratuitous jogs of memory for dates and background are often included.

In the face of a choice of usages a few practical decisions have been taken for the sake of consistency:

> — the time of day is in Continental form taking midnight as 00.01 and ending at 24.00 hours. Thus 13.00 is 1 p.m.; 19.00 is 7 p.m.

— the days and months follow the Continental order: first the number of the day, then the month. Months are spelled out to avoid the question of whether 4/6/23 is 4 June 1923 or April 6, 1923.

— the centuries are referred to by calendar dates. The era, 1600 through 1699, is not called the "17th Century" but the less-confusing "1600s".

— measurements are expressed in the metric system with occasional, erratic conversions into miles, tons, quarts, etc.

— money of former times is not converted to modern equivalents. No one really knows what Gold Swiss Francs 24,000,000 of 1873 would buy more than a century later.

— names, particularly first names, are in their French form for any French, Spanish, Italian, or German characters figuring in the cast. The principle here is to harmonize with the town of Geneva and use the spelling found on its street signs. Aberrations are tolerated. "William Tell" seems easier than "Guillaume Tell" but to refer to Rousseau as "John-James" would be ridiculous.

A few apologies would not be amiss.

First, please excuse any difficulties encountered in following the tour route. The geography of Geneva changes constantly. Through streets are paved over into pedestrian malls, street names change whimsically, two-way avenues become one-way, one-ways change direction. Few of Geneva's coordinates stand still for long.

Second, apologies to anyone who reads the full text and emerges with the feeling — to paraphrase James Thurber — "This book tells me more about Geneva history than I want to know". Another familiar phrase, "History repeats itself", applies here.

The book was written to explain Geneva to readers ranging from the quick visitor with little background about Geneva and Switzerland through the Old Hand of several years' residence and a passing if not profound interest in more details.

Thus the history is dished up both as chronology at first and then within the tour to help those who leapt directly into the visits.

The double helping is left on the table because no relatively detailed but still brief history of Geneva in English has been found and because knowledge of Switzerland is often confined to the clichés of chocolate, yodelers, and William Tell.

Third, apologies to scholars-in-depth who may differ on events and their presentation. Almost all aspects of Geneva are subject to continuing discussion and interpretation.

Scrupulous verifications of most facts and accounts have been undertaken. In cases of contradictory versions, the rendering chosen was the one combining the picturesque with the plausible.

Apocryphal items could have been hidden behind such phrases as "Some say..." and "According to certain sources..." Few attempts have been made thus to spread the responsibility.

Fourth, forgiveness is asked for omissions. They are not necessarily oversights but simply space limitations.

In truth the claim to cover "All" Geneva is at best unrealistic. For any locale so rich and complex that a 12-volume *Encyclopédie de Genève* has been compiled without exhausting the subject, no single tome will ever tell it "All".

In visiting Geneva's major points of interest, seek out any specialized brochures and pamphlets that describe the finer details of the place and its contents. Not even a decent percentage of such refinements could be fitted into these tightly rationed pages.

Geneva has its remarkable depths and facets. On the other hand, the claims of the town to major art works, overpowering architecture, and battlegrounds that changed the course of empires are modest.

The town's handsome setting, its odd corners, the rich variety of races and styles, the civilized pace and manner, and internationalism at work and play are among the Genevan elements to sort out and to savor.

Tailor your tour to your own pace, taste, and measures. Above all, enjoy it.

History of Geneva

The Six-Segment Approach

Of the five thousand years — give or take a millenium — of the existence of a recognizable Geneva, the starting date of its prehistory defies all estimating.

Two thousand years of its recorded history, however, can be dated and divided conveniently into four nearly-equal blocks of roughly five centuries each.

Outside any such tidy four volumes of time is the part that went before and the part that comes after. Thus the history of Geneva is force-fitted into six eras:

To begin: Prehistory: 15,000 B.C.-57 B.C.: From the Ice Age to the first written record;

Next: The First Era: 57 B.C.-460 A.D.: Through the Pax Romana to the advent of the Burgundians;

Then: The Second Era: 460-1032: The Dark Ages;

Next: The Third Era: 1032-1536: From the Jurassian Kingdom of Burgundy to the advent of Calvin;

Finally: The Fourth Era: 1536-1920: From small Republic to seat of the League of Nations;

And now: The Present Era: 1920 and on: An International Capital.

Prehistory: The Cavemen and the Tribes

Millions of years of seas and deserts and jungles and upheavals led to the Ice Age that gave this region its present form. A thick glacier extending back to the summits of the Swiss mountains to the east and the Savoy peaks to the south carved out this long valley.

About 15,000 B.C. the ice pack receded, scarring the mountain's wall and leaving behind the deep lake with a barren shore. Thousands of years later arctic flora and fauna appeared. Lone hunters wandered in, huddling through the nights in the caves of Mont Salève. Here the primitive men learned to chip stones into tools and weapons and to form larger boulders into still-mystifying monoliths.

Warmer, damper weather over the centuries nourished the valley floor into a thick forest through which a few pioneers made their way to the lake shore and set up camp as the first Genevese.

These early inhabitants evolved from the Stone Age to the Bronze and into the Iron Age in rudimentary communities, fishing, cultivating domestic animals and, for protection, building huts on pilings along the swampy shoreline. By 3500 B.C. the tribes had created a "ville lacustre" — Town of the Lake Dwellers.

Then, about 1000 B.C., human habitation along this end of the lake abruptly disappeared, possibly frightened off by a flood that may have raised the lake level as much as 10 meters (33 feet).

About 500 B.C. a migrating tribe of Allobrigians arrived from the Danube. They avoided the abandoned lakeshore site and settled instead on the strategically safer ovaloid hilltop — now Geneva's Old Town — above the junction of two rivers. The hill's steep sides down to the Rhone to the north and to the river Arve flowing past the southwest escarpment left only one side of their triangular settlement in need of barricading for its defence.

Added to this natural tactical advantage was a less apparent but even more strategic asset set in the throat of the Rhone near the apex of the triangular hill. Emerging from the river where it narrowed down from the lake were two hard-rock islands. These outcroppings served as natural pylons across which even the most rudimentary engineers could build a wooden span. The bridge built here in primitive times made this the only point in the length of the Rhone where travelers and their wares could cross its waters dryshod.

Prehistory: The Allobrigians and the Romans

The tribesmen from the Danube had been established with their village and their bridge for several centuries before the arrival of the Roman legionnaires. As the soldiers pushed northward the frontiers of empire they readily assessed the military value of the hilltop site and the river crossing and organized here an important fortified outpost.

After thirty years of Roman encroachment the Allobrigians in 120 B.C. rose up in violent protest. The soldiers summarily suppressed their outbreak and declared the settlement henceforth a Roman colony.

Across the Rhone to the north of the Allobrigians there lived long before the advent of the Romans another peaceful Celtic tribe, the Helvetians. With their quiet existence increasingly disturbed by raids of the Germanic tribes from the Rhine valley, the Helvetians about 60 B.C. prepared to emigrate en masse to southwest Europe.

Rome, however, preferred to keep the Helvetians in place as a buffer against the Germanics. Thus, when mass migration of the tribe began, Julius Caesar led an army to Geneva and blocked its passage across the Rhone bridge.

Forced to detour, the 360,000 migrants toiled over the Jura mountains and continued on their way towards Lyon and the south. To compel them to return to their plain Caesar pursued the slow-moving horde, slaughtered thousands, and drove the survivors back north.

Painfully the Helvetians restored the broad fields which they had, on leaving, scorched barren to discourage the faint-hearted from remaining behind. A century later the Romans spread north to annex the restored settlements between the Jura and the Bernese mountains and to develop the Helvetian towns into colonies that were among the most prosperous in the Empire.

The First Era:
Five Centuries of Pax Romana

The first mention of Geneva in history is Caesar's account in his "Commentaries" that begins, "Genua [sic] is the farthest town of the Allobrigians and the nearest to the land of the Helvetians..."

The Romans, having annexed Geneva and declared it a colony, granted its subjects full protection, rights, and obligations and encouraged their commerce. Under the governors of the Pax Romana, Geneva became busy, prosperous and, around 300 A.D., Christian.

The Roman Empire, however, had by 300 A.D. already matured and begun to weaken. As early as 270 A.D. bands of Alemanni tribesmen had pillaged the well-developed countryside near Geneva. Gradually the Roman gentry retreated from its landed estates and lakeside villas into the protection of the hill-top town behind thick stone walls.

Bit by bit the militarily impotent Romans lost control of their provinces north of the Alps. In 460 A.D. they conceded their domains in this area of the Jura and Savoy to the Baltic tribe called the Burgundians.

The Second Five Centuries: The Dark Ages

The second block of Geneva's recorded history opened with the century of the turbulent "First Burgundian Kingdom". With the arrival of the tribe from the north, one chieftain, Gondebaud, murdered his way to the leadership of the clan and established Geneva as the capital of his realm.

To secure his precarious throne Gondebaud bargained his orphaned niece and ward into marriage with the powerful Clovis, King of the Franks and conqueror of western Europe. After the death of Clovis, his far-flung Frankish Empire — including by then the Burgundian Kingdom — slowly disintegrated. Europe split up into a multitude of small estates as the Continent slipped into the Dark Ages.

While Europe in the 600s lay inert, Islam arose in the East under the Prophet Mohammed. In less than a century of Holy War, the Moslem armies swept the Middle East and crossed North Africa to turn north and conquer Spain.

Once across the Pyrenees, the militant faithful threatened France and all of Europe. The alarmed feudal lords combined their small armies into a single force under Charles Martel who, near Tours in 732, turned the tide and drove the Moorish invaders back into Spain.

Martel's son, Pepin the Short, visited Geneva in 755, thus becoming among the earliest of the town's celebrated guests. Martel's grandson, Charlemagne, was among the first to make Geneva an international meeting place. In 773 he called together his army commanders to meet in Geneva to plan his campaign into Italy.

In full control of that peninsula by 800, Charlemagne accepted from the frightened Pope Leo III the title and crown of the first of the Holy Roman Emperors. With this union of church and state at the summit, Geneva's bishops, the effective governors of the town, became bishop-princes.

The awesome title of "H.R.E." survived for another thousand years in a ragged succession of claimants, none of them notably holy, Roman, or imperial. Charlemagne's own conquests and realm dispersed soon after his death.

One segment of his short-lived empire became in 888 "The Second..." or "The Jurassian..." Kingdom of Burgundy — in any case, in no way related to Gondebaud's "First".

Geneva once again was a capital city in this latest kingdom, independent until its weak king, Rudolph III, bequeathed it to Holy Roman Emperor Conrad II.

The Third Era Begins:
Geneva as a Capital Once More

The third of Geneva's five-century-long episodes began in 1032 with the coronation here of Conrad as King of Burgundy. Accompanying the Emperor in his personal suite were two courtiers who looked on Geneva with acquisitive eyes. One was a Zurichois, recently titled by Rudolph III as the Count of Geneva. The other was from Arles, Humbert the White-Handed, the newly-minted Count of Savoy.

Both counts appraised Geneva as a promising asset. Each set about in his own fashion to appropriate the local government from the bishop-princes.

The succeeding Counts of Geneva established themselves in a central position by taking over the stone castle that Gondebaud had built, looming high over the marketplace of the Bourg-de-Four.

For its headquarters the House of Savoy besieged and captured the fort, tower, and tollgate recently built by the bishop-princes on the islands in mid-River Rhone.

The hard-pressed bishop-princes, driven into their palace on the hilltop, managed to retain a balance of control only through the stern intervention of Holy Roman Emperor Frederick Barbarossa.

While these three eminent contenders grappled for control, the people of Geneva in the 1200s developed their commercial skills and markets and organized their profitable trade fairs. Increasingly prosperous and politically astute, the technicians of the town began to unite in a "commune" which grew into a fourth and highly effective influence in the government of Geneva.

The Third Era: The Townspeople Take Hold

In 1291, the year in which herdsmen of the Three Forest Cantons to the east allied themselves into the seed of Switzerland, the citizens of Geneva first applied their own newly united strength. Exasperated by the struggle for control, they attacked one of their three antagonists by barricading themselves in their new Cathédrale de Saint Pierre and, from its lofty South Tower, rained down stones on the Château du Bourg-de-Four, routing its soldiers. By the early 1300s the Genevese had rid themselves of the Counts of Geneva and demolished their castle.

The 1300s were the hardest of times in Europe, beset by famines, the Black Death, the "Great Schism" dividing the Catholic Church, and England's battles for Continental land in the Hundred Years' War.

Geneva, however, was prospering with its trade fairs. The political strength of its townspeople increased in due proportion. The bishop-princes saw that cooperation with the "commune" could confront the Counts of Savoy with a daunting barrier. To effect a consolidation with the people, Bishop Adhémar Fabri issued his "Franchises of 1387", Geneva's own Magna Carta, recognizing in 79 articles the "... liberties, communities, usages, and customs..." of the people.

The renowned fairs of Geneva flourished in the early 1400s along with the other Continental markets profiting from English control and restraint of the great trade center of Paris. The Renaissance, begun in Italy in the 1300s and spreading in the 1400s, also aided Geneva. And, as a further boon to the citizens, the churchmen of the early 1400s were preoccupied with their divided Catholic hierarchy in the "Great Schism" and paid less attention to parochial affairs. The people were left in prosperity to govern themselves.

The Third Era Dilemma: Savoyard or Swiss?

The widened scope for self-government in Geneva diminished with the rise of the House of Savoy. In 1416 the family was elevated to a dukedom and, in 1439, Amadeus of Savoy became Pope Felix V. From this exalted position he assigned to his native parish of Savoy the privilege of appointing Geneva's bishops.

The alliance between the bishops and the citizens changed to a bond between the bishops and the will of Savoy.

This increase in Savoyard political pressure on Geneva was augmented by economic pressures. When the brother-in-law of the Duke of Savoy mounted the French throne as Louis XI, this wily "Spider King" in 1460 increased French trade and drove Geneva's commerce to the wall by banning French merchants from trading at Geneva's fairs.

Drained by the French boycott and with two centuries of affluence cut short, the Genevese turned to their second-best customers, the Swiss. For military protection as well as for trade, Geneva in 1477 signed treaties with several cantons of the Swiss Confederation, then at a zenith of its armed power.

Geneva's alliances with the Swiss cantons increased the town's military security but did little to offset its further loss of commerce in the late 1400s. In that Age of Discovery, the shipments over the routes that had long led traders through Geneva began to be carried in cargo vessels traveling the cheaper sea-lanes and bound for market ports.

In the early 1500s impoverished Geneva suffered under the continuing oppression of the puppet-bishops of Savoy. The only opposition to this corrupt government was a clandestine group of Genevese seeking to renew and extend the aid from the Swiss cantons to the northeast.

Switzerland by 1520 had, however, changed in two respects. First the French defeat of the great Swiss infantry at the Battle of Marignano in 1515 had altered national policy from rampant militarism to a new neutrality.

Second, the impetus of the campaign of Martin Luther for church reform was spreading fast and had carried into the cantons, particularly the influential center of Bern.

Bern looked on Geneva as a friend and ally but also as a useful buffer against Savoy. To assure a continuing understanding with its little neighbor, the Swiss protector sent its missionaries to preach the Reform. The fiery ex-priest Guillaume Farel and his associates from Bern adroitly persuaded the sophisticated Genevese of the validity of their new theology, of the evils and annoyances of Catholic bishops, priests, monks, and nuns, and of the political wisdom of following Bern's lead.

Braced against Savoy by their friends in Bern, the Genevese spoke out vigorously and frightened away the impious last Savoyard bishop-prince, Pierre de la Baume. The Town Council formally ordained the banning of masses and, in May 1536, the establishment of the independent Republic.

The Fourth Era Begins:
The Republic and Reformation

The most recent of Geneva's four major eras encompasses fewer than four hundred years. These latter centuries were, however, animated by a succession of changes tantamount to revolutions, beginning with those wrought by Jean Calvin.

With the inauguration in 1536 of the autonomous Republic, many citizens held high expectations of increased religious, political, and personal freedom. Little immediate notice was taken of the arrival of 27-year-old Jean Calvin and his recruitment by Bern's Preacher Farel to organize an entirely new way of life.

Calvin's piety, logic, personal authority, and diligence soon and profoundly altered the character and look of Geneva. Starting with this market town, where accomodating hosts had for centuries catered to roistering transients, Calvin, in fewer than three decades, converted it into the disciplined state whose stern government was based on the Reformer's interpretation of the literal Word of the Bible.

Anyone violating Calvin's precepts risked a heavy penalty as the theocrats condemned sinners and often mutilated, drowned, or burned the offenders in zealous efforts thus to save their souls.

The physical aspects of Geneva also changed and reflected the philosophical restraints as the Reformers built new and higher walls around their citadel to protect and confine the faithful.

The lusty visitors of yesteryear no longer lingered and dallied but hurried on their way, yielding their places to converts to Calvinism, the refugees from religious prosecution in other lands, who began to immigrate into Geneva well before the Reformer's death in 1564.

Théodore de Bèze succeeded the rigid Calvin and maintained the theocratic regime but with a more sensitive touch. Using his gift for diplomacy, Bèze steered the Calvinist revolution through the dangerous cross-currents of Europe's nine Wars of Religion, the waves of refugees fleeing from the massacre on Saint Bartholomew's Day of 1572 of thousands of French Protestants, and the infiltrations of the Jesuits' Counter-Reformation.

Bèze won for the Protestant cause the support of the sympathetic but pragmatically Catholic Henri IV of France who, in 1598, signed the "Edict of Nantes" and thus improved the lot of the Huguenots.

The Fourth Era: Resistance and Refugees

Savoy's interest in annexing Geneva revived during the Wars of Religion when Duke Charles of Savoy plotted with the militantly Catholic Philip II of Spain to crush the Reformation at its source. A combined force of Savoyards and Spaniards attacked Geneva's walls in December 1602. Geneva's resounding victory in this assault called "L'Escalade" won the town the gratitude and support of Protestant leaders in France, England, and Holland and a respite from the harassment of Savoy.

In 1610 the assassination of Henri IV and the subsequent rise of Cardinal Richelieu were hard blows to French Protestants. When in 1685 Louis XIV revoked the Edict of Nantes of Henri IV, the Huguenots fled in great numbers, many of them to Geneva. The arrival of these refugees caused immediate problems of housing but, in good hour, endowed the town with long-term assets in terms of the newcomers' diligence and marketable skills.

The Huguenot immigrants set up their shops for printing, textile manufacture, and particularly watchmaking, all industries that contributed to the restoration of Geneva's long-lost prosperity. Such commerce and the profits collected by the town's bankers financing the extravagant Louis XIV provided the Genevese gentry of the early 1700s with the means to invest in property. Residing now in substantial mansions, the new "Messieurs-du-Haut" enjoyed unaccustomed leisure, scrupulously directed towards serious discussion and scientific experiment. Geneva's less affluent, however, despite their great contribution to the civic well-being, found themselves with an ever-diminishing voice in their government.

Following Bèze's death in 1605 the administration of local affairs had evolved over the ensuing century from the inspired theocracy of the French preachers into a worldly oligarchy. The families of Geneva's elite from the heights of the Old Town intermarried, elected their sons to Council posts, and decided all issues with the arrogant benevolence of an "Ancien Régime".

The Fourth Era:
Local Revolutions Bring Limited Progress

The imbalance between the governing few and the unrepresented populace precipitated between 1707 and 1795 no fewer than five serious outbreaks of dissension and violence known variously as "Les Troubles", "Les Révoltes", "Les Insurrections", "Les prises d'armes", or — inclusively — as "La Petite Révolution".

The first episode occurred in 1707 when the recent immigrants met to protest against the oligarchy's disregard of all citizen's rights as defined under the ancient "Franchises of 1387". The ruling Council acted promptly. It quelled the oubreak with brutal force and ordered the execution of its leaders.

In 1734, 1763, 1781, and 1794 different issues and incidents set off yet other rounds of protest and violence. In each instance the incumbent Council called for the help of foreign troops. To appease the dissidents the Council regularly consented to a few minor Constitutional changes but control remained in the hands of the old families well into the 1840s.

While the firmly entrenched government of the mid-1700s repressed the democratic process, the townsfolk were increasingly influenced by two of the most persuasive philosophers of the Age of Enlightenment: the Geneva-resident Voltaire and the Geneva-born Jean-Jacques Rousseau.

Despite their conflicting views and their never once meeting, Voltaire and Rousseau together provided the intellectual and emotional inspiration for the revolutions in Geneva, America, and France.

The Fourth Era:
Revolutions That Made A Difference

The spirit of political revolution in the 1700s with its connotations of violence had a calmer counterpart in the Cartesian

Geneva's rivers and their drifting "Jonction"

The village that grew up to be Geneva began more than two thousand years ago on the hilltop overlooking the "Ile", the island where Lake Geneva narrows down into the Rhone River.

At the downstream tip of the "Ile" was the confluence — still called the "Jonction" — of the rivers Rhone and Arve.

The two waterways at the time lapped the converging slopes of the hill that separated them and served as a moat protecting two of the three sides of this natural strongpoint.

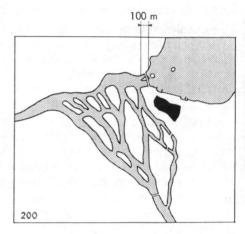

Early settlers completed their defences by closing the exposed side of their hilltop triangle with a ditch and palisade fence.

With the advent of the conquering Romans and the centuries of Pax Romana, Geneva had no need for static defences. The boundaries of the town spread naturally beyond the hilltop into the open terrain to the east.

The unfettered growth ended when Germanic tribes attacked the suburban villas and frightened their occupants back on to the hilltop.

Out of the debris of their former homes the townsmen built a wall around the crown of the hill. For a few more centuries this colony of Rome survived behind the protection of the wall and the waters of Lake Geneva and the Arve.

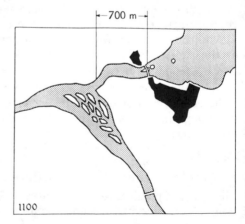

Through the Middle Ages and a succession of changing regimes Geneva was again able to expand, not only to the east as before but also to the south into land newly formed when silt and debris accumulated to fill in the delta of the Arve and nudge the "Jonction" westward.

By 1530 this enlarged Geneva faced new threats from neighboring Savoy. Among the first acts of the Reform was to order all outlying fields scorched and to recall the people within the confines of new and higher walls. Uninhabited and untended, the delta of the Arve continued to fill and rise as the "Jonction" inched farther to the west.

By the 1600s military artillery had grown more powerful. To defend against its batterings, many cities of Europe built ever more elaborate fortifications. Impressed by Geneva's repulse of the Escalade attack, the friendly Protestant rulers of Holland and England subsidized the building here of complex new bastions in the patterns first engineered by France's Vauban.

Two centuries later these massive, sprawling walls were outmoded and useless. At long last the old ramparts were demolished and in the 1850s Geneva broke out of its three centuries of confinement into an era of renewed expansion.

The rebuilding entailed construction of stone quaysides to control the line of the lake shore and the course of the rivers.

The "Jonction" thus was stabilized at its present location more than a kilometer and a half to the west of the point where, two thousand years before, the waterways crowded the hillside and served as Geneva's natural defences.

Plans de P. Fehlmann
d'après *Les origines de l'Homme et de Genève* Editions Georg.

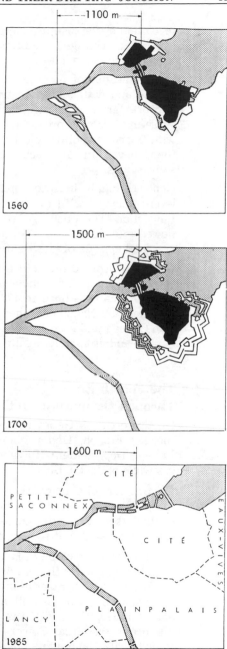

revolution of the scientific approach to thought. Analysis and experiment changed traditional notions and produced new tools for the modern era.

Communication of such new ideas improved with better postal service and with increased travel and even tourism as road networks grew and stagecoach services expanded. The Genevese in their new prosperity traveled widely. They returned with fresh viewpoints and lists of new foreign friends whom the Genevese in turn received graciously in the town's handsome salons.

Geneva's highly literate populace, politically sensitive at all levels, followed with fascination the events of the American Revolution. The ensuing French Revolution, however, overflowed into Geneva in 1794 as "La Petite Terreur", the fifth and final episode of "La Petite Révolution".

Geneva welcomed the return to better order in France under the initially popular Napoleon Bonaparte and hailed the General on his visit here in 1797. In 1798, however, the town's affection for Napoleon faded when French troops marched into Geneva and extorted a treaty making the Republic their captive and, ironically, again a capital.

The Fourth Era:
Through Occupation to Confederation

On this occasion Geneva became the seat of government of the new French "Département du Léman". The neighboring French "Département Helvétique" had as its capital Geneva's erstwhile protector Bern.

Geneva for fifteen years disdained its French occupiers, minded its decaying businesses, lamented as Napoleon drafted its youth for distant wars, and suffered under ruinous taxes, shortages, and restrictions.

In 1813 liberation came at last. Restored to its status as a free Republic and under the provisional protection of Swiss troops, Geneva forswore its tradition of independence and applied for acceptance into what is still, in Latin and officially, the Confoederatio Helvetica. With the support of the post-Napoleonic alliance of the Great Powers, Geneva on 14 September 1815 joined Switzerland as its smallest and most populous canton.

The Swiss Confederation in 1815 was a loose, insecure, and apprehensive aggregation of cantons. The group accepted Geneva's participation on the assumption of a continuing conservative town government. Thus reinforced, the veteran elite continued in control through the Restauration's "27 years of happiness" with the policies little changed from the two preceding centuries. The centuries of conservative control ended in 1846, a year of revolutionary change for both Geneva and Switzerland.

Within the Confederation in 1846 seven Catholic cantons in the east voted to secede. The liberal faction in the Swiss Diet favored preserving the Confederation whatever the costs. Geneva's conservative delegates to the Federal Diet refused to vote in support of taking up arms to keep the Confederation intact.

Incensed by their representatives' vote, the people of Geneva took to the barricades. The two-day revolution of October 1846 ended with the installation by acclamation of a new head of the Cantonal government, the liberal, controversial James Fazy.

Fazy's delegates to the Diet reversed Geneva's vote and thus provided the majority approval of the use of force to save the Confederation. The Federal Army under General Guillaume-Henri Dufour — a highly respected Genevese conservative — suppressed the secession in a month of skillful maneuvers with fewer than a hundred casualties.

In 1848 the reunited Swiss cantons approved a drastically revised Federal Constitution to establish a logical, coordinated central government. Switzerland, as it exists and functions today, began with that Constitution.

Geneva meanwhile had ratified its own new Constitution of 1847 giving Fazy's administration authority to change the look as well as the character of the town. The results were nearly as revolutionary as those Calvin had effected three hundred years before.

Fazy's regime removed Calvin's restraining fortifications, encouraged expansion into the suburbs, permitted broad freedom of religion, democratized the voting for the two Town Councils, and instituted popular banks to finance expansion of small businesses and industries.

The Fourth Era:
International Involvement Increases

Geneva's general reputation as an international center was based on its leadership in the Reformation and its trade location. In 1864 a specific initiative brought Geneva world renown when the delegates from sixteen nations met here to approve the First Geneva Convention of the Red Cross.

In 1872 the United Kingdom and the United States arbitrated in Geneva the "Alabama Incident" over the destruction of American shipping in its "War Between The States". Karl Marx's First Internationale held its annual meeting in Geneva and such groups as the League of Peace and Freedom attracted here an impressively polyglot participation.

Refugees fleeing the political clashes of the mid-1800s in Germany, France, and Russia, flowed once more into Geneva.

While Geneva thus stretched its political and social dimensions, its engineers were pioneering work in hydraulics and electricity for light manufacture and precision machining. These technical achievements brought commercial benefits but nothing comparable to profits from heavy industry, which had eluded Geneva.

Conservative resistance in the 1840s to a railroad connection diverted industrial development to the north of Switzerland with its superior communications. Belated efforts by Geneva's bankers and engineers to establish direct main-line service to Paris proved unsuccessful.

The Fourth Era Climax:
Geneva, Capital of a New World?

By the early 1900s Geneva's commerce lagged behind that of Basel and Zurich. With the outbreak of World War I Geneva faced more hard times. Its business curtailed for lack of outlets and with no prospect of revenues from armament-related industries or comparable sources, Geneva's involvement in that four-year-long conflict was largely through its services with the International Committee of the Red Cross (ICRC).

The Red Cross was a familiar and welcome sight on the battlefields of Europe. The part of its work that the ICRC directed from Geneva to control prisoner-of-war exchanges and mail deliveries and prison camp inspections was recognized and appreciated around the world.

When the war ended and the Great Powers gathered at Versailles to establish the ultimate peace treaty, they agreed to settle all future disputes through a League of Nations.

For that League's headquarters, the influential President of the United States, Woodrow Wilson, made his personal choice: Geneva.

The appointment as headquarters of the League of Nations caught Geneva by surprise. The war-weary citizens of this remote town recovered their balance, however, and soon learned how to provide the variety of services demanded to carry out an unprecedented international effort.

The Present Era: The League of Nations Experience

To house and service the League of Nations, Geneva set to work to improve its communications and accomodation. When some hotels were requisitioned for office space, others took up the slack by adding extra floors of rooms. To offset the regretted lag in rail connections, Geneva concentrated on developing air transport facilities. And, in response to the needs of a new species, the international civil servant, the authorities of the Republic adjusted laws and land deeds and, most important for Geneva's future, solved the vexing problems of siting and constructing that long-term fixed asset, the Palais des Nations.

The collapse of the League of Nations and the outbreak of World War II brought Geneva new hardships. With the end of the war in 1945 another blow fell. The United Nations invited into membership only countries considered as among the victors and thus excluded neutral Switzerland. Geneva watched in disappointment as New York assumed the role of "World Headquarters" that this Republic had enjoyed for twenty years.

The Present Era: Geneva's Luckier Second Chance

The UN Headquarters in New York concentrated, of course, on the demands of its active membership. On inheriting from the defunct League of Nations the rights to the Palais des Nations in non-participating Switzerland, the UN administration designated this unparalleled locale non-committally as "The Office of the United Nations in Geneva".

The Palais did not stand idle long as new entities sprang up to coordinate issues of health, refugees and migrants, telecommunications, and other tasks, and flooded the premises with more staff.

As they broadened their scope and increased their needs for communications and staff, many of the technical and specialized agencies of the United Nations, most of them with Switzerland as a contributing member, built in Geneva new and larger quarters. Non-governmental organizations such as the World Council of Churches and the YMCA joined the conveniently central official community. International businesses like Aluminium of Canada and America's Dupont, appreciating the same working climate, followed along shortly.

Four decades after its second start Geneva has combined the advantage of its central location and available space with dependable services, experience, and flexibility to make the work of the international community flow smoothly.

After its long and uneven history of good times and bad, Geneva's latest surge forward bids fair to be an extended run.

Geneva and Switzerland

A Recent Union

The name "Geneva, Switzerland" rolls so trippingly off the tongue that one feels that the combination must have existed forever. In fact it was as recently as 1815 that the Republic of Geneva and the Confédération Helvétique at last touched borders and joined destinies.

The Switzerland that the world knows as a nation today is considered to date only from its Constitution of 1848. And even this Swiss nation is still decidedly a confederation of unique cantons. Cantonal rights and interests take precedence over Federal concerns. Here a citizen is first a Genevois or a Bâlois or a Ticinese and, as an afterthought, a Swiss.

The family roots of the Swiss go back to a variety of semi-nomadic tribes of Celtic and Germanic origin. By 100 A.D. most of the land that today is Switzerland had come under Roman rule. Through the post-Roman times of the Frankish Empire and the Dark Ages, the hunters, herdsmen and farmers of this territory, with few natural resources beyond its beauty and its water, lived austere lives in isolated communities.

Geneva Came First

Geneva, by contrast, had by the late 1200s existed as an urban entity for two thousand years. The people of this bustling town were merchants and craftsmen, united by then into a political "commune" to compete with the alien Counts of Savoy and Geneva for control of their government.

In those same late 1200s three bands of mountaineers a couple of hundred kilometers to the northeast of Geneva were bestirring themselves to ally in resistance to the tyranny of the House of Hapsburg as depicted in the romantic Swiss legend of William Tell.

Before the "Schwytzers" Became Neutral

In 1291 on the shore of the Lake of Lucerne across which Tell reportedly escaped from Gessler's henchmen, the herders from three small and separate cantons secretly agreed to a loose alliance against their oppressors. The fighting men from those three cantons converted the accord into action in 1315 when they confronted and defeated the Hapsburgs in the Battle of Morgarten.

Five neighboring states, recognizing this potent force in their vicinity, joined the three early allies. The union enlarged to eight cantons was known by the name of its most powerful component, the Canton of Schwyz.

In 1388 the augmented "Schwytzers" again fought and again defeated the Hapsburgs, first at Sempach and later at Näfels. The cantons however, with the defeat of their ancient and common enemy, returned to their parochial ways and lost interest in their confederation. The union of fighting men regressed into an uncoordinated and often quarrelsome association.

The rise of a new foe in 1476 once more rallied the straggling cantons into a powerful entity. Within a ten-month span the revived Swiss army defeated at the epochal battles of Grandson, Morat, and Nancy the daunting legions of Charles the Bold of Burgundy.

While Switzerland Grows, Geneva Survives

This fresh display of Swiss power once again attracted more collaborators. Five other cantons joined the Confederation to bring the membership to a total of thirteen. And this enlarged coalition drew further strength from treaties between its individual cantons and eight additional neighboring states. Among these neighbors was Geneva, in 1477, impoverished, threatened by Savoy, and welcoming the protection of the cantons of Fribourg and Bern.

By 1481 Switzerland, lacking a military reason for being, reverted to its previous disorder and was rent by internal dissension until miraculously reconciled by another Swiss national hero — the soldier turned religious hermit, then diplomat, and eventually saint — Nicolas de Flue.

The army of this once-more-united Switzerland became for several decades the most potent military force in Europe. Swiss conquests extended to Dijon in the west and in the south beyond Milan before France's King François I turned the tide in 1515 at the Battle of Marignano.

Chastened by the defeat of its long-irresistible infantry, Switzerland signed the "Treaty of Everlasting Peace" and embarked on its traditional policy of neutrality.

The Reformation Divides Switzerland

As a nation, however, Switzerland found itself again divided not only by the absence of a common military target but also by the religious Reformation. While the Catholic Church remained strong in the mountain cantons, the rupture begun by Martin Luther in Germany in the 1500s was extended by Ulrich Zwingli in Zurich and Berthold Haller in Bern whose authorities sent Guillaume Farel to convert Geneva to Protestantism.

Once the cantons had returned to their autonomy the concept of Confederation paled. For more than a century between 1663 and 1776 the Diet of the cantons never met. When a degree of centralization finally returned it was in 1798 and on terms dictated in Paris after the occupation of the cantons by the armies of France.

Switzerland Expands and Geneva Joins

When the Allies finally overcame Napoleon and French rule in Switzerland ended, the Great Powers agreed on the desirability of creating a buffer state in mid-Europe. To provide this geographical cushion the Allies promoted the restoration of the Confoederatio Helvetica and reinforced it by the addition of the French-language cantons, Geneva among them.

The enlarged Switzerland of 1815 remained a decentralized and troubled confederation. Only after a civil war in 1847 did the cantons face the fact that a respected central government was the only hope for reconciliation of their wide individual differences. The adoption of the Constitution of 1848 mandated Federal control of a uniform currency, the postal and customs services, universal military service, and religious equality, and started Switzerland on its way to becoming a nation.

In 1874 a revised Constitution widened the powers of the central government in law, taxes, and education and established the uniquely Swiss system of allowing individuals to initiate important legislation and petition for its submission to the vote of the people in national referenda.

Swiss Contrasts and "Vive la Différence"

The early years of the new centralization were made difficult by divisions of sentiment between the German-speaking population and the French sector during the Franco-Prussian War.

Forty years later in World War I the differences persisted but were diminished. By World War II, however, Switzerland was as united in its resistance to the totalitarian philosophy as the nation's policy of neutrality and its geographical position between the Axis powers would allow.

Today the Swiss accept and constantly adjust to the inevitable differences between the industrial north and the service-oriented south, between the Protestant west and the Catholic east, and between the German-speaking majority and the Francophone and Italianate populations.

Geneva remains within this oddly-assorted Confederation as the embodiment of the extremes. It is the smallest canton, the most westerly, the most French with its long affinity for things Parisian, the canton farthest from the geographical center of Switzerland, the most heavily international — in short, if not a black sheep — sufficiently grayish to keep the others on guard.

The disparate Swiss have learned, however, after six centuries of hard experience, that whatever their individual preferences they get along best with the rest of the world by getting along reasonably with one another. When occasional family spats do arise, the cantons continue to compromise and cooperate and, thus, survive.

Seeing Geneva

Get On Your Mark...

Geneva is divided by the River Rhone into two major segments, identified by their river banks.

The Left Bank, the "Rive Gauche" in French, is on your left as you face the river downstream. In this area south of the river towards Mont Salève and Mont Blanc are the Old Town with its Cathedral, the fortifications, historic buildings, local government offices, and the University.

The Right Bank, the "Rive Droite", is the newer section towards the Jura mountains. This is modern or, at least, latter-day Geneva with its "International City" on its hill to the north, not far from such support services as the airport, railroad station, and most of the hotels.

Each of the two parts is treated separately in this guide. Each tour starts from the same place: The Right Bank or north end of the Pont du Mont-Blanc, the Mont Blanc Bridge.

Start with whichever tour you prefer. Historically, the Left Bank takes precedence.

The description of the route comes in three assorted formats, planned, first for the compressed, motorized, less-than-two-hour visit, next for the brisker walking tour, and lastly for the more leisurely sojourner or resident.

◆ The Large Type preceded by the mark ◆ is for Unvarnished Fact, the first category of information. Its editing is for quick reference to help the fast-moving visitor to note Geneva's high points as seen from an automobile, taxi, or bus. Visitors in this wheel-borne style are addressed in the text as The Driven. The term refers only to the travel status of certain guests, never to the psychological outlook.

The Medium Type, this 9^1/$_2$-point size, is for the Deeper Dip. Intended for the second category of tour, the text adds a few details to highlight the rudimentary first impression. It is intended for The Walker planning to cover the subject of Geneva in a matter of hours.

> The Small Type, this 8-point size, is for the Tantalizing Trivia, the third category of information. Here are the gratuitous details, addenda, and anecdotes for those Walkers who have time to be Strollers. These are Geneva's guests or residents fortunate enough to remain for longer stretches and under no pressure to absorb nine more cities in the next thirteen days.

And while considering typography, note that any item cited in the text in **Bold Face** letters is shown on the end maps by a number, arrows, or its printed-out name.

As to timing, The Driven can cover the full course in half-an-hour with no stops and in light traffic — say at 5 a.m. on a Sunday. But even on a frightful Friday at 6 p.m., a two-hour ride should easily cover the whole circuit.

The number of hours The Walkers need depends on the patience, practices, and distractability of the troupe or individual. Some sprint, some saunter, some thirst, some digress, some spell out the full text of wall plaques and guidebooks.

Averaging out the extremes, allow for the full Left Bank tour some three hours.

The Right Bank visit to modern Geneva can be covered by a walk combined with a bus ride of a kilometer and a half (one mile) in about two hours.

Short cuts plotted from the end maps can reduce distances, particularly in the Old Town.

Repose and recesses in cafés, parks, and squares for refreshment, reconnaissance, reading, and people-gazing are never discouraged. Benches, steps, and ledges abound.

Public-transport tram and bus service is available at almost every point along the route of march to return the foot-weary or rain-trapped to their Geneva base on payment of a single fare (page 229).

Fuss-budgety counsel concerning sensible shoes, protection from sunstroke, and clothing to encourage free circulation is omitted. One exceptional caution is offered and you'll see why soon enough: Use extreme caution in crossing any Geneva street.

Geneva Left Bank

◆ The **Start** for this visit to the Left Bank of Geneva is at the north (the railroad station) end of the **Pont du Mont-Blanc,** the Mont-Blanc Bridge. On the right-hand (downstream) side of the bridge is the River Rhone, bound for Marseille after having travelled some 200 kilometers from its source under a glacier high in the Swiss Alps.

The Rhone started as a drip and a trickle in a cave in the ice, picked up speed and volume as it coursed through the Canton of Valais, and slowed down on reaching the deep lake basin dug out of this valley by the Rhone's own glacier over fifteen millenia ago.

> The lake is shaped like a banana, 90 kilometers (60 miles) long, stretching from its Valais in the east past the Swiss Riviera resort towns of Vevey and Montreux westward to Lausanne and there bending south to Geneva.
>
> Snuggled inside the curve on the opposite short lies the French territory — the "Département de Haute-Savoie".

◆ The bridge is the line where the Rhone, having traversed the broad Lake Geneva (its synonym — Lac Léman — is generally disdained at this end of the waterway), contracts into its previous river form.

This lake-cum-river spread of water is the literal mainstream of Geneva — the divider between the newer Right Bank with its International City and the Left Bank spreading out from its core of the Old Town.

> On a fine summer day on the lake a single wide-angle camera setting can encompass lake cruisers, sailboats, windsurfers, paddlewheelers, harbor skiffs, swans, sun baskers, quayside strollers and, accenting it all with a giant exclamation point, Geneva's towering water fountain.

◆ The **Jet d'Eau [1]** is the high-rise geyser that animates Geneva's harbor on a varying schedule some 230 days a year from early March into mid-October.

The Jets d'Eau, 1886, 1891, 1947

Attractive as the Jet d'Eau may be, Geneva's municipal geyser has not yet lured to the town's quayside either the Statue of Liberty or Manhattan's United Nations building.

The photomontage showing two tall and widely recognized New York landmarks against the background of Mont Salève was made to give a scale of heights for the three generations of Geneva's Jets.

Jet I — to the right in this presentation — was the original spurt of 1886 rising up an honest 30 meters (98 feet), a pretty good thrust considering that the spout was a utilitarian pressure relief never intended as a scenic attraction.

Once the town's technicians realized that they had indeed created a work of art, they sought to improve upon their fortuitous masterpiece. Engineer Turrettini (page 131) forthwith produced a purely decorative assemblage of four auxiliary fountains projecting at an angle from the base of the higher-rising Jet II. This improved version of 1891 soared up to 85 meters (290 feet), a height rivaling that of the torch of the recently dedicated Statue of Liberty.

Two World Wars had come and gone before Geneva decided in 1947 to refurbish its aqueous logo with new motors and pumps set in a 16-ton caisson for its base. This augmented Jet III now starts its working day with a spurt that on occasions reaches as high as 150 meters, nearly 500 feet.

After its initial release Jet III settles down to its cruising altitude — variable according to wind conditions, humidity, and barometric pressure — of between 130 and 145 meters (425 to 475 feet), not far short of the 154-meters high (504 feet) United Nations building in New York.

The 1600-horsepower pumps of Jet III suck a steady 30,000 liters (8,000 gallons) of Lake Geneva through the intake grills each minute. The water picks up speed in the pump chambers and reaches 200 kilometers (130 miles) per hour by the time it roars out through the 16-centimeter (6-inch) double-concentric nozzle.

The volume of water thus dispatched suspends between heaven and the lake at any given moment more than seven tons of geyser, foam, and spray — a quantity held constant by the fact that the pump motor control has only two readings: "On" and "Off".

A technician in a quayside cabin monitors a bank of instruments gauging wind force and direction, harbor traffic, precipitation, and the other factors that influence his decision as to whether the Jet is to stop or go (map 1).

◆ This shimmering column of foam is as identified with Geneva as the Acropolis is with Athens and the Eiffel Tower with Paris.

The Jet d'Eau — locally pronounced "jeddo" — is not only as nicely proportioned and as distinctive as competing trademarks, it is also weatherproof, retractable, erosion-resistant, and composed of locally available raw materials.

Today's Jet is the third that Geneva's engineers have developed since producing unintentionally the first fascinating spout as the vertical discharge from a relief valve in a hydraulic conduit.

The second Jet the engineers planned as an elaborate decorative feature. They replaced Number Two in 1947 with this more powerful design rising 70% higher.

On the third time round the engineers were not content simply to reach new heights. They also fretted about the aesthetics of a simple upright/downright column of water. Seeking a more interesting plume of added breadth that would swirl, leap, and throb, the engineers designed concentric nozzles that produced the effect they wanted.

The engineers faced in this latest design a few problems not encountered with the earlier jets. Although only a sensitive few could hear it, a highpitched whistle accompanied the water from the nozzle. Fine tuning of the volume and speed finally suppressed the upper register squeal that had probably been driving Geneva's dog population out of its collective wits.

◆ Mont Salève is the broad ridge of mountain visible ahead and to the right of the bridge and resembling a mammoth slice of slightly squashed layer cake.

Salève's icing-striped strata were exposed after the glacier that filled this lake and valley tore away the rest of the mountain. The caves left in its side provided shelter for the early hunters whose descendants, moving from these grottos to the lake edge many thousands of years ago, qualify as the original Genevese.

◆ Although the early Genevese were the first to populate Mont Salève and the town has always considered the ridge's 1,000-meter (3,000-foot) wall to be its very own backdrop, this mountain and any others that you can see from Geneva are all in France.

The imminence of France on every side has prompted the more cynical Gallic neighbors to remark that "...the most beautiful feature of Geneva is its view of France".

And beautiful France is indeed all around Geneva. Of the 108 kilometers (65 miles) perimeter of the Canton of Geneva, 104 kilometers border France with the four remaining kilometers (a bit under three miles) touching the Swiss Canton of Vaud.

Geneva's contour is such that on maps the Canton appears in the shape of a buttonhook around the south end of the lake with its thin shank extending north into the solid handle of Switzerland.

During its centuries as an independent town-state Geneva was tightly circumscribed at the lake end, described as "... open only to the skies".

The pattern changed in 1815 as a result of the decision taken by the Great Powers of Europe. Meeting in the Congress of Vienna to arrange the boundaries of post-Napoleonic Europe, the Allies agreed that Geneva should be part of an enlarged Switzerland. Such a union was feasible, however, only if Geneva territory at some point touched an existing canton of Switzerland. At the time the two borders were 15 kilometers (10 miles) apart.

To arrange the consolidation the Congress of Vienna obliged France to concede to Geneva a long, narrow strip of lakeshore real estate. Once this corridor made Geneva contiguous to the Canton of Vaud the Swiss Federal Diet on 12 September 1815 admitted Geneva into the Confederation as its twenty-second canton.

The Genevese use the Salève as if they owned it and they have, on occasion, tried to acquire it. The strongest criticism of the Salève came — not from a Genevese — but from the French author Stendhal. He condemned the ridge as an eyesore, obstructing what otherwise would be from Geneva an inspiring view of Mont-Blanc.

The Genevese find the Salève reassuring to contemplate, tempting to ascend, whether by the traditional three-hour Sunday trudge up the roadbed of the abandoned railway, or by a challenging shinny up the rockface of the advanced climber's testing ground — La Varappe — or, more gently, by a vertiginous two-and-a-half minute lift in its cable car to watch the sunset over the Jura and the lights snapping on around the toy town and lake far below.

◆ Mary Wollstonecroft Shelley established Mont Salève and Geneva as literary landmarks in her Gothic parable *Frankenstein* wherein she describes the mountain as Geneva's adjacent "... nearly perpendicular ascent..."

In chapter 7 the author recounts the return to Geneva of Dr Victor Frankenstein and his visit in a violent storm to the park where, a month earlier, his father had found the corpse of the doctor's 8-year-old brother.

When a flash of lightning illuminates the scene Frankenstein perceives the strangler cowering nearby and recognizes him as The Monster whom the surgeon had pieced together and animated in the attic of his dormitory at Inglostadt.

The agile, 8-foot-tall Monster flees and in a matter of minutes Frankenstein sees him "... hanging amid the rocks..." of the "... overhanging sides..." of the Salève "... soon to reach the summit and disappear".

Frankenstein was written by 18-year-old Mary Wollestonecroft during her sojourn here in the storm-plagued summer of 1816. Mary had fled London with the otherwise-married poet, Percy Byssche Shelley and their newborn son. Accompanying them as nurse and interpreter was Mary's younger half-sister, Claire Claremont. Claire proposed a visit to Geneva as a way of their meeting Shelley's contemporary, George Lord Byron, with whom Claire hoped to extend her incipient love affair.

The Shelley and Byron parties arrived ten days apart in May 1816. The poets, once introduced by Claire at their hotel, decided to rent for the summer adjacent houses along the shore of the lake.

A frightening electric storm one evening inspired the literary coterie to try a competition for ghost stories. Mary's entry was a blend of the fantasy and philosophy that she later expanded into the full novel which was published anonymously. *Frankenstein* was an immediate success, more, however, for its bizarre plot than for the intellectual content its author intended.

The Monster as conceived by Miss Wollstonecroft represented the malevolent product of man's dabbling in science. Her Monster is not evil but misunderstood. After educating himself on the works of Plutarch, Goethe, and Milton's *Paradise Lost* he rationalizes his anti-social conduct in grandiloquent philosophical terms.

As to the element of horror, Miss Wollstonecroft would have been its most battered victim had she foreseen that her sociological morality tale would one day inspire a series of simplistic moving pictures while her apocalyptic symbol of the sensitive Monster became a shuffling, barely-articulate television clown.

◆ The sharp-prowed, artificial island on your right, midway across the bridge, was built in 1583 as a harbor defence against the armed galleys of unfriendly Savoy.

At that time Geneva began to experiment with the manufacture of its own gunpowder and prudently located the first factory on this island, well out of range of all habitation.

With the abatement of the Savoyard threat following Geneva's victory in the "Escalade" of 1602 (page 121), the town replaced the arsenal with a shipyard and the island became the "Ile des Barques".

◆ **The Ile des Barques changed to the Ile Rousseau [2] in 1834 when the town set here the bronze statue of the most influential writer-philosopher of the 1700s, Geneva-born Jean-Jacques Rousseau.**

Among Geneva's celebrated citizens and native sons, Rousseau is still the most famous. His writings launched the Romantic Movement that was for a century among the most important in art and literature. Despite his personal life, described as somewhat unsavory in his candid *Confessions*, Rousseau's often-conflicting but always persuasively expressed ideas won him ardent admiration.

Jean-Jacques was born in the prestigious Old Town in 1712, the time of its ascendency, but was by no means one of its select "Messieurs-du-Haut", those "Gentlemen at the Top" of both the hill of the Old Town and the social rankings of Geneva.

Rousseau's modest origins were forgiven by Geneva's conservative elite when the prodigal son returned in 1754, celebrated as a playwright and composer, well-received in the court of King Louis XVI.

The homage that Geneva's leaders paid to Rousseau then turned to wrath when his subsequent writings in defence of freedom of the spirit attacked certain hallowed concepts of property and privilege.

In 1762 the indignant Council ordered his books burned and the author condemned to exile as an irresponsible and morally dangerous agnostic.

Rousseau's reputation outside Geneva flourished and in 1794 a more liberal court here reversed the earlier judgment.

By 1828, a half century after Rousseau's death, his admirers in Geneva campaigned for his further recognition. Geneva's still conservative Council acquiesced in the financing of a statue even though their misgivings about extolling their rebellious "concitoyen" lingered on.

Even after accepting delivery of the cast figure executed in Paris by Geneva's James Pradier (page 104), the Council remained reluctant to accord its tacit approval of Rousseau and his principles. By way of compromise they decided to set his statue on this island but to screen it with poplar trees on three sides, leaving the philosopher visible only from the then-open lake.

Rousseau's semi-isolation lasted for thirty years. Then, in 1862, Geneva completed this Mont-Blanc Bridge, still the most heavily trafficked thoroughfare in town. After three decades of solitude Rousseau was exposed to more passers-by than any other figure in Geneva.

◆ Rousseau's statue is not only a tribute to Geneva's philosopher but also another literary landmark, the setting of an important scene in Joseph Conrad's 1911 novel *Under Western Eyes.*

Conrad wrote about Russian dissidents in Geneva and the morally bankrupt student, Razumov, who was forced by the Tsarist police to spy on these expatriate revolutionaries.

When Razumov must find a remote place in which to write his report, Conrad ironically chose as his screen the statue of Rousseau, the hero of every revolutionary, to shield the government's spy as he pens his treacherous letter.

While more cars traverse Mont-Blanc Bridge than any other roadway in Geneva, this is also the site of the town's most persistent traffic jams. Few of the exasperated motorists seem to pass their waiting time in contemplation of the now-revealed statue of Rousseau.

As to the philosopher, his bronze gaze in this likeness can hardly avoid the panorama of Genevese traffic chaos. The ghost of the bucolic Rousseau may very well consider this melancholy scene to be the perpetual Hell in which he so resolutely refused to believe.

◆ Beyond the poplar trees of the Ile Rousseau the Gothic spire and towers of the **Cathédrale de Saint-Pierre [3]** come into view atop the hill of the Old Town.

While Geneva began on that long, low ridge and has survived there for nearly three thousand years, the lakeshore you see to your left was a much earlier settlement and probably endured for an even longer stretch of time.

This Left Bank parkland was the downstream end of an extensive swamp and shallows. As long ago as 3500 B.C. a prehistoric "Town of Lake Dwellers" existed on pilings sprawled over some 300 acres, protected by the barriers of the water and a palisade of sharpened stakes.

About 1000 B.C. this ancient "Ville Lacustre" vanished for reasons still unclear. After a lapse of several centuries a Celtic tribe from the Danube, the Allobrigians, arrived but eschewed the lake edge to settle on the more secure ground at the top of the hill.

The original village on the ridge eventually overflowed and stretched down to the water edge as vineyards were cultivated on the slopes of the natural citadel.

Below the slopes tradesmen built shops and houses to cater to the itinerant merchants passing along the lake shore, bound for the bridge across the Rhone farther downstream. To attract the travelers the facades of these buildings faced the inner roads, leaving their less-sightly posteriors towards the lake, so convenient for the disposal of waste.

The squalid appearance of Geneva as seen from the lake became a pressing issue only in the 1820s when some more affluent and fastidious travelers abandoned the rough stagecoaches to try the new steamboat service that delivered the passengers to the dingy port area.

Among the celebrated travelers arriving by lake steamer was the American novelist, James Fenimore Cooper, with his four daughters. After spending a night at anchor in the harbor in 1828, Cooper added his voice to the other protests of Geneva's sights and smells along the waterfront.

In response to the growing pressures the Town Council granted Engineer Guillaume-Henri Dufour the means to build the stout stone quayside on the Left Bank, backed with earth to accomodate today's verdant parks and promenades.

With the handsome quayside in place the hovels of the waterfront gave way to hotels and houses whose facades now turned outwards toward the bright water and the mountains of the Jura.

The dissenting comment came from France's Victor Hugo. An enthusiastic admirer of Geneva and of its setting as observed on his visit with his wife in 1825, the novelist in 1839 returned with his friend Juliette Drouet (page 104) and testily noted that the Genevese — by prettifying their water-front — had ruined the town's most interesting feature.

◆ The Driven, approaching the end of the bridge, bear right into the traffic lane one away from the far right in order to enter the street heading inland at the Place du Port.

Walkers reaching the bridge-end must NEVER attempt to cross the motor roadway by hurdling the steel barrier. Turn right instead. Descend the stairs or ramp leading to the lakeside railing and walkway. Turn right again to go under the bridge through its glassed-in passage.

◆ The Driven, although busy selecting among an over-generous choice of traffic lanes, may note on the left of the bridge plaza the wooded park, Geneva's **Jardin Anglais,** the English Garden.

Walkers emerge from under the bridge into the English Garden. The term is a general one for a style made up of wandering paths, scattered trees and casual flowerbeds — the bosky natural look. French gardens, by contrast, feature formal plantings, symmetrical paths and geometrical trimmings.

> Continue along the lakeside promenade to the tenth lampost. Sighting across the harbor in the direction of the lighthouse at its entry you may see a large boulder a couple of hundred meters distant, projecting about two meters (six feet) out of the water — the **Pierre du Niton [4]**, Rock of Neptune.
>
> Engineer Dufour took his bearings from the crest of the Pierre du Niton, his geodetic benchmark in building these quays. Dufour assigned the rock an even heavier role ten years later when, as a colonel in the Swiss Army, he extended his Geneva plot to survey the entire surface of Switzerland's intricate topography on the superb, prize-winning maps still sold as the *Cartes Dufour*.

Birdwatchers wishing to identify the lake's waterfowl should return to the eighth lamppost on the promenade where a signboard on its park side depicts in colored drawings twelve different species.

In the middle of the English Garden is the massive fountain beneath whose spray bask bronze figures representing the "Four Seasons" — the work in 1858 of Louis Dorcière, a Geneva jeweler and engraver turned sculptor.

The fountain's finest hours are those of a warm summer evening when its light and sparkle serve as a setting for itinerant musicians, acrobatic roller skaters, and — returning towards the bridge — an **old-fashioned bandstand [5].**

This stage within the English Garden is one of the several locations where Geneva in warm weather offers free concerts by glee clubs, brass bands, yodelers, rock groups, Dixieland combos — to name but a few from a wide selection. Check the poster on the bandstand railing for the performers, schedule, and locations.

Continue to walk back towards the bridge plaza where you are unlikely to overlook on their lofty pedestal two stately larger-than-life ladies in bronze.

◆ The Driven, having settled into the right-bearing lane out of the bridge plaza into the Place du Port, may get a traffic-signal-stop glimpse to their left of the **Monument National [6],** Geneva's substantial acknowledgement of the years of its protection by Switzerland.

In this allegory cast in bronze, Geneva — the daintier of the two — cozies up to the stolidly maternal Confederation.

Geneva carries her age well in this representation, particularly as she is the elder of the pair by some fourteen centuries.

Geneva became a civic entity recognized by the Romans about 120 B.C. Only in 1291 did the men of the three Forest Cantons form the alliance that today is Switzerland.

That early nucleus attracted additional collaborators and by the middle of the 1400s had expanded to a union of eight cantons.

Geneva remained behind its restrictive defensive walls unchanged across the years — small and often in need of help. The cantons of the Swiss Confederation provided protection under the treaties of 1471, 1519, 1526, and 1584 as recorded on this monument in Roman numerals.

Switzerland and Geneva lived in this parallel independence until 1798 when the erstwhile allies found themselves compatriots under French occupation. At its end in 1815 Geneva joined the revived Confoederatio Helvetica (page 16).

The Confederation, however, continued to be so loose an alliance that in 1847 seven cantons attempted to secede. The nation survived by its victory in the "War of the Sonderbund" — a sort of Swiss "War Between The States" — in which Guillaume-Henri Dufour as General of the Swiss Army led the Federal troops.

To consolidate the restored state the Swiss adopted the Constitution of 1848 which remains the foundation stone of the present era of prosperity, unity, and high standing in the international community.

On this monument to four hundred years of understanding, two native daughters of Savoy, the state considered by Geneva and Switzerland as their common enemy, posed as models for the respective symbolic figures.

The Monument to the nation and canton was inaugurated in 1865 by the ever-useful General Dufour.

◆ Just inland from the Monument National, The Driven may catch a peripheral glimpse of Geneva's **Horloge Fleurie [7]**, the Flower Clock, with its 4-meter (13-foot) dial.

For seven months of the year the clock's face and borders are a riot of botanical color. The decorative plants are actually grown in the municipal hothouses as the gravelly glacial moraine on which the town rests is not the richest of soil for conventional gardening.

◆ The Driven, once more in motion, pass by the Place du Port and its fountain — one among some 150 placed throughout Geneva — across the **Rue du Rhône** into the **Place Longemalle.**

This quite solid ground is now well away from the water's edge but, before being filled in, the area was Geneva's busiest port.

Walkers cross cautiously the perilous **Quai Guisan** and continue into the **Place Longemalle.**

When this plaza's borders were actually the quaysides of an inlet from the lake, travelers and merchants arrived here by boat and by shore road to trade at Geneva's markets.

Originally a rank of casual stalls, the market developed in the late 1200s into the organized, four-times-a-year fairs on which Geneva's economy thrived for centuries.

The profitability of the fairs declined seriously in the 1460s as a result of King Louis XI's order to French merchants to patronize his fairs at Lyon. Economic conditions in Geneva deteriorated further in the late 1400s when the Age of Discovery expanded ocean travel and commerce shifted from the cumbersome trails across the Alps to sea lanes and ports far from this marketplace.

Trans-European travelers often chose the route via Geneva where such celebrated guests as Cellini, Machiavelli, Rabelais, Servet, Walpole, Tiepolo, Casanova, Mozart, and Goethe stayed in the lively inns of the Longemalle neighborhood.

◆ At the plaza's inland end beyond another massive stone fountain the street to your left is the **Rue de Rive,** the Riverbank Street, once the site of the Franciscan Monastery of Rive.

> The religious retreat was the scene of the historic "Dispute de Rive". In 1535 the contentious preacher Guillaume Farel and two fellow missionaries for the Reform came from Bern to debate with the Catholic monks. After 25 days of relentless argument Farel's eloquence and logic persuaded the Franciscans to join the Reform.

◆ To your left at this intersection the street name changes from Rive to the **Rue de la Croix d'Or**, the Cross of Gold Street.

> The cross of gold was the ancient trademark of the banking guild. In the 1300s Geneva's burgeoning trade fairs attracted from Lombardy men skilled in finance to provide currency exchange and interim funding. Their stalls were identified by the sign of a cross of gold. Not surprisingly, a nearby tavern was duly named "Croix d'Or".

Another tavern of the quarter was the "Tête Noire", the Black Head. The 1773 version of its signboard remains posted and visible high on the wall above the door at 25 rue de la Croix d'Or.

◆ On the corner of Croix d'Or at number 34 stood in the late 1780s the pharmacy of Henri-Albert Gosse (page 102). Here, Gosse and two associates originated today's soft drink industry.

The three partners experimented for ten years developing a "health drink" consisting of plain, potable water laced with a few minerals and many bubbles of carbon dioxide. Finally successful in confecting an artificial "effervescent water" the trio found Geneva totally uninterested in their product.

> One partner, however, refused to give up. He moved to England and there marketed this "natural cure" under his own name, John Jacob Schweppes.

In London his drink was a quick success. Schweppes soon sold out his interest to return to Geneva with his family. The new owners expanded their product line by adding exotic — presumably medicinal — herbs such as ginger (as in "ale") and quinine (as in "tonic").

The trade name, however, was never changed from the original catchy "Schweppes". Today the world-wide soft drink industry recognizes as its pioneer J.-J. Schweppes, a Genevese jeweler turned amateur chemist who began it all where the "Cross of Gold" intersects the "Street of the Fountain".

◆ **Rue de la Fontaine,** the Street of the Fountain, is a short slope up toward the Old Town. Looming over the **Place de la Fontaine [9]** ahead is the highest section remaining of the oft-rebuilt town walls.

Those bishop-princes who ruled Geneva through the Middle Ages built on top of this segment of the town's bastions a formidable stone palace known as "L'Evêché", the Bishopric.

Shortly after the last of the bishops retired in 1532 in full flight through a secret passage in the walls, the Reformers converted the massive structure into the town prison. The cold, unsightly block hung over the lower town like a threat until in 1911 the Council condemned the obsolete eyesore to demolition.

When Geneva in 1940 at last got around to removing the blockhouse, this photogenic view of the Cathedral's imposing Gothic tower and steeple rewarded the effort.

◆ At the turn left from rue de la Fontaine a traffic-light-hold may allow The Driven to glimpse on the right the **Church of the Madeleine [8],** the temple in which the proselytizing Farel preached the Reformation creed in the early 1530s and where Michel Servet, an early proponent of unitarianism, was arrested as a heretic in 1553.

On Farel's arrival from Bern in 1528 he preached in homes and stables and any other place where people would gather to listen. Finding at the Madeleine a congregation already assembled for Catholic services, Farel — a tiny but wiry man — threw the priest out of the pulpit and delivered his own evangelical message.

Using the pseudonym "Ursinus" (from his mother's name "d'Ursiéres" — meaning the "place of the bears"), Farel eluded the frequent threats and bans issued by the Catholic hierarchy to stifle his Protestant mission. Farel persisted valiantly and on 21 May 1536 prevailed when the Town Council adopted the Reformation by official edict.

Farel recognized that his talent was for evangelism rather than for the administration that the new regime henceforth required. He considered as an Act of Heaven his meeting in July 1536 with a passing refugee, Jean Calvin. Farel soon persuaded the young Frenchman that God had willed Calvin to remain in Geneva to consolidate His Reform.

Calvin, trained as a lawyer, had infinite faith in the written word, whether in his approach to his work or to the Bible. He undertook his new duties by writing for Geneva an exhaustive set of laws and codes on every aspect of human behavior and of theology. He devoted particular attention to the sin of heresy.

Michel Servet — or by his Latin name, Servetus — was a Spanish aristocrat and physician who harbored outspoken doubts about the value of baptism, the immortality of Christ, and the existence of a Holy Trinity.

For his expression of such opinions, France had convicted Servet of heresy and forced him into hiding. Undaunted, he wrote to Calvin who replied that such thoughts were unitarian and mortally sinful. Servet believed he could persuade Calvin by direct discussion and imprudently came to Geneva.

Servet found that in Reformed Geneva attendance at the several-times-daily religious services was compulsory. He was, therefore, in the Church of the Madeleine when the town guards recognized and arrested him. Calvin personally directed his trial for heresy and handed down the sentence.

On 27 October 1553 the public executioner burned Servet at the stake (page 94), an episode that has long perturbed Calvin's reputation.

The street to the right of the Madeleine Church is the Rue du Purgatoire, Purgatory Street, one of the Rues Basses, the Lower Streets, which were a century ago among Geneva's most odoriferous slums.

The denizens of this quarter used spade-calling candor in designating their squalid alleys as Rue d'Enfer — Hell Street — which intersects at the next corner with Rue du Purgatoire.

Mark Twain on a stroll about Geneva during his 1878 visit found himself first in "Hell" and then in "Purgatory", moving him to remark that he "... seemed to be going in the wrong direction."

Directions, also confusing and intriguing, are set in a work of art on the paved terrace below the town wall.

On the **Place de la Fontaine [9]** Genevese artist Ducimitière has installed "The Water Ring", a stone circle level with the ground and bisected by an elongated rectangular stream of water.

Alongside the rectangle are the names of all the waterways that this miniature flow would cross if its vector were extended all the way around the globe.

◆ The left turn near the Madeleine leads into **Rue du Vieux-Collège,** the Old School Street, so named for the school donated to Geneva in 1428 by a public-spirited apothecary, François Versonnex, as an annex to the sprawling Monastère de la Rive.

Geneva might have had an institute of higher education even earlier. In 1328 Emperor Charles IV offered to enfranchise Geneva as a university town as he had Prague and Vienna.

Geneva, fraught with misgivings concerning the conduct and malevolent influence of students in general, declined the Emperor's offer.

◆ Ahead, across Rue Verdaine and high on the wall to your right, a plaque notes the death in 1629 in a mansion on this site of Emilie of Nassau.

This princess was the daughter of William the Silent (page 108), the Protestant statesman who consolidated many small estates of northwestern Europe into the nation of Holland.

Emilie, the daughter from the second of William's four marriages, moved to Geneva to escape the vicious feuds raging within her large step-family.

Geneva has traditional ties to Holland in religion and education and was pleased to welcome royally the pious, intellectual Princess of Orange and Nassau and her six daughters. On her death three years after her arrival, the Republic showed its esteem by providing Emilie a tomb in its Cathédrale de Saint-Pierre (page 75).

◆ Further along the Rue du Vieux Collège, about a hundred meters beyond Rue Verdaine, look high on a wall to your right for another marble **plaque [10].** The inscription is in an artificial language and explains that this marks the residence of the inventor of Esperanto, **Ludovic Lazarus Zamenhof.**

Zamenhof was an opthalmologist from the Baltic regions where multilinguality is common. Having known the problems of writing in the Roman, Cyrillic, and Hebrew alphabets, Zamenhof sought to solve the world's communication problem with one logical, readily pronounceable, easy-to-learn language available to all.

An even earlier inventor of an artificial language was a citizen of Geneva, Peter Mark Roget. The name is English because Peter Mark was the son of a Genevese pastor assigned to the French Protestant Church in London. The diligent and versatile Peter Mark spent twenty of his ninety years compiling that English language "triumph of logic" — *Roget's Thesaurus.*

Roget was, by profession, a doctor. He worked with Sir Humphry Davy (page 126) on anesthesia, Jeremy Bentham on sewage recycling, the London authorities on water supply, and the Manchester Clinic on tuberculosis. Outside of the medical field Roget served as secretary to Foreign Minister Earl Grey and as secretary of the Royal Society. He was among the founders of the Society for the Diffusion of Knowledge and the University of London.

In addition to inventing an artificial language, Roget devised a slide rule and rudimentary computer. He wrote numerous entries for the *Encyclopedia Brittanica,* technical articles on ants and bees, books on physiology, phrenology, and electricity. To this abbreviated summary of the multilingual Genevese's working activities add his pastimes of setting chess problems for the *London Illustrated News* and working on the *Thesaurus.*

This unique reference tool has enriched both English literature and several unscrupulous publishers who have pirated the original, which, in the authorized edition alone, has sold thus far more than 20,000,000 copies.

◆ The Driven continue to the traffic signal and there turn right into the Boulevard Jacques-Dalcroze. A hundred meters along, take another very sharp turn to the right into the ramp that is the Rue Théodore-de-Bèze. At the top on your right is the **Collège de Calvin [11],** Calvin's High School.

Walkers who trekked to the Zamenhof plaque return to **Rue Verdaine.** Walk up to the **Rue de la Vallée** and the headquarters of the Salvation Army.

The Salvation Army is in Geneva thanks to the persistence of Marshal Caroline Booth, the daughter of the Army's founder, Commander-in-Chief William Booth.

For eight long years in Geneva the Marshal waged her battle against prejudice and ignorance before winning in 1890 her sect's right to pursue here its evangelical, humanitarian mission.

Some two centuries earlier at this same corner, Geneva lost an even graver challenge to its religious integrity. In 1679 in a mansion here a Catholic Mass was said openly for the first time in the 130 years since the town had "temporarily" banned this rite by its edict of 1535. The occasion was the installation of one Monsieur Chauvigny in provisional quarters to represent France's Louis XIV as his "Résident" - not an ambassador but an overseer assigned to report on the Genevese and their intransigence.

Looking across Rue Verdaine to Number 12, note on its wall the **plaque [12]** marking this as the birthplace of the "Promoter of the Red Cross", **Henri Dunant.**

Dunant was a sincere, ultra-pious eccentric humanitarian. He vigorously espoused and promoted not only the concept of the Red Cross but many other causes including the International YMCA, the abolition of slavery, the founding of a Jewish homeland, international arbitration, an international library, and the use of Esperanto.

To earn his living Dunant became manager of a Swiss bank's agricultural project in France's Algeria. Confronted with a local political problem, Dunant carried it directly to the highest level — French Emperor Napoleon III who, at the moment, was conducting a war in Northern Italy.

On his arrival at Solferino Dunant found himself swept into one of history's bloodiest battles. He undertook to help the 40,000 sick and wounded of the day by organizing a group of civilian volunteers.

Durant's vivid account of his experience in *Souvenir of Solferino* inspired the organization in 1863 of the original International Committee of the Red Cross — the ICRC.

This committee of five Genevese in turn persuaded sixteen nations to accept in 1864 the First Geneva Convention under which each would respect the neutrality of civilians engaged in the care of soldiers wounded on the field of battle.

The Red Cross won universal acclaim and Dunant entered happily into a heady world of honors, royal receptions, and the espousal of still other worthy causes, all at the expense of his commercial affairs in Algeria.

The subsequent bankruptcy of the Crédit Genevois bank, in which his fellow-townsmen had invested heavily, left Dunant condemned and disgraced. In May 1867 he left Geneva, never to return.

For two decades the earnest humanitarian wandered about Europe, living on charity and dreams, writing, lecturing, and petitioning for every good work he heard about or could conceive.

Exhausted at last, ailing and impoverished, Dunant settled in 1887 in the remote village of Heiden, as far away from Geneva as he could go and still remain on Swiss soil.

A journalist's "discovery" of the reclusive Dunant in 1896 awakened widespread sympathy and interest. Renewed activities and appointments revived his energies and improved his fortunes with grants, donations, and purses, including in 1901 a half share in the first Nobel Prize for Peace.

In the years before his death in 1910 Dunant wrote his autobiography, replete with unflattering references to his former associates in Geneva. His bitter comments were fresh in the minds of the Town Council in 1919 when his nephew appealed for a memorial for Dunant's birthplace.

With the petition refused, the family financed from its own funds this plaque commemorating Henri as the "Promoter of the Red Cross".

Walkers now continue up the Rue de la Vallée into a Husband's Heaven — for the next half hour of your stroll your route will pass not a single shop window.

◆ Calvin's **"Collège" [11]** at the hilltop, where The Driven meet The Walkers again, is not a degree-awarding institution of higher education. In Europe a "collège" is a secondary school.

The higher-level institute here was the "Académie", founded simultaneously with the Collège. As the Académie expanded, it moved from this site to various locales. In 1872 a medical faculty was added, elevating the status of the Académie and making it the University of Geneva, housed in new buildings in the Bastions Park (page 110).

Calvin's classic institutions opened in 1559 with the inauguration of the central building. At the opening of the South Wing in 1560 Dean Haller of Zurich remarked that the new schools of Geneva "... were obviously for their own people since the local cost of living and the quality of the staff made it unlikely that anyone with a choice would ever enroll."

The Dean underestimated the attraction of Calvinistic discipline. Courses taught entirely in Latin and Greek throughout a schoolday of ten hours, six days a week, earned the Collège its reputation as a sort of Gallic Eton with an international accent.

Its graduates include most of Geneva's elite and a broad spectrum of foreigners ranging from Benjamin Franklin Bache, grandson of

America's first Ambassador to France, through Argentina's Jorge-Luis Borges, among the most respected of modern writers.

Also educated here was John André, born in London but a citizen of the Republic by virtue of his Genevese parents.

As an officer in the British Army, André first distinguished himself against the French in Canada in 1775. He later served as a special agent of the British forces attempting to suppress the American Revolution. The conspiracy with the traitorous General Benedict Arnold for the betrayal of the strategic fort high above the Hudson River — West Point — was thwarted by the capture of André with the plans in his boot.

In the face of strong British protestations, overridden by the personal order of General George Washington, Major André was hanged as a spy. The English showed their high regard for this citizen of Geneva by according him full military honors and entombing his body in Westminster Abbey.

Citizen-General Napoleon Bonaparte made 22 November 1797 a memorable date at this Collège on an official visit arranged to pass the time while his coach was being repaired.

Still the "Hero of the People" in 1797, Bonaparte turned his social call into a political triumph by reading aloud verses hastily improvised by student Louis Malan, followed by the General's assurance that "... France would never come to Geneva as masters". On 15 April 1798 — fewer than six months after this pledge — French troops occupied Geneva and forced upon it the treaty altering the "citizens of the Republic" into subjects of France.

◆ At the top of the ramped street in front of the Collège is the wide **Promenade de Saint-Antoine,** a former gun emplacement once renowned for its view across the countryside and up Lake Geneva.

The plain on this side of the approximately triangular Geneva hilltop — the only side not naturally protected by the steep banks of the two rivers — was cleared of all life and obstacles in 1535.

The Town Council, having just defied Savoy, ordered all those living outside the wall to raze their houses, barns, crops, and trees and to move inside the town. The resulting wide desert left no possibility of an invader's advancing unperceived.

As the most vulnerable sector of the ramparts, Saint Antoine remained guarded by the heaviest guns until 1799 when the town's French occupiers requisitioned the cannon for Napoleon's war. Once disencumbered of its artillery the terrace developed into a chic residential quarter.

◆ By the 1820s the house at 14 Promenade de Saint-Antoine was the private elementary school directed by Rodolphe Toepffer, the son of a popular Geneva painter. As a pastime the young teacher created the story-book format that has become a major medium of communications — the French "bande dessinée" or "bédé", called in America the "comic book".

Beginning with sprightly sketches illustrating his notes of walking tours with his students, Toepffer progressed to writing and drawing entire volumes of whimsical stories narrated in a series of from 600 to 1,000 interlocking scenes.

Toepffer, working alone to produce thousands of drawings, completed seven books. His friend Soret in Germany showed one of the handcrafted volumes to Johann Wolfgang von Goethe, the intellectual leader of the age.

Goethe's generous praise of the ingenious form and of the talent, wit, and inventiveness of its originator encouraged Toepffer to allow publication of an edition that quickly spread the popularity of his novel style.

◆ At 16 Promenade de Saint-Antoine there resided from 1826 to 1831 Rodolphe Kreutzer, the originator of the "French technique" for violin, the conductor of the music for a series of royal courts, and the composer of forty operas, and numerous ballets and concerti.

The name of Kreutzer is preserved today by a sonata he never performed and a book he never read.

Kreutzer in 1798 met the young Ludwig von Beethoven, who in 1803 dedicated to the violinist his impassioned *Sonata for Piano and Violin in A Major, Opus 63*. Kreutzer, however, disliked all of the music of Beethoven and never even attempted to play the work.

Many decades later Leo Tolstoy termed this same Beethoven *Opus 63* a "... musical call to the destruction of all morals..." The composition disturbed the Russian novelist to such a degree that he used the title *The Kreutzer Sonata* for his novella which condemned matrimony so bitterly that the Russian censor in 1890 banned the sale of the book.

◆ 18 Promenade de Saint-Antoine was the town house of Ninette Duval-Toepffer and her husband François, the generous patron of her artistic family (page 168).

Voyages en Zig-zag (1827)

Toepffer, inventor of the comic strip

Rodolphe Toepffer learned to draw from his father, a professional painter of scenes of local life. A congenital eye disorder obliged young Rodolphe to turn to literature and schoolmastering (page 47).

At holiday time Toepffer led his students on week-long outings – "Voyages en Zig-zag" – through the Alps, each duly noted in his journals with supplementary sketches. Favoring drawing as his medium of expression, Toepffer invented a method of presenting long stories by hundreds of sketches, each with a few lines of text – the original form of the French "bandes dessinées", referred to in English as the "comics".

In the many sketches composing each of his stories Toepffer was careful to keep his characters unmistakable in appearance and consistent in character. He drew each figure in good proportion and in attitudes that were loose and natural except when creating such still-current "comic-strip" conventions as people expressing surprise by falling backwards or by their hats flying off their heads.

Toepffer's simple plots are in the 1830s tradition of theatrical comedy, rife with mistaken identities and complex misunderstandings, but seasoned with satires of bureaucratic idiocy, exaggerated formalities, the mindless conformity of the military, and the vagaries of the latest technical advances, of which Toepffer was personally sceptical.

Monsieur Vieux-Bois (1827): A parody of the hapless lovelorn so popular in Romantic literature, the ardent Monsieur Vieux-Bois pursues his "Well-Beloved" (no other name supplied) to prevail over his suspicions, multiple mishaps, suicide attempts, and a rival to attain the Happy Ending.

Le Docteur Festus (1829): A satire on "travel for improvement" in which an accident-prone bachelor endures his misadventures with the militia, a bureaucrat, a hapless English couple, and an institute of astronomers. On his return home, he gathers his family to hear his account only to realize that he has nothing to say.

Monsieur Cryptogame (1830): A tale of the conflicting amours of a 35-year-old nature lover traveling for adventure and to elude his sticky fiancée. After catastrophes of Biblical and Voltairean proportions, Cryptogame marries a widow with eight awful children, leaving his frustrated fiancée to explode – literally – in rage.

Monsieur Crépin (1837): A commentary on educational methods wherein this father of eleven sons is badgered by his flighty wife to engage a series of eccentric tutors, each with a bizarre system of instruction. Faddish doctors and phrenologists aggravate matters until Crépin triumphs with simple methods predicated on common sense.

An earlier generation of Duvals had gone to Saint Petersburg in the early 1700s. There the family prospered as jewelers to the Russian Court through the reign of Empress Catherine the Great, allowing grandson François to return to Geneva in some luxury as a gentleman-artist and connoisseur.

◆ The **Place Franz Liszt** is the intersection of five streets at the south end of the Promenade. A wall **plaque [13]** marks the house where Liszt, the seminarian turned pianist and composer, lived with the Countess Marie d'Agoult during their Geneva idyll of 1835-1836.

> Marie d'Agoult at the age of 29 deserted her family and her fashionable Paris salon to flee with the 23-year-old Liszt. The society of Geneva at that epoch did not eagerly welcome even the most celebrated "irregular couples". Among their few friends was James Fazy, later the leader of Geneva's first liberal government. On the birth of the couple's first child in 1835, young Fazy joined in certifying in Geneva's civil register the customary misrepresentations concerning the details of such parentage.

> Another friend was Major August Pictet, son of Charles Pictet-de-Rochemont who represented Geneva at the Congress of Vienna (page 98). The young officer was Professor of Esthetics and Literature at the Académie, an authority on Indo-European languages, the inventor of the percussion shell for artillery, and the author of the *Encyclopedia on Science, Linguistics, and Philosophy.* "Monsieur l'Universel" was also a useful extra man.

> In this latter capacity Pictet accompanied on strolls through Geneva a Parisian intimate of the Liszt ménage, George Sand. The renowned novelist and feminist impressed the citizens less with her literary fame than by appearing in Geneva's streets in men's clothing and smoking either a pipe or one of her custom-made, opium-leaf-wrapped cigars.

Marie d'Agoult, Liszt, and their infant Blandine left Geneva in 1836 and had returned to Paris for the birth in 1837 of the second child, Cosima.

> Thirty-three years later this headstrong second daughter, by then married to conductor Hans von Bülow, arrived in Geneva to take up her life with Richard Wagner, first as his mistress, later as his wife, and finally as his musical executrice and the dictatorial controller of Wagner's artistic legacy (page 182).

After a dozen tempestuous years Agoult and Liszt separated. The saga of their relationship became, however, an enduring plot line in romantic literature.

George Sand recounted her version of their affair to Honoré de Balzac who wrote from it his "roman à clé" *Béatrix*. Balzac's work
inspired poet Charles Baudelaire to relate a similar tale in his only
novel, *Le Farfarlo*.

Marie d'Agoult herself, under her pen name of Daniel Stern,
published in 1846 her own embittered account in *Nélida*. And
George Sand, who in later years quarreled sharply with the Countess, avenged herself by caricaturing d'Agoult as the unattractive
Viscountess of Chailly in *Horace*, a major work among Sand's some
eighty novels.

◆ From Place Liszt turn left to cross the first of two
short bridges separated by a land island. In the park
on your right is the sculpture of two fast-striding
women approaching a point of collision.

The work by Koenig is a memorial of obscure relevance to the prolific and popular Swiss artist, Ferdinand Hodler (page 90).

◆ In number **5 Promenade du Pin [14]**, a mansion
bequeathed to Geneva by Madame Plantamour-Dio-
dati, are two superb reference centers: the 80,000-
volume **Library of Art and Archæology** and the
Museum of Art's **Archive of Engravings and Prints**
housing more than 300,000 works.

The art library with its remarkable range of research material in
many languages is open to all.

The "Cabinet des Estampes" presents small exhibits on specialized
themes in addition to maintaining row after row of cabinets from
which the staff will on request cull engravings, plates, and litho-
graphs of the masters, including Rembrandt, Piranesi, Dürer,
Hogarth, Daumier, and Picasso.

◆ The two short bridges forming this Promenade
cross the ancient, stone-lined moats of fortifications
now converted into sunken thoroughfares.

By the early 1800s the deep protective trenches had become useless
hazards, too costly to fill or to level or to bridge with the usual
arches of keyed stonework.

A way across the moats was finally devised with a new technique
imported from the United States whose numerous rivers required
light, shore-based bridges. Engineer Dufour in 1824 strung across
these trenches Switzerland's first cable suspension bridge.

The lacy span not only allowed the Genevese to traverse their abandoned ramparts but also inspired the longer, stouter structures that made railroading feasible through the mountains of Switzerland.

The problem of spanning the deep gorges between the Alps was solved by the suspension bridge for the Swiss rail network which requires, on average, two bridges for every mile of track.

◆ At the end of the Promenade du Pin on your right is an example of the last word in 1860 town houses. The **Petit Palais [15],** the Little Palace, is a 1968 addition to Geneva's growing complex of small museums and houses modern works collected by a Tunisian resident in Geneva, Oscar Ghez.

For an entry fee you may inspect first in the Victorian salons of the Palace and then in its several stone subcellars, reconstructed from the casemates of the old fortifications, various paintings by Chagall, Kisling, Foujita, Renoir, and Mané-Katz.

◆ Continue from the bridge on to the **Rue Saint-Victor.**

About 480 A.D. Princess Clotilde (page 62) and her sister Chrona built outside the walls of Burgundian Geneva their Priory of Saint Victor, hallowed by relics of the saint, a Roman soldier martyred in the Valais two centuries earlier.

The priory endured for more than a thousand years, free of any control by either Geneva's Councils or its bishops. The coveted secular post of managing prior passed in 1510 to a convivial 17-year-old, François Bonivard. Bonivard became involved in Geneva's political factions and joined Philibert Berthelier (page 129) and Besançon Hugues in opposing the town's annexation by Savoy.

Because they favored alliance with the Swiss Confederation — in German "Der Eidgenossens" — they were called in Geneva pâtois the "Eidguenots", eventually compacted into the "Huguenots".

The Savoyards considered political dealings with the Swiss as acts of treason and on several occasions trapped the leaders of the Huguenots, killing some, imprisoning others. In 1530 they caught Bonivard and chained him to a pillar in the dungeon of the lakeside Castle of Chillon. The Genevese navy freed him in 1536.

On Bonivard's return to Geneva young Calvin assigned him to establish the town library and to write a history.

Bonivard's vernacular style, however, offended the classical taste of the formally-educated Calvin who refused to allow publication of the manuscript. Bonivard's work stayed on the shelf for some 300 years.

At last, in 1816, Byron's narrative poem *The Prisoner of Chillon* aroused new interest in Bonivard. In 1831 his *Chronicles* were retrieved and published.

◆ Three blocks along on the Rue Saint-Victor turn left on the far side of the parkway street. Ahead you see the church with an unmistakable set of onion-shaped domes at the end of **Rue François Lefort.**

François Lefort was from a Genevese family of Scottish origin. After military service in several countries he took a commission in the Russian army. His help in suppressing a military mutiny brought Lefort to the attention of Peter the Great. The 18-year-old Tsar appreciated the Genevese's unusual attributes, particularly as a drinking companion but also as a counselor on social reform, women, mythology, pyrotechnics, seafaring, and western manners.

Tsar Peter advanced the 33-year-old Lefort rapidly, first to Lieutenant-General of the Army and then to Grand Admiral of his non-existent Fleet. To fill the gap Lefort built a shipyard on the river Don and there constructed Russia's 28-vessel navy eventually based in the Black Sea port of Azov.

Peter showed his gratitude by appointing Lefort to the posts of Viceroy of Novogorod and President of all his Councils. Lefort was also the First Ambassador Extraordinary for the management and diplomatic details of the Tsar's educational two-year tour of western Europe for observation, alliances, and the absorption of culture. Following this expedition's hasty return to Moscow to suppress another army mutiny, Lefort audaciously upbraided the Tsar for his eruptions of outrageous cruelty.

The chastened Peter, anxious to show "no hard feelings", built for his mentor a splendid palace—Lefortovo. For its inauguration Lefort laid on so strenuous a party that his celebratory exertions and old wounds sent him to his grave, at the age of 43.

However exalted a role Lefort played in Russia, he loyally retained his ties with Geneva. He corresponded with his brother for technical assistance in designing Peter's beloved fireworks, sponsored a series of Lefort nephews in careers in the Russian army and, in the famine year of 1694, succored the Republic with a cargo of Russian grain.

For the world Lefort is still the man who introduced into an isolated Russia western techniques, philosophy, and customs. In the Soviet Union the name of the Genevese remains as part of that of Peter's gift palace, Lefortovo, a place still referred to in news bulletins.

According to an official USSR encyclopedia, Lefortovo is a hospital; according to the *Journal de Genève*, Lefortovo is the headquarters of the KGB security service.

Lefort helped wipe out one cliché about Switzerland by attaining the loftiest naval rank extant and thus making a mockery of the hoary jokes about land-locked "Swiss Admirals".

Lefort, in the arts, is unique as the only Genevese yet to inspire a character in an opera.

"Admiral Lefort, Russian Ambassador to Holland", is a substantial bass role in Albert Lortzing's *The Tsar and The Carpenter*, a work ever popular in the German repertory since its Leipzig premiere in 1837.

◆ Connoisseurs of Oriental art consider that the **Baur Collection [16]** of Chinese and Japanese porcelains, jades, lacquers, and more is among the finest and the best-presented extant and simply "not to be missed".

The collection is in a converted mansion just off the Rue Lefort at the third street on your right, **Rue Munier-Romilly.**

◆ The **Russian Church [17]** at the head of Rue Lefort is a Byzantine jewel in Geneva's diadem of eclectic architecture. The interior, rich in icons and even more ornate, is worth a visit.

James Fazy, the leader who in the mid-1800s radically changed the style and look of Geneva, provided in his Constitution of 1847 both for religious freedom and for territorial expansion of the town.

To accomodate the worshipers of the newly-sanctioned sects, the Council made allotments to each congregation of 100 "toises" — about 700 square meters (a bit less than one-fifth of an acre) — of terrain that had recently been cleared of fortifications.

The Roman Catholics received the town's first grant in 1850. The Anglicans were next in 1851. The Jewish community got their temple ground in 1853, the Freemasons their plot in 1857, and the Russian "Orthodox Christians" this site in the re-opened suburbs in 1859.

The sponsor of the Russian Church was a longtime Geneva resident, the dowager Grand Duchess Anna Feodorovna Constantia, sister-in-law of Tsar Alexander I and, through her

Saxe-Coburg family, the aunt of both Queen Victoria and of Victoria's Consort, Prince Albert.

A less regal but still familiar name on the church register is that of the daughter of Dostoevsky, the author of *Crime and Punishment.* Sophie Dostoevsky, born in Geneva, was baptised here in 1868.

◆ The **Museum of Ancient Musical Instruments [18]** in the house across the street from the Russian Church owns well over three hundred examples of European, Oriental, Indian, Middle Eastern, and African instruments dating from the 1500s through the 1800s.

Most of the exhibits are in working order and are often played in specialized concerts. Inquire here both about the opening times and the current concert schedules.

◆ From the intersection of Rue Lefort and Rue Toepffer, turn left in to the latter towards the Old Town. On your right in a small square is the bust sculpted by Jean-Charles Toepffer of his father, Rodolphe, the innovator of the "comic book".

The appreciation of Toepffer's picture stories that began with Goethe's praise was shared after their publication by profiteers engaged in wide-spread pirating, counterfeiting, and imitation.

Toepffer's narrative-by-pictures technique influenced several more serious artists. Gustave Doré, the engraver of powerful illustrations of classic writings, was a frequent visitor to Geneva and acknowledged readily his artistic debt to Toepffer.

Pablo Picasso also studied Toepffer's art form. In his early days in Paris Picasso bartered his sketches for the "funnies" from American Sunday newspapers. Critics today discern the influence of such graphics even in works as serious as his mural "Guernica".

◆ At the dead end of Rue Toepffer turn left towards the **Rue Charles Galland,** which — simply by its name — earned millions of gold francs for Geneva.

Banker and art patron Galland willed Geneva more than Sfr 8,500,000 with the sole request that the town assign his name to one of its streets. Geneva lost no time in scrubbing from the town maps the name of the "Rue de l'Observatoire" to replace it with "Rue Charles Galland".

◆ The Galland bequest financed the building of the **Musée d'art et d'histoire [19],** the Museum of Art and History, reached by a turn to your right and the crossing of the short bridge to confront Geneva's largest gallery.

> This Beaux Arts hall was planned in 1910 to concentrate under one roof the best of Geneva's works of art and objects of interest, scattered at the time among many smaller collections.
>
> That commendable program collapsed under the sheer volume of high quality donations pouring in. Overwhelmed by its surfeit of treasures, Geneva has reverted to the use of specialized museums — natural history, ethnography, watches and clocks, history of science, prints and drawings, musical instruments, botany, regional history, manuscripts, ceramics, and the long list goes on.

Even with such dispersal there remains here display space for less than ten per cent of the museum's inventory. The permanent exhibits include archæology, armor, guns, a guillotine, sculpture, coins, porcelains, and six rooms from historic dwellings, as well as the galleries of paintings.

> The most cherished of the paintings is "La Pêche Miraculeuse", the Miracle of the Fishermen, depicting Christ walking on the waters — not of Galilee — but of Lake Geneva.
>
> This segment of an altarpiece from the Cathedral is the only signed work among the twenty existing paintings attributed to Conrad Witz, a seminal artist whose technique is said to be a hundred years ahead of his 1400s era.
>
> The painting collection includes works of Picasso, Monet, Sisley, Renoir, many Corots (page 152), several rooms of portraits by Geneva's Liotard (page 58) and candy-box-cover landscapes by Genevese and other Swiss Romantics.
>
> Their lush pastures and mountains contrast sharply with the cold, stark Swiss scenes in a room devoted to the turn-of-the-century works of Ferdinand Hodler.

In the museum's center court is a beguiling bronze fountain in the form of a chubby boy grappling with a small crocodile. This sculpture was given by King Ludwig I of Bavaria to the Irish beauty, Lola Montez.

> Lola, a pseudo-Spanish dancer, had by the age of 28 traveled everywhere and known everyone including Liszt, Dumas, and the Tsar Nicolas I before totally captivating the 60-year-old King Ludwig.
>
> During her fifteen-month management of Bavaria, Lola garnered from her enthralled Ludwig substantial royal assets and the titles of

the Canonness of the Order of Saint Theresa, Countess of Landsfeld, and Baroness of Rosenthal.

Lola dubbed Ludwig her "little crocodile", inspiring the king to
commission this fetching statue for his inamorata. When
Church and State combined in February 1848 to purge Munich
of the disruptive influence of Lola, she departed for Geneva in
regal dudgeon and included in her considerable baggage this
hefty bronze statue.

Disappointed by the failure of Ludwig to follow her as promised and
betrayed by the reports of August Papon, her perfidious "man of
confidence", Lola remained in Geneva for a few eventful months
(page 163), then left for London and America.

The crocodile work of art passed into the custody of a local industrialist. When he went bankrupt the bronze cherub and his cayman
playmate became town property.

After its display in the Bastions Park and, later, in the Botanical
Garden the fountain settled in the center of the out-of-the-way inner
court of the Museum of Art and History as a slighted memento of a
colorful visitor.

◆ Across Rue Charles Galland, well outside the
walls of the Museum, stands the most prestigious
sculpture of its collection, Henry Moore's larger-than-
life representation of "Reclining Figure With Arched
Leg".

Moore's work has occupied since 1974 the abandoned site of the last
of Geneva's series of celestial observatories.

Astronomer Jacques-André Mallet built the first in 1772 for purely
abstract study of the heavens. Within a few years practical use was
made of its readings for the celestial calibration of Geneva-made
chronometers for marine navigation.

In 1790 Marc Pictet offered the "Observatory Prize" for the most
accurate timepiece tested here. The trophy from Geneva was once
the most cherished award in the watchmaking industry.

Timepieces in great variety are on display in the town house Musée
de l'Horlogerie, the Clockwork Museum nearby.

◆ Proceed across Promenade de Saint-Antoine into
the Rue des Chaudronniers, the Boilermakers' Street.
The view from the head of the street is a striking
glimpse into the Old Town.

The street is named for the boilermakers and coppersmiths who practised their noisy craft in what was once a quarter remote from the rest of Geneva.

◆ **16 Chaudronniers on your left was formerly a hospital and, from 1757, the studio of Jean Liotard, portraitist to the European elite.**

Liotard's pastels and paintings may be seen in almost every museum in Europe. The widest exposure of his work was, however, on millions of American breakfast tables.

Liotard's full-length portrait of "La Belle Chocolatière", the Viennese serving girl who became the Countess of Liechtenstein, labeled every package of the cocoa sold by the non-Swiss Baker's Chocolate.

◆ **At the foot of the Chaudronniers, six roads into central Geneva meet to form the two-thousand-year-old market place, the Bourg-de-Four — a distortion of the Latin for the "Forum of the Burgundians".**

The Bourg-de-Four was the public meeting ground, not only by reason of the crossroads, but also because of the availability here of fresh water.

The Romans supplied water high on this hilltop by an aqueduct twenty kilometers (12 miles) long. Its two-foot-wide channel carried the flow over valleys and through hills from springs on the slopes of the Voiron Hills about 130 meters (400 feet) above the level of the Old Town.

The street to your left is the **Rue Etienne Dumont,** a name chosen not just to honor a most proper pastor and statesman but rather to replace, in a spasm of Grundyism, the explicit and sardonic but no longer relevant name of "Rue des Belles Filles", the Street of the Pretty Girls.

For examples of Old Geneva at its most picturesque, walk up Rue Etienne Dumont to number 20. Turn around and consider from there the street framing the view against the sky of the Cathedral's steeple and its North Tower, both recent reconstructions in the neo-Gothic style.

For a glimpse at Geneva's less-flaunted charms walk through the passageway into the courtyard of 20 Rue Etienne Dumont to appreciate the neat woodwork of its balconies.

Number 16 has a courtyard of similar style. In this house — as the wall plaque confirms — the Pellet family of printers worked with Geneva-resident Voltaire in the publication of both his own work and of later editions of his friend Denis Diderot's controversial *Encyclopédie*.

At 14 Etienne Dumont, General Dufour resided for twenty years. Among the visitors soliciting his highly regarded counsel was Queen Hortense of Holland, simultaneously Napoleon's step-daughter as Josephine's child and his sister-in-law by the dynastic marriage to brother Louis Bonaparte.

Hortense's son, Louis Napoleon, was among Dufour's students at the Swiss military academy. In 1836 the young Bonaparte lived with his mother in Geneva prior to his political rise to eminence as France's Emperor Napoleon III from 1852.

The narrow, picturesquely refurbished Rue Chausse-Coq on your left is a further example of civic tidying. The street's commerce today is devoted to stylish shops with its former impolite-in-French name sanitized by a manipulation of its fourth and final letters.

◆ On the left of The Driven is a small park with its statue of the wispy "Clémentine". Behind the shy girl in bronze is the down-sloping Rue Saint-Léger. On its facades are still posted the signs of the ancient inns.

Above number 19 note the "Cheval Noir", the Black Horse; at 21, "La Coquille", The Shell; and at 22, "La Pomme d'Or", the Golden Apple.

Walkers returning from Rue Etienne Dumont may look down the Rue Saint-Léger on their left.

Hugo de Senger, conductor of Geneva's symphony and director of the rebuilding of the Geneva opera (page 119), resided here in 1875 at the time of the visit of his friend Friederich Nietzsche.

Nietzsche fell so in love with a fellow guest, Mathilde Trampedach, that on the third day after their meeting he proposed matrimony. Mathilde refused the philosopher, however, as she preferred Senger whom she wed shortly after his divorce from his first wife.

◆ Continuing a clockwise look from Rue Saint-Léger around the Bourg-de-Four you see the Librairie Jullien. Before Jullien opened in 1839 this was the print shop of the *Journal de Genève*, still one of Europe's most esteemed "newspapers of opinion".

The *Journal's* first edition in 1826 printed an article by the young journalist James Fazy and set forth as its slogan the principle: "Let no man hold office without the consent of the people".

Two decades later the *Journal* — grown more conservative — disagreed sharply with the liberal Fazy. In 1846, when the same "people" of the paper's slogan propelled Fazy into office by armed revolt, then reaffirmed "the people's choice" by popular election, the *Journal* updated its declaration to the present principle, "We shall stand firm".

◆ In one of the houses farther to the right facing the Bourg-de-Four the French painter Gustave Courbet stayed after his escape from a Paris jail in 1873.

During France's civil strife of the "Commune" Courbet was said to have threatened to dynamite the Column to Napoleon in Paris' Place Vendôme. When the tall monument was in fact toppled, the French court accepted Courbet's foolish boast as grounds for sentencing the painter to jail and to the payment of the cost of a new column.

Courbet escaped to Geneva before moving on to Vevey where a production team turned out paintings for Courbet to sign and sell as originals to pay his debt. For repose from his autographing Courbet returned often to Geneva for the absinthe in which he drowned his sorrows. His sorrows, he noted ruefully, were very strong swimmers.

Continuing to the right towards the lake, you see the street is lined with former stables and granaries transformed into today's chic shops and studio apartments.

◆ Across the street, facing uphill, is the **Lutheran Church [20],** a town house of deliberately unchurchly appearance.

The Republic of Geneva in 1760 tolerated the construction of so alien a place of worship as long as it was for private use and was bereft of all ecclesiastical identification.

Calvin was so convinced of the absolute truth of his own creed that he saw no reason to confuse his flock with alternative dogma. Calvin's bias extended to the sect of Martin Luther, the German priest who had protested against Rome with his Ninety-Five Theses nailed to the Wittenberg church some twenty years before Calvin arrived in Geneva.

The theological technicalities that separated Calvin from Luther were never reconciled. By the 1700s, however, their respective ministers could agree on practical matters such as the care of refugees. When certain German states welcomed homeless Huguenots, Geneva in turn countenanced the presence here of German visitors including princes and diplomats with their chaplains accompanying them.

In the mid-1700s the Council authorized the building of a Lutheran temple provided, first, that it in no way resembled a church and, second, that its congregation looked after not only its own needy but also the hardship cases of all other non-Calvinist sects.

Today this still discreet Lutheran Church and its workshop provide a range of community activities. Three pastors conduct its services in English, French, German, Swedish, Danish, Norwegian, and Finnish.

To the right of the church, across Rue Verdaine, is the house in which Henri-François Guizot lived while studying in Geneva. From the Académie, Guizot went on to his Paris career as lawyer, professor of history and, in 1847 under Louis Philippe, as France's last royalist prime minister.

◆ The **Palais de Justice [21]**, Geneva's Courthouse, is in the Bourg-de-Four next to the police station.

On the site of this Palais the Catholic Convent of Saint Clara stood until the Reformation made it into an "hôpital", not only for the care of the sick but also as a shelter for the indigent and for refugees.

During the prosperous 1700s Geneva added the present facade and converted the building into a medical hospital with a chapel. With the end of the Napoleonic Wars and the return of an English colony, the chapel became Geneva's church for Anglican services.

Here in 1820 the English Protestant Mary Ann Birch married Catholic Alphonse Lamartine, the French Romantic poet and lover and eulogist of Geneva.

In 1848 Lamartine, in the Paris governed by Louis Philippe and Henri-François Guizot, existed in a curious mixture of sentimental poetry and moderately liberal politics. When the "February Revolution of 1848" overran the parliamentary monarchy and replaced the government of Henri-François Guizot with France's Second Republic, that Republic's first president was Alphonse Lamartine.

◆ Leave the Bourg-de-Four by way of its main thoroughfare, the **Rue de l'Hôtel-de-Ville,** Town Hall Street.

◆ At the point where you would enter the "oppidum" — the walled, hilltop town of the Romans — a thick stone portal for the town gate stood until 1843.

On the days when the door to 11 Hôtel-de-Ville is unlocked, the walkers may enter and see, about 15 meters (50 feet) down the passage, part of the old **Roman ramparts [22]**.

The massive stonework, 3 meters (10 feet) thick and 8 meters (25 feet) high, left by the Romans became the foundations of the Burgundian castle known variously as the Château Gondebaud or the Château Clôtilde.

The pious Clotilde came to Geneva after her Uncle Gondebaud had murdered her father and made the princess his ward. In 493 A.D. Gondebaud saved his throne of the First Burgundian Kingdom from the onslaughts of Clovis, King of the Franks (meaning "free" — from the Romans), by arranging for Clovis to marry Clotilde.

When Clotilde converted her conqueror-husband to her Christianity, Clovis shepherded most of western Europe into his new faith. For this great conversion, for her establishment of convents and churches, for her help to the poor, and for her forbearance in her personal tragedies, the good woman was canonised by Pope Pelagius II, thus establishing Geneva's claim to its own saint Clotilde.

Five hundred years after Princess Clotilde left Geneva and her quarrelsome family of the First Kingdom of Burgundy had accomplished its self-extinction, the Holy Roman Emperor Conrad II arrived in Geneva for his coronation as King of Jurassian Burgundy.

Among his attendants at the ceremonies in 1032 were the Counts of Savoy and of Geneva, new to the area but soon to become contenders against the bishop-princes appointed by Rome to rule over Geneva.

About 1100 the Counts of Geneva built upon the ancient foundation of Château Clotilde a castle of their own. In 1291 a fourth faction interested in governing Geneva — the recently organized and aroused "commune" of townsfolk — expelled the Counts of Geneva and in 1320 demolished their Château.

◆ The portal at the walls which dated from Roman times was removed in 1843 to make way for the mansion at 14 Hôtel-de-Ville.

The plaque [23] on its wall refers to Théodore Agrippa d'Aubigné, resident on this site in the early 1600s. This Protestant hero of the nine Wars of Religion was not only a soldier but also a poet, a leader of the Huguenots, and the confidant of France's Henri de Navarre.

Henri's conclusion that "... Paris is worth a Mass..." and consequent conversion to Catholicism led to his coronation in 1589 as Henri IV. Agrippa d'Aubigné remained staunchly Protestant and managed to persuade his patron to sign in 1598 the Edict of Nantes to protect political rights of French Huguenots.

The assassination of Henri IV in 1610 shattered all hope of religious tolerance in France. Agrippa d'Aubigné retired to Geneva for meditation, occasional conspiracy (page 75), and daily attendance at the Cathédrale de Saint-Pierre where he was entombed on his death in 1630.

The granddaughter of the piously Protestant Agrippa d'Aubigné was raised in the Catholic faith. After surviving a miserable childhood the Marquise de Maintenon served as governess at the Court of Versailles to the offspring of Madame de Montespan and Louis XIV.

The Sun King, greatly impressed by her loving care of his children and frustrated in his efforts to bed her short of marriage, wed La Maintenon morganatically in 1684 and tempered his life style in response to her strong-willed religious devotion.

In 1685 the influential Maintenon brought disaster to the Huguenots of France when she induced Louis to sign his Revocation of her grandfather's treasured Edict of Nantes.

◆ The ornate door at 12 Hôtel-de-Ville is embellished with a heavy knocker, cast in the style of Benevenuto Cellini.

This souvenir of Italy on the town house of collector Gustave Revilliod is only one among thousands of acquisitions culled on his travels in the mid-1800s.

When his gleanings overflowed this house Revilliod undertook the construction of a private museum, the "Ariana" (page 166), on the family estate to the north of Geneva.

◆ Above the door of 10 Hôtel-de-Ville a **plaque [24]** commemorates **Jean Capodistria,** who migrated from his native Corfu to Russia where he rose to the top of both the Tsarist military and foreign service. He retired to Geneva until 1827 when he went to newly-independent Greece as its first president.

Capodistria joined the Russian army in the 1790s and by 1812 had risen to a post on its General Staff. Moving on to diplomacy he represented Russia at the Congress of Vienna where he proved a great and useful friend of the delegation from Geneva.

From 1822 he concentrated all his efforts on the struggle of Greece for independence from Turkey. With the establishment of the Greek Republic, Capodistria served as its president from 1827 until his assassination in 1831.

◆ As you turn right at the next street, notice 8 Hôtel-de-Ville, a long Italianate mansion dating from 1620. This was the residence of the Turrettinis, a Protestant family from Lucca in Tuscany.

> This distinctive name threads its way through many aspects of Geneva's history where the descendents have made their marks in religion, teaching, law, and engineering (page 132).
>
> Field Marshal Joachim Murat of the Grand Army of France accompanied his brother-in-law, Napoleon Bonaparte, to Geneva in May 1800 en route to the Battle of Marengo. Murat billeted himself in the Turrettini house while Napoleon requisitioned the mansion of Madame de Saussure (page 83).

◆ The turn to the right takes you into the short Rue de la Taconnerie. In 5 Taconnerie lived Jean Huber, described by Goethe as "l'homme complet" — the all-around man.

> Huber was a literate man-of-the-world, soldier, linguist, artist, ornithologist, naturalist, poet, and musician. As a trusted friend of the Mozarts he looked after the musical family when their travels brought them to Geneva in 1766 (page 90).
>
> Huber's friend Voltaire called him a "genius" and allowed Huber to make the amusing sketches that today preserve glimpses of the philosopher in his daily routine.
>
> Huber's "découpages" — the scissoring of black paper into scenes and silhouettes — are so admired that he is sometimes credited with having invented the technique.
>
> François Huber, son of Jean, although blinded at 15, directed his wife's observations to compose his definitive treatise on the habits of bees. François was called "Huber of the Bees" to distinguish him from his son "Huber of the Ants".
>
> The son, Pierre Huber, grandson of Jean, was a physician , painter, and naturalist. His reports of the habits of ants included claims of feats so incredible that decades passed before later entomologists confirmed and accepted his findings.

◆ Over the door at 8 Taconnerie the keystone is engraved with the letters "IHS", the initials associated with the Reformation in their Latin context to represent "Iesus Hominum Salvator".

Actually, well before the Reformation, the bishop-princes ordained that all Geneva houses be marked with "IHΣ" representing the "IHΣU" as the name "Jesus" is spelled in Greek.

The presence of the Reformation mark on this house has led to the conjecture that this is where Calvin first lodged on his arrival in Geneva in 1536.

Calvin said that when he arrived in Geneva "... people were interested only in seeking and smashing idols. There was no Reformation".

Calvin restored order from this anarchy by drafting a code of laws and enforcing them rigorously, much to the disappointment of those urbane and independent townsfolks who had looked forward to more relaxed times in a Geneva free of its Catholic bishop and priests. Some such disenchanted citizens formed a dissident group called the "Libertins" — the origin of the still-pejorative term "libertine" — and succeeded in 1539 in forcing Calvin and Farel to leave Geneva (page 80).

◆ The house at **6 Taconnerie [25]** stands at the highest point of the Old Town and rises to an unusual seven stories in height, making it the "Most Lofty Residence in Geneva".

In 1854 Eugène Süe lived at 6 Taconnerie in the apartment with the balcony. The author of *The Mysteries of Paris* and *The Wandering Jew* was himself a wanderer at the age of 53 after his political exile from the France of Napoleon III.

Sharing the apartment was the 21-year-old Countess of Solms, née Marie Wyss-Bonaparte. This granddaughter of Lucien Bonaparte, brother of Napoleon I, was equally unwelcome in the Paris of Napoleon III, not for her political views but for her clamorous ways which embarrassed her imperial cousin and earned her the soubriquet of "Princesse Brouhaha", roughly "Princess Uproar".

The young beauty's affair with Süe ended in 1857 when the novelist died suddenly from food poisoning after a lunch with the Countess at the country house of James Fazy.

The irrepressible energumen went on to engage in 1860 both arms of Italy's new parliamentary monarchy. She captivated the parliamentary element by marrying the nation's first prime minister, Urbano Ratazzi. As to influencing the monarchy, Madame Bonaparte-Solms-Brouhaha-Ratazzi agitated Italy's King Victor Emmanuel II to the point that on his deathbed he sent up a fervent prayer for admission to Heaven only because, he said, in Hell he would certainly again encounter the Princesse Brouhaha.

From the end of the Taconnerie to the left is the Rue du Soleil Levant, the Street of the Rising Sun, named for a tavern that once stood here.

> Halfway down the street you see the sculpture **"Jeremiah" [26]** by "Rodo" the pseudonym of Auguste de Niederhausen, a student and admirer of Rodin.
>
> This representation of the Old Testament's unlucky prophet of doom moved one commentator to verse:
>
> > Don't you know why Jeremiah
> > All his life was sad and gloomy?
> > As a prophet he foresaw,
> > "Rodo will sculpt a statue to me".

◆ The **Auditoire [27]**, the Lecture Hall, on the right at the end of Taconnerie, was recently restored to its austere style of 1555, the year in which Calvin assigned this former chapel of the Catholic bishops to John Knox and the band of refugees driven from England and Scotland in the oppressive reign of Catholic "Bloody Mary" Tudor.

> John Knox led his two hundred Protestants first to Germany, then to Geneva. His congregation included such contemporary intellectuals as Thomas Bodley, later the founder of the Bodleian Library at Oxford, and Miles Coverdale, the publisher of the first popular Bible in English, derived from the classic German text of Martin Luther's translation.
>
> Coverdale directed here the preparation and publication of a more advanced English-language version, the Geneva Bible designed for household use.
>
> This innovative edition featured chapters, divided in turn into short verses, chapter-head summaries, marginal notes by Calvin, maps, woodcuts, and a simpler typeface — the refugee printers having abandoned in their flight their Gothics fonts — all in a manageable size at lower cost. The Geneva work is sometimes called the "Breeches Bible" since in its version of the Book of Genesis Adam and Eve sewed together "... fig leaves to make breeches..."
>
> The edition went through two hundred printings before the King James Version of 1611, incorporating many of the features of the Geneva Bible, replaced it.
>
> John Knox, a hardened veteran of bloody political wars in Scotland and of a year of slavery in the French galleys, supervised the production of the Geneva Bible and at the same time refined his own stern Presbyterian doctrine.

Although the irascible Knox was pampered in Geneva by his solici-
tous wife, an intimidated mother-in-law, and a devoted maidservant,
he composed here his *First Trumpet Blast Against the Monstruous
Regiment of Women.*

His mysogynist text did little to reconcile Knox with Scotland's new
monarch when in 1560 he returned from Geneva to confront the
charming and redoubtable 18-year-old Catholic Mary, Queen of
Scots.

◆ Bearing to the right around the Auditoire turn into
the Rue Farel. At the end of the street is number 8,
La Maison de la Bourse Française [28], the House of
the Huguenot Stipend Bank.

The trickle of religious refugees arriving in Geneva in the 1550s
increased to a steady flow with the start of the Wars of Religion.

The floodgates opened after Saint Bartholomew's Day 1572 when
the massacre of Protestants in France drove Huguenots to Geneva
by the thousands.

The town did its best to provide the refugees with food, housing, and
work but soon exhausted its charitable resources. The Venerable
Company of Pastors helped, however, by improvising a fund for
loans to finance refugees during their resettlement.

The honorable borrowers from the non-profit "bank" that Geneva
established in this building repaid their debts so conscientiously
that on liquidation of the fund centuries later in 1846 the assets
account showed a gratifying surplus.

The garret of 8 Rue Farel was divided by the painters Firmin
Massot and Adam Wolfgang Toepffer into their respective
homes and studios.

Massot was a one-man factory of portraiture. He turned out in his
lifetime 5,000 likenesses including — in a single fortnight — 28
heads of Empress Josephine. Toepffer, the father of Rodolphe and
Ninette (page 47), painted and drew scenes of Geneva life and rural
landscapes. In addition, the elder Toepffer tutored Empress Josephine in drawing and design and taught art at his son's private
school.

◆ Following Rue Farel around to your left you reach
the walk and wall above the grassy Terrasse
d'Agrippa d'Aubigné, planted in 1940 after the demolition of the 800-year-old Evêché, the Bishops' Palace.

The Reformation, although having no hierarchy of bishops, still left unchanged the name "Evêché" when it converted the former churchmen's stronghold into a prison complete with torture chamber and "oubliettes".

Three hundred years later, in 1840, the Genevese were in the forefront of prison reform. They tempered the lot of their convicted with the installation of heat and running water and by encouraging Bible classes conducted by volunteers like Henri Dunant.

While unsullied citizens deplored this "coddling", the social workers rejoiced in such symptoms of rehabilitation as the inmates' contribution of SFr 134 to aid the victims of the floods in Lyon in 1872.

The ungainly prison building was officially condemned in 1911. Actually, it remained in place for three more decades as the depot and auction house for property seized in foreclosures and bankruptcies.

◆ At the lower end of the terrace a turn to the left takes you by the house at number 7, the family residence of Pierre d'Airebaudouze du Cest, author of Geneva's *Chronicles of 1545*.

A stone set in the wall just inside the doorframe is engraved "PAB Cest" and the date 1606.

The narrow, cobbled Rue du Cloître, Cloister Street, at the next left took its name from the compound of church walks and gardens adjoining the Bishops' Palace and the Cathedral.

Across on your right the Rue des Barrières slopes sharply down through the heavy walls. This access path to the Old Town changes direction every few feet, not because of bad survey work but as a defence measure.

The zigzag form of the passage is called a "Chicane" — a devious way, as in "chicanery".

The changing angles prevent ascending invaders from getting a clear shot at defenders while the marksmen posted above pick off any enemy caught peeking around the bends.

◆ Emerging into the **Cour Saint-Pierre** you arrive at the center of the area assigned to Geneva's religious community until the Reformation.

Two thousand years ago at this crest of the "oppidum" a temple was dedicated to Apollo by the early Romans. Their Christian descendents replaced the pagan shrine about 400 A.D. with a basilica garnished with relics from Rome and attributed to Saint Peter.

In their turn the Burgundian successors, converted by King Clovis from Aryan to Roman Christianity, rebuilt the basilica as a church.

In the Middle Ages the bishops added their palace and cloister and in 1160 Geneva joined the many European centers caught up in new enthusiasm for religious structures and laid the foundations for its own Cathedral. As long as the Catholic Church dominated Geneva, the Cathedral, cloister, and palace were isolated and scrupulously maintained.

When the Reformers seized control in 1535, however, they opened the church premises to the citizens. Intensive public use and haphazard maintenance as an item of the town budget rather than from rich church funds led to the deterioration of the entire area.

By the 1700s the Cour Saint-Pierre was an agglomeration of ruins, shacks, and crumbling stonework. In those same early 1700s, however, Geneva began to reap the financial fruits of the seeds sown by John Calvin.

First, the "Calvinist ethic" of diligence and frugality provided a base for prosperity. Second, "Protestant banking" changed the earlier interpretations of the Bible which considered lending money at interest as usury.

Calvin's reading found lending acceptable as long as the loan imposed no oppression or hardship. While steadfastly condemning hoarding, price-fixing, usury, and improvidence, Calvin sanctioned commercial financing and removed a major obstacle to capital formation and modern banking.

The early 1700s were the latter years of the reign of Louis XIV, the French monarch who unintentionally made useful contributions to the economy of Geneva. The Sun King's "Revocation" order drove out of France the skilled and often affluent Huguenot migrants who provided Geneva with fresh resources. Then the heavy interest that Louis' regime paid on loans to support his extravagant court and wars enriched the lenders of Geneva. And finally the "Mississippi Company" was a windfall for the town's more agile speculators (page 77).

Geneva by the 1700s was prosperous and, with its increasing culture, interested in architecture. An era of vigorous construction began.

Private citizens bought land from the town's holdings on the hilltop thus enhancing the municipal finances and soon improving Geneva's appearance with well-designed, stately mansions.

◆ Number 5 on your right was the site of Geneva's first "Casino". Although the term evokes visions of Monte Carlo and Atlantic City, in Italian and as intended here by its donor François Bartholoni, "Casino" simply means "Little House".

> By extension Geneva's present day "Grand Casino" (page 147) means literally its "Large Little House".
>
> The Casino on the Cour Saint-Pierre began in 1825 as meeting rooms for discussion groups and a lecture hall for the serious Genevese of whom it has been said, "Give a Genevese a choice between Heaven and a lecture about Heaven and he will hesitate but for a moment..."
>
> In November 1835 the rooms of the Casino were used for the first Conservatory of Music, whose faculty included Franz Liszt.
>
> The Director was the Geneva-born musician Nathan Bloc — sometimes spelled Bloch — the promoter of the work of Hector Berlioz. Ernest Bloch, another Genevese composer (and no relation to Nathan) also directed the Conservatoire. He became in the 1920s the conductor of the Cleveland Symphony Orchestra.

◆ At 3 Cour Saint-Pierre a marble **plaque [29]** marks the library and laboratories where successive generations of the **Candolle family** worked as botanists.

> The study of herbs for their curative effects — for 5,000 years a sideline of medicine — was changed by the development of the microscope in the 1700s into the science of botany.
>
> Augustin-Pyramus de Candolle was a medical student in Paris when he became interested in the work of the pioneer botanist Linnaeus. Candolle worked on the cataloguing that Linnaeus had begun and devised a new approach to classification.
>
> The Candolle system reduced the contradictions that arose from the Biblical assumption that all existing plants remained unchanged since the Day of Creation.

Alphonse de Candolle, son of Augustin-Pyramus, continued the research and noted that ferns of some regions had developed more fully than similar species growing under different conditions.

> Ascribing the differences in their characteristics to the factor of time, Alphonse developed a plausible hypothesis of evolution in plant life. His book, the 1855 *Géographie Botanique*, caught the attention of the English naturalist, Charles Darwin.

The two scientists speculated in their correspondence on the possibility of a similar evolution affecting animal life across the ages. Darwin spelled out his theory of such changes in his *Origin of Species* published in 1859.

◆ 1 Cour Saint-Pierre was the Candolle residence. In its salons the gregarious, multilingual family introduced the sociable Genevese to a broad spectrum of international visitors.

The letters and journals of foreign guests visiting Geneva in the post-Napoleonic "27 years of peace" report warmly on the Candolle charm and hospitality.

Novelist Honoré de Balzac mentions his gratitude to Pyramus de Candolle for technical counsel concerning the mind-altering herb "flora Danica", an important element in Balzac's novel *Serafita*.

In addition to his scientific work and his role as unofficial host to half of Europe, Pyramus de Candolle planted the town's botanical garden, organized its first museum and reading rooms, edited the technical journal *La Bibliothèque Universelle*, and transformed the "Society of Physics and Natural History" from a polite dining club into a serious discussion group.

Acknowledging in his personal journal an innate talent for organization and management, Candolle noted his feat in arranging a shipment of household goods and books. So precisely did he plan the loading of forty mountain-wagons of personal effects that on the day that caravan arrived in Geneva Candolle had the contents off-loaded, sorted, and set in place, in all respects ready for use on the following morning.

◆ The mansion at 2 Cour Saint-Pierre was built in 1702 for Henri Duquesne, a Huguenot naval officer who inherited the prize money amassed by his father during Abraham Duquesne's career as commander of the Mediterranean fleet of Louis XIV.

The Catholic King refused to award the rank of Admiral to the Protestant mariner but did make Abraham Duquesne a marquis and exempted him from the terms of the Revocation of the Edict of Nantes.

Son Henri Duquesne, a rich and zealous Protestant, in his youth assembled in Holland ten ships to carry Dutch Calvinists on a colonizing mission to a supposedly deserted island in the Indian Ocean.

Shortly before setting sail Duquesne chanced to learn that his destination, the "Ile des Bourbons" — today Reunion Island — was far from uninhabited but had in fact been in the firm control of a

French garrison since 1712. Pessimistic about the prospects of evan-
gelizing both the natives and the French coast-guardsmen,
Duquesne cancelled the mission and returned to Lake Geneva.

◆ By a complete 180° turn you now come to face the
Cathédrale de Saint-Pierre [30].

◆ The towers and steeple of the Cathedral have been
pointed out on your way here as being Gothic in
architecture. The structure you now face is clearly
not Gothic but a facade of Greco-Roman columns.
The anomalous west front of the church dates from
its reconstruction in the 1700s.

In 1160 the initial concept of the Cathedral was Romanesque. The
architecture evolved, as in the case of so many other cathedrals
built in the transitional 1200s. As the structure's walls rose higher,
the design of the upper reaches melded into lighter, loftier Gothic
patterns.

However hybrid the Cathedral's style may be, its construction was
solid enough to serve through four centuries of Catholic care and a
further hundred and fifty years of hard use by the Calvinist congregation.

After five hundred years of so vast a weight of heaped-up stone
pressing down on the gravelly terrain of the hilltop, the Cathedral in
the 1600s developed a disquieting forward tilt.

The benign neglect of the next hundred years during which succeeding Town Councils pondered the problem of repairs did nothing
to straighten the plumb line.

The Council finally agreed to the restoration work at roughly the
same period when the world of art became enthralled by the
recently excavated remnants of ancient Pompeii. Architects and
builders everywhere swarmed to reproduce the styles of classic
Rome.

The Geneva Council of the 1750s welcomed for its Cathedral a
new facade of columns supporting a dome, modelled after the
Roman Pantheon which France's Louis XV copied in his fashionable Church of Saint Genevieve in Paris.

When the fever for antique architecture subsided, the disparity
between the Cathedral's Greco-Roman front and its Gothic corpus
required fresh rationalizations. Its apologists changed tack, pointing
out how nicely the more formal columns harmonized with the
facades of the new mansions in the Cour.

If architectural purists have reason to be confused by the Cathedral,
seekers of ecclesiastical consistency may be equally startled by the

Catholic cardinals' hats capping the high wall of the adjoining Protestant chapel.

Actually, the smaller temple attached to the south side of the Cathedral is a remarkable conjunction of not two but three religions.

◆ The **Chapel of the Maccabees [31]** was built by and
for a Catholic cardinal, is named for a family of Jewish heroes, and is dedicated to an early Protestant
martyr.

Jean de Brogny, the Catholic cleric who ordered the chapel in 1405
for the use of the priests and to serve as his own tomb, was a pro-
tégé of Robert, the last Count of Geneva.

In 1378 the Catholic Church had split in the "Great Schism" between
one hierarchy in Rome and a strong opposing faction in the city of
Avignon. The French contingent elected Robert of Geneva as its
Pope Clement VII.

The contending parties in the "Great Schism" continued with
parallel popes until 1414 when they met in the Council of Constance. Brogny presided over the four-year-long meeting
which at last agreed to a single pope to be seated in Rome.

The same Council of Constance, however, unwittingly opened
another breach in the universal church when it tried and
burned for heresy an early reformer, the protesting Czechoslo-
vak, John Hus.

Following Brogny's death in Rome in 1425 and his reburial in
this chapel, Pope Felix V sent to Geneva religious relics pur-
porting to have been derived from the Maccabees.

The Jewish family of Judas Maccabee led the revolt against the
pagan Antiochus IV of Syria in 167 B.C. and drove out of Jerusalem
the Greek priests who had desecrated the temple of Solomon. The
Maccabees purified and restored the sacred premises and then celebrated there the first "Feast of Channukah", the year-end Jewish
holiday concurrent with the Christmas season and today an occasion for exchanging seasonal gifts.

In accepting for Geneva the holy relics sent from Rome, the bishop-
prince placed them near Brogny's tomb and named the priest's private temple the Chapel of the Maccabees.

The relics and bodies and all of the chapel's ornamentation disappeared with the Reformation which in due course assigned the
building first to refugees from Italy and then to the Académie as
supplementary classrooms. Later and harder use as a granary during the Wars of Religion and as an arsenal for the storage of a hundred tons of gunpowder in the "Troubles of 1781" further deteriorated the deconsecrated chapel.

By the middle of the 1800s its advanced state of decay made demolition seem inevitable until the prestigious French architect Viollet-le-Duc encouraged its restoration as a work of art. Geneva launched an eleventh-hour campaign and raised the funds to salvage the venerable structure.

As restored in 1898 the chapel built to be the tomb of the Catholic Cardinal de Brogny retained the Jewish name of the Maccabees. Geneva then added the element of a third religion by dedicating the edifice to the Protestant martyr, burned by Brogny's order, John Hus.

◆ The interior of the Cathedral is remarkable for its clean, spare lines and comparatively uncluttered look. Such was not the case during the Catholic regime when the Cathedral accumulated over the centuries considerable elaborate ornamentation.

The rich impedimenta disappeared in 1535 as departing priests salvaging holy relics vied with zealous Protestants casting down graven images and icons. Souvenir hunters seized the occasion to loot the hangings, altar pieces, communion plate, and even the church's twenty-three altars, some of which reappeared in private homes as ponderous washstands.

Under Calvin's stern regime religious services were held several times each day. Compulsory attendance as mandated by law and enforced by the police guaranteed an overflowing congregation. To accomodate the increasing number of faithful as new refugees arrived, the town built a series of galleries above the main floor of the Cathedral.

The size of the audience was more a tribute to the discipline of the worshipers and the efficiency of the constabulary than to the eloquence of the pastors. No matter how pertinent and appealing the preaching might be, few in the Cathedral could make out his words let alone appreciate the subtleties of the text.

The confusion of pâtois, dialects, and accents of the preachers from various regions of France was compounded by the poor acoustics, the wailing of children, and the noise of dogs whose barking reached such volume that in 1600 a rule forbade the presence of pets at services.

In addition to its primary function as a house of worship the Cathedral has served as the town meeting hall and chamber for the Grand Council, a "Temple of Law" under the French "Cult of Reason" and as an improvised hockey field for neighborhood youth until 1700 when they were officially ordered to cease and desist.

Preservation and restoration work on the Cathedral has been going on for enough centuries to make the premises seem a permanent worksite. A major rehabilitation begun in 1973 had by 1976 turned up so many unexpected archaeological finds that the program of excavation and study was extended indefinitely.

Among the enlarged objectives is the conversion of a large crypt beneath the Cathedral into a subterranean museum covering the 2,000-year history of the site.

If your concern for nave, apse, narthex, and transept extends beyond crossword puzzle solutions and you are visiting in July or August, consult the multilingual, well-informed attendant present during the afternoon hours.

For the more casual visitor objects of visual interest are frankly limited. Under the rigorous sumptuary laws neither the Cathedral nor indeed any Reformed Church is rich in ornamentation. The original Romanesque columns supporting the arches are cited by scholars for their decorated capitals depicting some 210 mystical symbols and scenes from the Old and New Testaments.

The choir stalls are also fine examples of pre-Reformation art with grotesque figures carved beneath the wooden seats which are hinged to bring the figures into view.

The sole effigy allowed since the Reformers removed earlier images and likenesses is the white, life-size statue of the Duke of Rohan watching over his ducal crown and red marble tomb.

Rohan, the successor of Henri of Navarre (page 62) as the leader of the Huguenots, died in battle in 1635 at Rheinfelden and was brought here for burial.

His tomb and all others in the Cathedral were vandalized in the 1794 episode of the "Petite Révolution" (page 13), an emotional outburst against all things deemed "aristocratic". The tomb of Rohan was rebuilt in 1890.

After the desecration of the tomb of Agrippa d'Aubigné (page 63), who conspired with Rohan in an aborted coup against Cardinal Richelieu of France in 1620, the old Protestant warrior was memorialized by a plaque in the south wall of the Cathedral. Memorials of Princesse Emilie of Nassau (page 42), entombed here alongside her daughter, Maria Belgia, are now limited to wall plaques on the north side of the nave.

The extent of the refurbishment of the stripped Cathedral by the Reformers seems to have been the addition of "Calvin's Chair", a carved wooden seat preserved near the north wall and the steps to the pulpit. The sign designating the chair has for years provided the date "1535" in contradiction to the fact of Calvin's first arrival in Geneva in July 1536.

◆ Agile and adventurous visitors who regularly scale pyramids, campanile, and lookout points will find the Cathedral's North Tower irresistible, easy and, panoramically speaking, well worth the effort.

Climbers may appreciate not only the long view but also a closeup examination of the huge bells dating back to the 1400s.

The melodies produced by the carillon every hour on the hour are changed eleven times in the course of the year. The efficient but mundane electronic control that now operates the system replaced an ingenious, wide, wooden drum which rotated and made its projecting pegs strike the clapper levers like an oversized Swiss music box.

The old control drum is preserved in the Museum of the History of Science (page 157).

The electronic operation of the bells can be overridden to allow manual keyboard performances by a carilloneur. The sound of these bells on holidays and for visits of dignitaries adds a uniquely Genevese tone to such occasions.

The neo-Gothic of the Cathedral's steeple and accessible tower is in contrast to the late-Gothic style in which the South Tower was rebuilt after the fire of 1430.

For early detection of Geneva's frequent and disastrous fires of yore, the town posted a 24-hour firewatch in the South Tower.

Communication from towertop to ground was through a five-foot-long megaphone. In 1911 the never-precipitate Genevese authorities deemed the telephone sufficiently reliable to replace the horn which is, however, kept handy in the Town Museum (page 79) just in case...

◆ As you are leaving the Cathedral you should pause for a look inside the Chapel of the Maccabees. Its small door is almost hidden at the south side of the Cathedral portal.

The chapel is used today for weddings, baptisms, and similar smaller ceremonies. The stained glass windows omit any references to either the Maccabees or to John Hus but are a source of local satisfaction in their distant resemblance to those of the illustrious Sainte-Chapelle of Paris.

◆ On emerging from the Cathedral note at the lower end of Cour Saint-Pierre another substantial town-house, number 9. The mansion was designed in 1721 by the architect Jean-François Blondel for the banker Gédeon Mallet, one of the several Genevese who profited from their investments in France.

As the art of banking matured in the late 1600s, developing new institutions like the Bank of England, 1694, and the London Stock Exchange, 1698, Geneva's adaptable financiers were centrally situated to prosper in due proportion.

The ravenous appetite for cash of the bankers' client of the century, Louis XIV, seemed insatiable. To look after his financing the King in 1710 appointed as Director of France's Royal Bank the ingenious Scottish goldsmith, John Law.

Among King Louis' most solid assets were the vast territories in North America which the explorer Robert La Salle had claimed for France in 1682 and loyally named "Louisiana". Three decades later Law sought to finance the development of these holdings with his "Mississippi Scheme", one of the first ventures in corporate finance.

When the capitalization of the promising project grew into the ill-famed "Mississippi Bubble" of speculation and the perfidy of local managers brought the company to bankruptcy in 1720, history's first stock market crash ruined thousands of hapless plungers.

Many of Geneva's prudent and better-informed investors, however, sold out before the collapse. Mallet used part of his profits to build his family this town house and to construct on a high cliff overlooking the Rhone the country villa, "Les Délices", which Voltaire acquired in 1755.

The mansion which became famous then as Voltaire's residence in Geneva is now the principal museum, research center, and archive dedicated to the French philosopher.

◆ The Mallet town house served from 1919 to 1921 as the office of the League of Red Cross Societies, organized after World War I by the American banker, Henry P. Davison.

The League coordinates the activities of the national societies − the independent American Red Cross, the British Red Cross and the others which in peacetime help the victims of flood, fire, earthquake, and other disasters.

This relief work of the League members is not the same as the wartime work on behalf of the wounded and captured combatants. In a war the opposing factions will accept the good offices of only a truly disinterested and proven neutral — i.e. the Swiss. Thus the official organization for overseeing the observance of the four Geneva Conventions is the all-Swiss group confusingly named the "International Committee of the Red Cross".

The ICRC and the separate but complementary League of Red Cross Societies cooperate closely enough for them to receive jointly in 1963 the Nobel Prize for Peace.

◆ From Cour Saint-Pierre go into the short Rue Balaban directly opposite the broad steps of the Cathedral. A few steps along is another open area, small but with a large fountain, the **Puits de Saint-Pierre [32],** the Wells of Saint Peter.

On your right, stone steps lead to a Belgian-block-paved incline, the **Rue du Perron,** named for a Cardinal of Evreux.

For centuries the only access from the Lower Streets to the enclosed Cathedral compound was up this steep path lined with stands hawking religious objects to the faithful.

Many transformations later, this busy passage is still dedicated to shopping but with a less aggressive sales force discreetly offering a choice of devilish temptations out of elegant boutiques and galleries.

Visible at the foot of the slope is a large "brutal" sculpture named "5", a tantalizingly cryptic title until demystified by the explanation that the work stands opposite Number 5 Rue du Perron.

In the 1740s the Genevese family of the mother of the French Revolutionary, Jean-Paul Marat, lived on the Perron.

Marat was born in Boudry on the Lake of Neuchâtel. In his boyhood his family frequently visited relatives in Geneva where the children played in the Rue du Perron. His brother Jean Marat remained here as a watchmaker in the Place Molard. The more ambitious Jean-Paul, however, left for England and France and a career as a doctor, hydraulic engineer, publisher, and — until knife-wielding Charlotte Corday assassinated him in his bathtub — the intellectual leader of the French Revolution.

Above the art gallery to the right on the Perron stairs is set high up on the building's edge an odd window installed on a bias. It opens into a room on the rear of 3 Cour Saint-Pierre, the workshop of A.-P. de Candolle.

The botanist was, in addition to his other activities, a conscientious town councilor. He had this window installed so that he could keep watch from his work-table over any activity of interest in front of the Town Hall, a hundred meters away.

In the street up the slope from the Wells of Saint Peter is the round tower of the **Maison Tavel [33]**, a house dating back to the 1300s, the oldest in Geneva in continuous existence and now rebuilt as the Museum of the Town of Geneva.

In addition to rooms full of mementos of Geneva and a three-dimensional model of the town, the Museum has an impressive cistern, 10 meters (33 feet) across, built centuries ago in the back court to hold both catchwater and the river water pumped up to supply the Old Town when its needs increased sharply with the new construction of the 1700s.

◆ Above the ornamented wellhead look high up on the wall angle over the Perron for the wrought iron holder for a "pot au feu", literally a "bucket of fire", more specifically, of burning pitch that once served to light this junction of four streets.

Jean Calvin passed here regularly on his way from the Cathedral to his home on Rue des Chanoines, the Street of the Canons, now **Rue Calvin.**

On the wall of 17 Rue Calvin a plaque marks the house of lawyer Pierre Fatio. His concern for the rights of all Genevese set off in 1707 the first of five civil outbreaks that rent Geneva over the ensuing nine decades of the 1700s.

Variously referred to as "Les Révoltes", "Les Troubles", "Les prises d'armes", or simply "La Petite Révolution" Geneva's civil strife began after the conservative "Ancien Régime" had governed for nearly a hundred years with steadily diminishing regard for the rights of later arrivals and residents to a vote and to representation on the Councils.

When the politically deprived met in 1707 to claim their classic rights, Geneva's Little Council burned their petitions. Fatio, himself one of the privileged "Messieurs-du-Haut", defended the petitioners. The Council called in troops from Bern to suppress the protests, then tortured, condemned, and executed Pierre Fatio and his fellow "provocateurs" on the premise that the "...health of the state is more important than due process of law".

The harsh repression and a few amendments to Geneva's Constitution restored order for a quarter of a century. In 1734 a former ally of Fatio, Jacques Micheli-du-Crest, protested new heavy taxes of the people levied to pay for more fortifications. His trials precipitated the second round of violence and another call for alien troops to keep the "Ancien Régime" in power.

◆ The Maison Buisson at 13 Rue Calvin was in 1707 an example of daring extravagance as the first townhouse in Geneva with a courtyard broad enough to allow the entry of a horse and carriage.

Today the courtyard provides precious Old Town parking space for civil servants.

◆ 11 Rue Calvin bears the **plaque [34]** identifying the site where **Jean Calvin** and his family resided from 1541.

◆ The modest structure in which the Reformer and his family lived in no way resembled the present mansion in the Louis XIV style, now used by the Office of Education.

Calvin's career in Geneva was in two parts. On his first arrival in 1536 he succumbed to the arguments of Guillaume Farel and undertook the organization of the new religious movement. He remained for fewer than three years as the "Libertins" forced the departure of both Calvin and Farel before the Easter services of 1539.

The two Reformers went from Geneva to Strasbourg. There, in 1540, Farel officiated at the marriage of Calvin to the widow Idelette de Bure.

In 1541 the frantic pleas of the Town Council for Calvin to return to Geneva to save the disoriented populace from sliding back into Catholicism persuaded the Reformer to make one further attempt. On 13 September 1541 Jean Calvin arrived with his two step-daughters and his wife at the small house where their son Jacques was born on 28 July 1542.

The death of Calvin's wife in March 1549 added the management of the family to the Reformer's already overwhelming religious and governmental responsibilities. The accumulated pressures led to Calvin's long illness and, in 1564, his death from overwork and exhaustion at age 54. Calvin was buried as he ordained with neither ceremony nor marker to provide a shrine for future pilgrims.

In response to the yearnings of his followers for some tangible relic of the Great Reformer, the *Répertoire des Personalités* published by the Plainpalais Cemetery makes reference to Grave 83-I, marked by a plain stone about the size of a shoebox and roughly inscribed "J.C."

The humble house at 11 Rue Calvin passed to Théodore de Bèze, Calvin's successor as leader of the Reformation.

Bèze was a French aristocrat, respected as an intellectual, poet, dramatist, and an authority on the Bible.

More flexible than Calvin, Bèze guided the fragile new faith and the vulnerable Republic through their forty critical formative years: – the nine Wars of Religion, the massacre of the Huguenots on Saint Bartholomew's Day and a heavy influx of refugees, the attacks by neighboring Savoy, the encouraging Edict of Nantes, the incursions of François de Sales and his Jesuits of the Counter-Reformation, and Geneva's astonishing Escalade Victory (page 121).

After Bèze's death in 1605 the house at 11 Rue Calvin deteriorated. With its demolition in 1707 to make room for the present fine mansion, even the memories soon faded of the whilom modest residence of Calvin and Bèze.

The tenant of this town house in the early 1800s was a newcomer to Geneva but quite aware of the significance of 11 Rue Calvin to the Protestant faith. This later resident was Catholic Abbé Vuarin, assigned to Geneva under the protection of Napoleon I, the town's nominal Emperor, when Bonaparte reopened the churches of France as part of his 1801 Concordat with Pope Pius VII.

The aggressive Vuarin arrived fully intent on forcing the capital of the Reformation to accept his militant revival of the Catholic Church in Geneva.

The Abbé's strategy included the installation in Geneva of a chapter of the "Little Sisters of the Poor", the Catholic service order founded by Vincent de Paul. The order flourished in Napoleon's era under its Vatican-appointed patronne, the Emperor's pious, peasant mother, Letitia Bonaparte. The first contingent of the "Little Sisters" ordered to Geneva was dispatched from the town of Noyon in Picardy – Calvin's own birthplace.

The mansion at 11 Rue Calvin was the residence of Abbé Vuarin from 1806 until his death in 1834 when it became the home and headquarters for the "Little Sisters of the Poor".

More than one Protestant pilgrim seeking at Calvin's old address some vestige of the pioneers of the Reformation were startled by the sight here of the severe coiffes and robes of the sisters of the Catholic order.

◆ 9 Rue Calvin was the town house of Baron Necker, Minister of Finance for France's King Louis XVI. Necker's daughter, Madame Germaine de Staël animated here and at their family Château de Coppet the salon described by the admiring novelist Stendhal as "The Headquarters of European Opinion".

Plain, energetic, imaginative Germaine de Staël knew everyone, traveled extensively, loved generously. She wrote novels and political analyses, talked incessantly, and organized in Geneva and at Coppet the most international, scandalous, and influential social gatherings of the early 1800s.

◆ At the end of Rue Calvin turn left into the Rue de la Pelisserie, the Street of the Fur Trade.

◆ **16 Pelisserie [35]** was the home during the winter of 1849-50 of Mary Ann Evans, author of *Silas Marner* and *Middlemarch* under her pen name of **George Eliot.**

Eliot in 1849 traveled through Europe to recover from the blow of her father's death. Attracted to Geneva by her admiration for the works of Rousseau she settled for a lengthy stay with the family of D'Albert-Durade. Although D'Albert-Durade had suffered as a child an injury that left him a dwarf he did not let his four-foot stature deter him from becoming a theologian, an accomplished musician, the director of the "Athénée" (page 101), a portraitist who painted the definitive likeness of Eliot, and a linguist who in the 1870s translated into French her novels *Adam Bede* and *Mill On The Floss.*

Eliot's recollections of her winter here provided the Geneva background for her 1859 novelette, *The Lifted Veil.*

The second **plaque [35]** on the wall at 16 Pelisserie recalls the **"Société Economique",** the group of astute Genevese who salvaged three precious intellectual assets from France's annexation of the Republic in 1798. Marc Pictet's negotiation of the treaty terms reserved to local leaders the continuing control over the town's churches, hospital, and schools.

◆ At the end of the short Pelisserie, turn right into **Grand'Rue,** Main Street, and pause at the Maison Pictet, 15 Grand'Rue, to appreciate the carved door, a masterpiece of 1600s wood sculpture.

11 Grand'Rue is still called the **Maison du Résident de France [36],** even though Geneva has had no French "Résident" for nearly two hundred years.

This mansion in the Louis XIV style was finished in 1743 as the permanent headquarters of the representatives assigned by the French monarchy to monitor the behavior of this otherwise independent Republic (page 44).

Louis XIV initiated this unwelcome control with his dispatch of his first Résident in 1679. As succeeding envoys grew in self-importance they demanded housing more prestigious than Geneva had originally made available. The town acquiesced by constructing this elaborate town house. The Council then suggested to the French court that some sort of rent payment might be in order.

To this impudent proposal the French Foreign Minister replied that "..Geneva will certainly find ample repayment in their knowledge of the pleasure they have given the King..."

The post of "Résident" and of his successor, the French prefect during the occupation, ended in 1813. The spacious "Maison" was converted in 1816 under Pyramus de Candolle into the laboratories of the Society of Physics and Natural History, supplemented by one of Europe's first museums and by Geneva's "Reading Society", continuing today with its original stacks intact.

◆ The fountain at the next corner marks the **Place du Grand-Mézel [37],** the name derived from the Latin "macellum" meaning "slaughterhouse" and describing the main business of the area in the 1300s.

From the foot of Grand-Mézel you can see downhill the facade of 24 Rue de la Cité, the home of Horace-Bénédict Saussure. The name of Saussure, one of the last "Universal Scientists" in the tradition of Samuel Johnson and Benjamin Franklin, has long been associated with the conquest of Mont Blanc.

Actually Saussure was not the first man to reach the top of Europe's highest peak. Long fascinated with the mountain in his geological explorations, Saussure offered a cash prize for the first climb. The guide Jacques Balmat collected the award for his ascent in 1786 and in 1787 led Saussure's own ambitious scientific expedition to the summit.

In Saussure's vivid account of his purposeful climb the human drama overwhelmed the technical substance. His book aroused more public interest in mountains and travel and in the town of Geneva than it did in his meteorological and geological observations.

Saussure's mansion was requisitioned in 1800, a year after his death, as the personal quarters for Napoleon on a second visit to Geneva (page 46). In the course of his three-day sojourn Bonaparte contemplated eventual retirement to Geneva's Villa Beaulieu, assessed the increasing discontent of his reluctant subjects, and completed his plans for the forthcoming Battle of Marengo.

Six women from Geneva's album

470

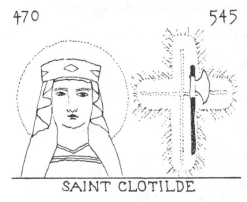

SAINT CLOTILDE

545 **Princess Clotilde** was the grand-daughter of the Burgundian king to whom the Romans in 470 A.D. ceded Geneva and Savoy. Raised piously in Geneva, Clotilde married Clovis, King of the Franks, and converted him and his empire to Christianity. Clotilde helped Clovis establish Paris on the ruins of the Roman city of Lutetia, then devoted herself to the spread of her religion. The Roman church elevated her to sainthood in recognition of her piety and achievements (page 62).

Germaine Necker-de Staël was the daughter of the Genevese banker who for many years managed the finances of France. Germaine at an early age abandoned Baron de Staël for a life of society, romance, and the political intrigues for which Napoleon exiled the hyperactive heiress from Paris. With her native Geneva as the new base for her travels, writings, and amours, she reigned at the family's Château de Coppet over the most animated salon of the era (page 81).

1765

CHÂTEAU DE COPPET

1817

GERMAINE NECKER-de STÄEL

1797

MARY WOLLSTONECROFT-SHELLEY

1851 **Mary Wollstonecroft-Shelley,** the daughter of a famed English feminist, ran off to Switzerland at 16 with poet Percy Byssche Shelley. In 1816 they came with their child to Geneva to meet the poet Byron. Here Mary wrote her Gothic novel *Frankenstein* in which The Monster escapes capture by agilely scaling Mont Salève. Mary married Shelley in 1817. After his accidental death in Italy in 1822, she worked quietly in London, returning to Geneva in 1840 for a brief, nostalgic visit (page 31).

1818   1861

LOLA MONTEZ

Lola Montez was born Eliza Gilbert in Ireland and grew up in India, Scotland, and Paris. The multilingual beauty became the "Spanish dancer Montez" and enjoyed a "succès de scandale" and a series of famous and infamous lovers before enthralling the King of Bavaria. Expelled eventually from Munich Lola waited in Geneva for Ludwig I to join her. Ditched but undaunted, she went on to new loves and careers before espousing evangelism and dying in rags in New York City at 43 (page 56).

George Eliot was born Mary Ann Evans in Warwickshire. In her late 20s she visited Geneva and remained through the winter of 1849-1850. On her return to London she edited the *Westminster Review*, lived with fellow editor George Henry Lewes, and wrote the great works for which Herbert Spencer hailed her as "... the female Shakespeare". In a visit to Geneva in 1860 she arranged for the translation into French of several of her novels by D'Albert-Durade, director of the Athenée (page 82).

1819   1880

GEORGE ELIOT

1819   1899

CARLOTTA GRISI

Carlotta Grisi, hailed as one of the three finest classical dancers of all time, was trained at La Scala. Her years of triumph throughout Europe as a prima ballerina ended when an affair with a Polish prince left her with a child. Retiring to Geneva, Grisi bought a mansion overlooking the Rhone and there raised her daughter, passed her days in genteel anonymity and, on her death, was buried nearby in the Châtelaine Cemetery (page 114).

◆ The Driven pass by the Grand-Mézel to turn sharp left down the narrow Rue de la Tertasse. At the foot of the ramp drive ahead into the counter-clockwise traffic flow on the **Place Neuve,** passing on your right the Rath Museum, the Grand Théâtre, and the Music Conservatory to arrive before the gates of the **Parc des Bastions.**

◆ If you are among The Driven aboard certain tour buses in summer, you may debark here for a visit afoot to the park and its Reformation Monument (page 105).

◆ If you are not in a position to leave your vehicle, continue the tour of The Driven by turning to page 115.

Walkers at the Place du Grand-Mézel turn left up the residential street which six centuries ago housed Geneva's bordellos. On the trade's transfer to the livelier Rue des Belles Filles (page 58) this became the town ghetto until a Council order in 1488 banished all Jews from Geneva.

> The well-entrenched meat market continued in this dilapidated district for centuries before its removal to the edge of the lake to make room in the 1700s for this row of handsome town-houses.

At its upper end the Grand-Mézel meets the **Rue des Granges,** the Street of the Barns. In the 1600s the residents of the Grand'Rue, Geneva's smartest avenue, kept their horses in this alley behind their houses. Today their "Barn Street" is one of the most prestigious addresses in the Old Town.

> 2, 4, and 6 Rue des Granges were built in 1723 in the Louis XV style with a common facade to unite the three houses, the original residences of three branches of the Boissier family. The only child of the Boissiers in 2 Rue des Granges was a daughter. By her marriage the house came into the Sellon family and five generations later Count Jean-Jacques Sellon founded here in 1830 Geneva's first Society for Peace.
>
> The Count's daughter Adelaide married the Piedmontese Count Michel Cavour and was the mother of Camille Cavour, who spent much of his youth here with his Genevese family.

The **plaque [38]** on the portal of 2 Rue des Granges commemorates **Cavour,** the statesman renowned for his unification and modernization of the Italian nation.

The energetic and progressive young leader of his northern principality of Piedmont used the revolutionary trends of the 1840s to install a liberal constitution in his region and under its terms he became its first prime minister. Cavour then expanded his efforts to encompass neighboring principalities. Through his deft diplomacy Cavour cleared them of their foreign occupiers and by 1861 consolidated them with his own Piedmont into the Parliamentary Kingdom of Italy.

2 Rue des Granges became in the 1950s the property of the town of Geneva whose officials wished to use it for official receptions. Lacking appropriate furnishing for the extensive premises, Geneva welcomed the civic gesture of the Zoubov family to contribute the decor as a memorial to their daughter, killed in an automobile accident at the age of 18.

Over the main entry from the inner count of 2 Rue des Granges is a plaque recognizing the Zoubov Foundation, formed in 1973 to provide the mansion's present furniture and paintings for municipal use and for the delectation of the public on conducted tours according to the schedule listed in most Genevese publications.

7 Rue des Granges [39] was the birthplace in 1761 of **Albert Gallatin,** who migrated to America during its Revolution and became a leading statesman, diplomat, and financier in his adopted land.

Left an orphan in Geneva and seeking a career at age 19, Gallatin declined a commission in the Hessian Army, deciding instead to go to America where he joined the Continental Army. After a stint teaching French at Harvard University Gallatin moved to western Pennsylvania.

In 1787 he served on his state's delegation to draft the Constitution and in 1794 helped to preserve it and the Union when he dissuaded his mountaineer neighbors from seceding in the "Whiskey Rebellion" over the issue of a Federal excise tax on their domestic distillants.

As a member of Congress Gallatin showed such financial expertise that President Thomas Jefferson made him Secretary of the Treasury. Gallatin not only liquidated the staggering public debt incurred in the Revolution but even managed to raise an additional $11,000,000 to finance the purchase of France's Louisiana Territory (page 77) from cash-short Napoleon I and thus to double the area of the United States.

After thirteen years in the Treasury post Gallatin undertook a decade of diplomacy on missions to Russia, France, and England. On his return to America Gallatin was William Crawford's running mate for the vice presidency in the 1824 presidential campaign.

In 1828 Gallatin went into private business in New York. Among a variety of achievements there he founded the Gallatin Bank — today the Manufacturers Hanover Trust Company —, the American Ethnological Society, the Historical Society of New York, and New York University.

Ahead in the middle of Rue des Granges is Geneva's oldest Christian church, **Saint Germain [40],** dating back to 400 A.D.

In 540 the construction of the larger Basilica of Saint Peter relegated Saint Germain to the status of a parish church for the next millenium. In 1536 the Reformers assigned Saint Germain as a chapel for Flemish refugees and later used it as a hall for town meetings.

With the completion of the Town Hall, Saint Germain served such purposes as a butcher shop and, in the times of the "Petite Révolution" of the 1700s, was a supplementary barracks for troops overflowing the guardhouse at the head of Rue des Granges. With Napoleon's Concordat with Rome and the arrival of Abbé Vuarin in 1806 (page 81) the Société Economique (page 82) succumbed to the pressure and ceded Saint Germain as the principal church for Vuarin's Catholic congregation.

By 1857 the Abbé Gustave Mermillod, a successor to Vuarin, had provided for Geneva's Catholic worshipers his ambitious Basilique de Notre Dame (page 185) and had returned Saint Germain to its parochial status.

In 1871 the mother church in Rome suffered another internal conflict, a breach less profound than the "Great Schism" (page 73) or the Protestant Reform but a still bitter division. The split called the "Kulturkampf" — the "War of the Ideologies" — arose from the rejection by some Catholics of the dogma of Pius IX concerning the infallibility of the Pope.

A portion of Geneva's Catholic congregation sided with the dissenters. Geneva, a church-state in 1872, assigned to these so-called "Old Catholics" all of the municipally-funded Catholic property including Saint Germain.

After 35 years of political maneuvering Geneva in 1907 voted to remove its churches from government control and the Roman Catholic hierarchy reacquired its real estate. The congregation of Saint Germain, however, refused reconciliation with Rome. This tiny church remains today a bastion of the diminished but still-protesting cult of the "Old Catholics".

From the front of Saint Germain turn left and walk through the narrow, nameless alley to arrive again in the **Grand'Rue.**

The sign showing a half-dozen lawyers outweighed in the balance by Justice hangs over the door of 25 Grand'Rue to identify the offices of a law partnership.

An earlier residence here was that of Jean Diodati who in 1605 succeeded Bèze as the spiritual leader of the Reform. Diodati's translation of the Bible into Italian is still considered one of the masterpieces of that nation's literature.

Among Diodati's functions as leader of the Reform community was that of receiving its distinguished guests. During John Milton's stay en route from Italy in 1639 when the 31-year-old poet was already inclining away from the Anglican church towards his eventual Presbyterian faith, Diodati conferred with Milton on each of the ten days of his visit.

The country house of the Diodati family at suburban Cologny has been occupied by a wide variety of tenants: Giuseppe Motta, a President of Switzerland and of the League of Nations Assembly, Balthus, a modern painter, and — dating back to 1816 — the poet George Lord Byron (page 154).

During the working hours of his summer at Villa Diodati Byron wrote most of *Manfred*, the third canto of *Childe Harold*, and the popular *Prisoner of Chillon*.

The present mansion at 25 Grand'Rue with its courtyard and stone fountain was built in 1722.

In 1833 the lovely Claudine Potocka, a Polish aristocrat and refugee from the Russian annexation of her country in 1831, invited the French novelist Honoré de Balzac to move out of his stuffy pension room and into her comfortable apartment here.

Claudine's compatriot, Madame Evelyne Hanska, declined the invitation on Balzac's behalf. Hanska had just exerted great efforts to make the writer's acquaintance and had no intention of sharing the company she was enjoying in Geneva at such times as she could elude her accompanying husband and children.

27 Grand'Rue was the birthplace in 1895 of the star of French films, Michel Simon. His legal name was François Simon. In 1924 he usurped for professional use the Christian name of his son Michel.

To restore the balance the son baptised Michel took as his professional name for his performing career in Swiss film and theatre the one that his father had abandoned and became locally renowned as "François Simon".

At 29/31 Grand'Rue a plaque notes that André Grétry, the French innovator of the "opéra comique", resided here in 1766-67. Grétry's first exposure to a work of opera was at Geneva's "Théâtre Rosimund" (page 113).

> On hearing the *Isabelle et Gertrude* by Charles Favart, Grétry returned to these rooms and composed his own version of the same work, his first of some fifty contributions to "opéra comique" repertory.
>
> Grétry's journal for August 1766 mentions a recital of chamber music at the Hôtel-de-Ville. The French musician was not greatly impressed by the violin performance of a 15-year-old named Anna Maria Mozart accompanied on piano by her 10-year-old brother, Wolfgang Amadeus.

The Mozart children were into their fourth year of a concert tour launched by their father Leopold in June 1763. He brought his prodigies to Geneva in the hope of their impressing Voltaire, whose opinion on any subject was the most influential in Europe.

> For three weeks the Mozarts remained in Geneva under the aegis of Jean Huber (page 64) giving only two recitals as Leopold tried without success to arrange a performance before Voltaire.
>
> The Mozarts found their visit as harrowing as it was frustrating, according to Leopold, who reported their survival of a "civil war" — actually the third episode of the "Petite Révolution", the one ignited by Jean-Jacques Rousseau (page 91).

33 Grand'Rue housed the studios where painter Ferdinand Hodler worked from 1881 to 1902. Hodler broke away from the long Swiss tradition of scenes of misty waterfalls and browsing cattle of the Romantic School with his depictions of stark landscapes and heroic murals in hard lines and sharp colors.

> Hodler, a struggling artist in 1886, earned 200 francs by painting a series of canvases for the proprietor of Geneva's Taverne du Crocodile to glue onto the walls of his pub.
>
> By 1910 the painter was far better known. In that year a Bernese entrepreneur bought the bistro "Crocodile", had Hodler's murals steamed off, framed them — signed by the artist — and auctioned the lot for a tidy capital gain.

40 Grand'Rue is marked by the **plaque [41]** as the site of the house where **Jean-Jacques Rousseau** was born.

The writings of Geneva's erratic but oft-venerated philosopher were among the most influential of the late 1700s. With his literary eloquence Rousseau supplied seductively simple responses to the challenges of the Age of Science and to the logic of its intellectual defender, Voltaire. Rousseau's back-to-nature appeals beguiled several generations into sentimental Romanticism and resistance to technological innovation.

> Rousseau's beginnings were not auspicious. His mother died at his birth in 1712. His father was a ne'er-do-well. The boy's early education was negligible and his apprenticeship unproductive. With the emptiest of prospects at 16, Rousseau had little reason not to drift away from Geneva in aimless wanderings.
>
> He survived by ingratiating himself with a series of indulgent protectors, working sporadically as a tutor, secretary, and music copier while educating himself through intensive reading and observation. Two decades of such exposure developed in Rousseau the talent for the writing of the essays, plays, and music that by 1749 had won him prizes, royal recognition, and critical acclaim.

Geneva, gratified at this native son's renown, welcomed Rousseau back to the community in 1754. After a few months of basking in local adulation the philosopher was lured back to France by the offer of the use of "L'Ermitage" at Montmorency.

In his borrowed cottage Rousseau wrote over the next few years *The New Héloise, Emile,* and the *Social Contract,* each expressing liberal concepts that infuriated the conservative governments in both France and Geneva.

> The indignant Councilors of this Republic in 1762 condemned their philosopher to exile and his books to burning (page 95). Rousseau's "open letter" of response inflamed the populace in his favor against the Council and precipitated the town's third outbreak of the "Petite Révolution". The Council called in troops from France to maintain order.
>
> Rousseau's sweeping pronouncements covered a wide range of subjects. They were — like the Bible and Shakespeare — rich in quotable phrases in support of either side of almost any argument. The leaders of the French Revolution combined bits of Rousseau's impractical philosophy with scraps of the logic of the diametrically opposed Voltaire and merged these mortal enemies into the mismatched "twin deities of Revolution".
>
> When the Genevan, American, and French Revolutions of the 1700s subsided into the more tranquil years of the early 1800s, Rousseau's sentimental counsel remained a potent influence on art and literature with such later Romantics as Byron, Chateaubriand, Shelley, Stendhal, and Eliot in their turn visiting Geneva and its shrine of the birthplace of Rousseau.

From the Rousseau house look ahead to the arcaded building at the jog in the street. High up, just below its eaves, is a running fresco recounting in twelve colorful murals the story of Geneva from the arrival of Caesar in 57 B.C. through the ratification of the Constitution of 1848.

> To follow the story from its beginning, go through the arcade and to your left, back into the Rue du Soleil Levant. From there, at a neck-wrenching angle, you may see the first four panels.
>
> The second set of four panels faces the Rue du Puits-Saint-Pierre and Geneva's Museum of Town History — the **Maison Tavel [33]**. Geneva's oldest building was once the guardhouse of the gate that controlled access to the Old Town through the wall at the head of Rue du Perron.
>
> Two disparate ornamental features project from the Tavel house: a series of small carved stone heads, the "mascarons", set in the wall in the 1400s, and, on its upper floors, the first iron balconies ever seen in Geneva, an Italian novelty introduced by the Calandrini family in the early 1600s.

This area on the crest of Geneva's hill was from Roman times an open market-place within the fortifications. The arcaded structure was built only in 1588 when the Wars of Religion threatened Geneva with siege and a granary was needed to stock emergency foods. The Escalade victory of 1602 reduced the menace of siege and food shortage and the loft space was cleared for the storage of gunpowder and arms — hence, the **Arsenal [42]**.

> In the Arsenal are, appropriately enough, five cannon, souvenirs of the more-than-two-hundred that once guarded Geneva's ramparts.
>
> Napoleon requisitioned for his wars most of Geneva's artillery; the conquering Austrians in the course of liberating the town in 1813 borrowed the rest. In 1923 the Vienna Military Museum, after long negotiations, handed over to a diplomatic mission from Geneva these five handsome pieces from its collection.
>
> Four of the guns, decorated with animals, are the work of the Dresden craftsman, Georg Münch. The cannon ornamented with dolphins was cast in Geneva in 1680 by the master founder, Martin Emery II.

The three mosaics on the back of the arcade are the recent works of a Geneva artist, Alexander Cingria. They depict, from left to right, Caesar's arrival in Geneva, the Geneva trade fairs of the 1300s, and Geneva welcoming religious refugees.

> The stone stairs to the right of the murals lead to the old granary and gun lofts, today converted for Geneva's Archives. In addition to

the records of births, deaths, and real estate deeds, the Archives maintain displays of old registers and documents, including some in Calvin's own handwriting as well as the original of the precious "Franchises of 1387" (page 9), this Republic's counterpart of the Magna Carta.

The third set of four panels of the frescoes of the Arsenal face the **Hôtel de Ville [43]**.

When this hilltop was the market place it was also the natural meeting ground and center for discussion. It followed that, when the "Franchises of 1387" affirmed the rights of the people to participate in their own government, the "commune" chose to build its own meeting hall on this familiar terrain.

2 rue de l'Hôtel-de-Ville [43] was the people's starting point and today houses the Council Chambers and a few offices of "L'Etat" — the Republic and Canton of Geneva. 4 Hôtel-de-Ville is for the "ville" — the town or municipality — much of whose administration works out of other quarters.

Note the lintel with its bas-relief eagle carving above the door of 2 Hôtel-de-Ville. Inside the Cantonal headquarters, open officially only during business hours, are thirteen Tuscan columns supporting decorative vaults and seals.

Straight ahead through the door is a fine Renaissance portal of carved stone framing the entry to the cobbled ramp. To the left at the foot of the ramp is the "crotton", a small cage for the interim restraint of troublesome drunks of yesteryear.

The cobbled ramp, reminiscent of a Swiss mountain trail, permitted the more sedentary early functionaries to ascend directly to the Council chambers by horse, mule, litter, or sedan chair.

Across the courtyard to your left is a double door marked "A L A B A M A". The name is that of an armed ship built in Britain and described on the brass plaque beside the door as a "vaisseau corsaire" — a "pirate vessel".

The "*Alabama* Incident" in America's "War Between The States" led to an important international arbitration held in these rooms in 1872. Actually the setting was by then already historic, having served in 1864 for the signing of the First Geneva Convention on the Red Cross.

Should you wish to visit the *Alabama* suite consult the guardian in his booth in the door near the entry from the street.

The first room of the three is a small reception hall opening into a richly furnished salon with a handsome view. The third room was the dining room of Geneva's Council until its expropriation in the summer on 1864 to seat the delegates of the sixteen nations meeting to consider the care of the wounded in battle.

The Red Cross, or more concisely, the ICRC (page 78), began its official existence with the signing of the Geneva Convention here late in the afternoon of 22 August 1864.

While the elite of Europe and Geneva met on the ground floor Geneva's newly-elected Town Councilors on the floor above were held hostage by the partisans of James Fazy who had just lost a closely-contested election. As the Red Cross meeting adjourned below and the Councilors seethed overhead, a posse of Fazy's supporters raided the Arsenal for guns to carry their battle into the streets.

Bloody skirmishes were raging throughout Geneva as Gustave Moynier, freshly confirmed as head of the Red Cross, scurried to his home amid the gunfire. Hidden under his frock coat was the signed original of the Convention to reduce the suffering caused by violent conflict. The well-intended paper provided Moynier with very little protection.

Eight years later in the same meeting room the United States and Great Britain settled their serious conflict without violence through their arbitration of the *Alabama* claim.

During America's Civil War of 1861/65 a British shipyard built the raider *Alabama* for the Confederate Navy. Under Admiral Raphael Semmes she accounted for sixty-seven Union ships before the *Kearsage* sunk her in June 1864.

At the close of its war the United States claimed reimbursement from Britain for the losses incurred from the neutral nation's intervention in an internal conflict. The arbiters awarded the United States $15,500,000 in gold.

The *Alabama* meeting room is heavy with memorabilia. Reasonably relevant ship models, portraits, and battle scenes are supplemented by such miscellany as a plowshare forged from officers' swords and — from a melted-down American cannon — a brass Liberty Bell. The bell, dedicated to keeping order at meetings in the service of peace, was rung on 15 November 1920 to open in Geneva the First General Assembly of the League of Nations.

Leaving the Hôtel de Ville, turn left along the sidewalk with half its width taken up by a stone bench. From a platform here the justices of Geneva once handed down their verdicts. Among the condemned were Michel Servet, Pierre Fatio, and Jean-Jacques Rousseau.

The Spanish physician Servet (page 41) was found guilty of heresy for his unorthodox beliefs.

The court took the measures deemed essential for the salvation of the soul of a heretic and ordered Servet burned at the stake.

Sentenced on 27 October 1553 Servet was led forthwith to the "Champs du Bourreau", the Executioner's Enclave — the present site of the Cantonal Hospital — and burned alive on the road now named "Rue Beauséjour", the Street of the Pleasant Visit.

The site of Servet's execution is marked with a rough-hewn boulder placed in 1903 by — as its plaque declares — "respectful and grateful sons of the church of Calvin..." condemning an error of the times of Calvin and offering by this monument to make amends.

Pierre Fatio was found guilty of sedition and incitement to revolt (page 79) in the first outbreak of the "Petite Révolution".

For his punishment Fatio was "arquebussed" — shot and killed by a firing squad using long-barreled, small-bore rifles — in secret in the inner court ot the "Evêché" prison beside the Cathedral.

The justices of 1762 found Rousseau and his writings guilty (page 91) of offence to morals and of tending to destroy the Christian religion and all governments.

Following the judges' sentencing of the writings, the public executioner burned in this square a pirated copy of Rousseau's *Emile* and an abridged version of his *Social Contract* since copies of the original edition were no longer available.

Rousseau himself, tried and sentenced in absentia, remained first in the Canton of Bern and then in Neuchâtel. From his exile the convicted philosopher wrote the letters that inctied his partisans in Geneva to the third round of the "Petite Révolution".

Rousseau's defenders fought the charges and some thirty years later won their case. In 1794 a court assembled during the fifth and final episode of the "Petite Révolution" reversed the 1762 verdict and exonerated and rehabilitated Rousseau a scant fourteen years after his death.

Turning left into Rue Henri Fazy you meet again the Rue des Granges at the top of the entry road and gate built by the Reformers through the high wall against the south side of the Old Town.

Before the Reformation the last building on the Rue des Granges was the Chapel of Saint Aspre. The Reformers converted the chapel into a guard-house and during the eruptions of the "Petite Révolution" the Town Council billeted here the contingents of foreign troops called in to protect them. The barrack's demolition in 1788 made way for the mansion at 16 Rue des Granges, the only one in the row designed in the fashion of Louis XVI.

Six citizens of Geneva, men of the world

1656

1699

FRANÇOIS LE FORT

François Lefort, a statesman prominent in Russian history, was born into a merchant family in Geneva and went to Moscow as a soldier-of-fortune. Befriended by the young Peter the Great, Lefort became the Tsar's mentor on Western customs and commerce and his principal aide in military, political, and diplomatic affairs. In his single decade of influence, Lefort made Russia receptive to Continental ideas and increased substantially the impact of the Tsarist empire in world affairs (page 53).

Jean-Jacques Rousseau, philosopher, left Geneva at 16 to venture abroad. Success in France in literature, drama, and music reconciled him with Geneva until his later writings on liberal themes led to his condemnation and exile. Despite his tawdry personal life Rousseau wrote lyrically of the The Noble Savage, The Common Will, and education through self-realization – concepts that kindled revolutions and inspired the Romantic movement in art and literature (page 90).

1712

1778

JEAN-JACQUES ROUSSEAU

1761

1849

ALBERT GALLATIN

Albert Gallatin, the American financier, born and educated in Geneva, was still a recent immigrant in the United States when he was elected to the first Congress and then named Secretary of the Treasury to manage the nation's troubled post-Revolutionary finances. Turning later to diplomacy Gallatin served as Minister to France and as negotiator of peace with Britain. In 1828 he began in New York a distinguished private career in banking and philanthrophy (page 87).

1779 1869

PETER ROGET

Peter Mark Roget, English scientist and man of letters, was the son of the Genevese pastor of a London church and thereby a citizen of the Republic. After medical studies, Roget worked in public health, research, and hospital administration. Active in the intellectual life of England as an inventor, organizer, and writer on a wide range of subjects, Roget in his leisure time compiled over a 20-year span his masterful reference work, *Roget's Thesaurus* (page 43).

Camille Cavour, who forged the many small states of Italy into a modern nation, was the son of Count Cavour of the principality of Piedmont married to Adelaide de Sellon of Geneva. The widely-traveled, well-educated Camille reformed his state's economy, wrote its Constitution, and became its first prime minister. Cavour mobilized with masterful diplomacy the forces that ended the military occupation of neighboring principalities and united Italy into a parliamentary democracy (page 86).

1810 1861

CAMILLE CAVOUR

1828 1910

HENRI DUNANT

Henri Dunant, the universal humanitarian, born in Geneva, conceived and laid the groundwork for the Red Cross. Acclaimed for this and other worthy initiatives but discredited here for his role in a financial disaster, Dunant left Geneva to campaign for his many causes. After decades of thankless effort, miserable poverty, and, eventually, resignation and reclusion, Dunant emerged in 1901 to reap the recognition and material rewards of the first Nobel Prize for Peace (page 44).

On the left side of Rue Henry Fazy is the Café Papon, a revival of the tea terrace that served the "crème de la crème genevoise" in the high society of the 1770s.

> By the 1820s, however, Papon's was abandoned to the handful of Geneva's veterans of Napoleon's armies who lamented Bonaparte's loss and lounged here, soddenly awaiting their Emperor's return from exile.
>
> The Little Corporal's hard-drinking men of war would have even more to lament if they faced the bill of fare of the recently revived Café. From this Papon's list of now rigidly-non-alcoholic offerings, the troopers could choose among forty varieties of crêpes and fifty flavors of ice cream.

The arch across Rue Henry Fazy supported by Ionic columns replaced in 1783 the heavy stone portal and gate that guarded the head of the ramp leading up from the drawbridge over the moat below the ramparts.

The **statue [44]** beyond the arch is that of **Charles Pictet-de-Rochemont,** the brother of Marc Pictet (pages 57 and 82). This gentleman sheep farmer and organizer of Geneva's militia was the Republic's delegate to the 1814 Congress of Vienna of the Great Powers meeting to restore the map of Europe after its disruption in Napoleon's wars.

> Pictet-de-Rochemont negotiated so adroitly the joining of his Republic of Geneva to the Confédération Helvétique that the diplomat's new homeland of Switzerland promoted him to the leadership of its delegation.
>
> Acting on behalf of Switzerland, Pictet-de-Rochemont persuaded the Allies to include in the Treaty of Paris, as a matter of international doctrine, a statement that the neutrality of Switzerland was in the best interests of all of Europe — a principle that has served both the Confederation and the Continent so well for so long.

La Treille, the Trellis, a south-facing slope, was a vineyard from time immemorial. In the 1500s the newly-fledged Republic of Geneva bought the sunny hillside, cut away the vines, and replaced them with a steep stone wall.

> The Treille, transformed into a gun emplacement and parade ground, stood guard over the delta of the river Arve until the 1700s when the threat of attack had abated. As the Old Town developed, the terrace was widened, planted with its double row of chestnut trees and, in 1767, embellished with Geneva's pride — *The Longest Park Bench In the World* — 120.21 meters (351 feet) of uninterrupted sitzplatz.

On the inner side of the Treille stands the Tour Baudet, built in 1473 as a combination watch tower, strong point, and town hall.

Most of the stones used to build it came from earlier structures and even ruins dating back to Roman times. You can see below the Geneva seal two blocks whose markings identify them as the gravestones of one Rufia Aquilina.

The plaque set in the tower recalls 31 December 1813, the day the French occupying troops took flight and a new Town Council announced the "Restauration de la République".

Two among the dozens of sundials in time-conscious Geneva are set high on differently-angled walls of the Tour Baudet. In the retaining wall below is a calibration chart to assist mathematicians in the reconciliation of the sun readings of the moment to the nearly exact (standard only) time in Geneva for any cloudless day of the year.

At the far end of the Treille is Geneva's "Official" chestnut tree — "Official" because its first budding each year proclaims "L'Eclosion", the commencement of Geneva's natural, as contrasted with solar-calculated, Springtime.

For instance, by the bud's botanical instincts, Spring is known to have begun here on 10 January in 1982, 20 April in 1837.

The sighting of the first official bud — a ritual as solemn and arcane as America's Vigil of Groundhog Day — is celebrated by an outburst of dancing school-children, speeches, a marching band, and the local television news team.

The Official Tree is recognizable by its brass plaque, its metal crutch, and precarious angle. An apprentice tree is on standby close at hand in the event of collapse or early retirement of the incumbent.

From this far end of the Treille descend the cobbled ramp and face the **International House [45]** of the University of Geneva.

The chaste vases in the niches of its facade replaced the statues of a nude male and a nude female, each under five years of age, when the mansion of Mademoiselle Pictet was made fit to serve as a meeting place for the foreign students who make up a majority of the University's enrollment.

Cross Rue de la Croix-Rouge, Red Cross Street, a dangerous traverse for pedestrians, at the yellow "zebra" crossing a few meters down the slope.

Returning up the slope you pass on your right the ramp into the park and then the Bastion Mirond, another remnant of the Reformers' defences.

In 1748 Geneva built on these foundations of the abandoned Mirond its first School of Art which guided several generations of painters and designers at this site until 1825 when it moved to improved studios in the Rath Museum (page 118).

The owners of the structure at the Mirond thereupon added several floors to convert it into a banal apartment house, the Calabri.

The apartment on its top floor was in 1835 the modest residence shared by the deposed Queen of Holland, Hortense Beauharnais Bonaparte (page 59) and her son, Louis Napoléon.

In 1908 the town bought the "Calabri" apartment house, planning its early demolition to clear the surroundings for the Reformation Monument and to straighten out a murderous bend in the adjacent streetcar tracks. The Calabri was indeed duly removed in 1932.

The mansion in the Greek style, the **Palais Eynard [46],** was built in 1821 for the banker-diplomat Jean-Gabriel Eynard.

Eynard set out at age 22 to recoup the fortunes of his bankrupt parents. He succeeded so well as a banker in Tuscany that by the age of 35 he had paid the Eynard family's debts and retired to Geneva where he married the niece of Charles Pictet-de-Rochemont and moved into the Mallet house at 9 Cour Saint-Pierre (page 77).

When Pictet-de-Rochemont was sent to the Congress of Vienna (page 98) Eynard accompanied his wife's uncle as secretary of the Geneva delegation.

At the Great Powers' "Dancing Congress" Eynard was persuaded by Jean Capodistria, the Russian delegate although a native of Corfu and a Greek patriot (page 63), of the justice of Greece's struggle for independence. Eynard became a major sponsor of the Hellenic cause, formed committees to send food and funds, arranged substantial loans, and exerted his influence as the appointed representative of Greece to all the governments of Europe.

In Geneva, meanwhile, Eynard promoted vigorously the improvement of the swampy, slum-ridden area between the Reformers' walls and the River Arve and in 1816 donated the ground for a scientific garden to nurture Pyramus de Candolle's botanical specimens.

The construction of this personal "Palais" outside the Old Town walls was a considerable departure for Geneva. Its unusual setting expanded the horizons of the old families as Eynard's showplace became the cultural center for the meetings and lectures which were of such importance to Geneva's social life.

> In 1891 Geneva bought the Palais Eynard to use as a combination art museum and reception hall. When, in 1910, Galland's all-encompassing Museum of Art and History absorbed the public art collections, this mansion became an annex of the Museum of Natural History at the University.

> The natural history collection in turn moved to its own new building at Place Guyénot in Malagnou leaving Palais Eynard for renovation into offices and reception rooms for the executive arm of the municipal government.

Further up the slope, beyond the Bastion Saint-Léger, is the **Athénée [47]**, a meeting place and gallery financed by Eynard in 1860. The building was for the use of the Society of the Arts, a group formed in 1776 by Horace-Bénédict de Saussure and watchmaker Louis Faizan to foster interest in art and in the humanities among Geneva's artisans.

> The busts in the niches around the upper frieze commemorate nine Genevese men of distinction — from left to right:

> 1. Adhémar Fabri, grantor of the "Franchises of 1387" (page 9);
> 2. Bésançon Hugues, chief of the Huguenot advocates of ties with the Swiss in 1519 (page 52);
> 3. Jean Calvin, the personification of the Reformation of 1536;
> 4. Michel Roset, negotiator of the "perpetual alliance" with Switzerland in 1584;
> 5. Jean-Jacques Rousseau, the Romantic philosopher, born 1712;
> 6. Charles Bonnet; the "natural scientist", born 1720;

> And, on the side of the Athénée toward the park:

> 7. Horace-Bénédict de Saussure, founder of the Society of the Arts, 1776 (page 83);
> 8. Ami Lullin, head of the government at the "Restauration", 1813;
> 9. Charles Pictet-de-Rochemont, Swiss delegate to the Congress of Vienna, 1814 (page 98).

The Athénée opened in February 1863 with the meeting of the "Committee of Five", convened to convert the broad ideas set forth in Dunant's *Souvenir of Solferino* (page 44) into a practical plan for the presence of neutral civilians on battlefields to provide care for suffering casualties.

> The Committee's plan received the unanimous approval of its First International Congress, meeting in October 1863 to draft a "Convention". The Congress further agreed that those civilian non-belliger-

ents who were to be exempted from the conflict should wear a distinctive insignia. The badge chosen was the flag of Switzerland with its colors reversed — hence, a Red Cross on a white background.

Continue around the Athénée to its east wall to see the plaque commemorating this as "The Cradle of the Red Cross".

From the street at the side of the Athénée turn right down Rue Eynard and cross Rue Saint-Léger to reach on your left the **Parc des Bastions.**

The area around the gates has been paved to permit parking of tour buses bringing passengers to visit the Reformation Monument here.

◆ Those of The Driven who are traveling in buses may at this point be joining The Walkers for a visit afoot.

Uncommitted walkers take the path to the left leading to a monumental **grey sculpture [48]** set on a large stone cube. This work depicting an angel guarding a few cowering humans commemorated **the centenary of the ICRC,** the International Committee of the Red Cross.

Dunant's reputation in Geneva had so mellowed a hundred years after the signing of the Geneva Convention that he is mentioned twice on this memorial to the occasion. From his family's 1919 nomination of Henri (page 45) as "Promoteur..." of the Red Cross, he is here elevated to "Initiateur..." of the work of the ICRC with added mention on the other side as "Promoteur..." of the Geneva Conventions.

To recognize the centenary occasion an all-Swiss committee raised some Sfr 200,000 by public subscription and commissioned a sculpture intended to grace the Treille overlooking this park.

After inspecting artist J. Probst's symbolic tribute, the organizing committee declared the piece too large for the prominent site on the town terrace and assigned it to this corner of the Bastion park.

Proceed next on the path to your left towards the University, passing on your left an unhewn **boulder with a brass plaque [49]** of appreciation of the founder of the Swiss Society of Natural History, **Henri-Albert Gosse,** the amiable, eccentric pharmacist-partner of John-Jacob Schweppes (page 39).

The theatrically cloaked Gosse with unfashionably long hair below his shoulders, traversing Geneva astride his donkey "Drin-Drin", was a familiar sight in the 1790s. In Gosse's pharmacy there dangled within a disemboweled grandfather's clock a human skeleton that he had personally disinterred while a student in Paris.

In 1802 Gosse went out of business and moved to Mont Salève in Savoy. There, in his seven-sided Château Mornex, accessible only by rope ladder, he experimented with the occult, tended his zoo, and sought to perfect a perpetual-motion machine.

Gosse's unique conventional act seems to have been that of October 1815 when he convoked from Geneva six respectable savants to form his Society of Natural History.

On Gosse's death in 1816 the lease to his château passed to his son Louis, a physician further distinguished as one of the founders of the Geneva Dispensary and later the *Journal de Genève*. Louis Gosse, a Protestant, was forbidden by the laws of Catholic Savoy to buy the Château de Mornex. Saintly intervention, however, provided the miracle.

The skeleton that old Henri Gosse had kept in his pharmacy clock was certified by an ecclesiastical expert as the earthly remains of Saint Benoît. The Cardinal of Turin, informed of this sacred relic, coveted the hallowed bones. In exchange for the skeleton Doctor Gosse acquired the right to purchase the property, known thereafter as Mont Gosse.

The learned society begun by Henri Gosse continued as a forum for scholarly papers, some of appreciable merit. The later members of the society expressed their gratitude for Gosse's initiative by arranging in 1888 for this commemorative boulder to be hauled from Mornex to the Bastions.

As you continue down the path observe that most of the trees are identified with a sign spelling out their name and place of origin. The Bastion Park is also an arboretum with a rich dendrological (from the Greek as in "rhodo-dendron" for "red-tree") collection of several hundred species of carefully selected trees.

The path ends at the Bastion's hard-surfaced promenade, stretching out under four lines of trees from the wrought-iron gates of Saint Léger to their counterparts at Place Neuve.

Turn left towards Place Neuve and then right on the next path to approach the ornate fountain with four cast-iron caryatids surrounding a thin flow of water for hyper-hygienic consumption. These odd structures are a common sight in Paris but are rarely seen this far afield.

Paris owes its ample inventory to England's Sir Richard Wallace, a Francophile connoisseur of art who, during the Franco-Prussian War, contributed a fleet of ambulances to the French Army. In 1872 Wallace concluded that Parisians drank too little water. To remedy

the shortage he ordered installed in the French capital some fifty of
these elaborate dispensers which are still referred to as "Les Wal-
laces".

The next **bust [50]** along the path is that of **Augustin-Pyramus
de Candolle** (page 70), the founder of Geneva's Botanical Garden.

> Two centuries ago this flatland outside the fortifications was the
> swampy vestige of the moat and a cleared terrain, protected, how-
> ever, by the hill from Switzerland's icy wind "la bise". The fertility of
> this plain attracted farmers who had immigrated from the south of
> France and had made here their "Petite Languédoc" of garden plots,
> expanded in 1816 by the planting of Candolle's Botanical Garden.
>
> The garden was a civic project that combined popular interest in a
> new science with the town's need to create jobs for the unskilled in
> the hard winter of 1816-17.
>
> Under the direction of Professor Pyramus de Candolle — abetted by
> Eynard's purchase of the land and the town's supply of manual
> labor — the garden soon flourished. Additional support came from
> official subsidies supplemented by individual gifts of more than
> three hundred items ranging from packets of seeds to benches,
> fences, and wrought-iron grillework.

The bronze bust of Candolle is the work of James Pradier, the
Geneva-born sculptor responsible for the Rousseau statue
(page 34) on the island in the Rhone.

> In preparing the Candolle memorial Pradier blended his private life
> with his art. Among the four dancing girls embellishing the pedes-
> tal, the nude pose was that of the delectable Juliette Drouet. When
> this mistress of Pradier became the mother of his daughter Claire
> in 1828, the ruthless artist turned the pair out into the streets. Victor
> Hugo retrieved them and two years later obliged Pradier to
> acknowledge his daughter with Hugo standing in as Claire's god-
> father.
>
> Hugo, meanwhile, took Juliette as his own mistress until, inevi-
> tably, he found younger replacements to take over her original
> assignment. Hugo thereafter retained Juliette as his traveling com-
> panion and copier of manuscripts, housed near to his lawful family
> for the next fifty years.
>
> Pradier, meanwhile, married the widow Louise d'Arcet Dupont, a
> frivolous woman who helped to make the sculptor's studio a popular
> Paris rendezvous. There Gustave Flaubert met the promiscuous,
> extravagant Louise and later used her as his model for the anti-
> heroine Emma in his classic novel *Madame Bovary*.
>
> At Pradier's studio Flaubert also met, in 1846, the poet Louise Colet,
> a collector of literary lions. Colet engaged the novelist in an affair

that endured for most of a turbulent decade before she set her sights on Alfred de Musset and left Flaubert to his tranquil, sunset friendship with George Sand.

Pradier at 51 died from a heart attack in the course of a picnic in the company of 16-year-old Mademoiselle Adeline.

The Botanical Garden begun by Candolle still exists but in 1904 was transplanted to broader fields north of Geneva (page 162). Most of its trees were left in the Bastions including, on your right, the towering Giant Sequoia redwoods from California.

At the souvenir stand near the Candolle pedestal during summer months you can buy an excellent paperback directory to a selected 150 of the trees growing here — each pictured, identified, and located by a map.

◆ Since the **Reformation Monument [51]**, which you are now facing, is 100 meters (330 feet) long and 10 meters (33 feet) high, it needs very little pointing out.

The wall commemorates the entire Reformation movement. By means of its panels and statues the monument recalls events and individuals prominent or influential in Protestant affairs through the 1500s and 1600s with, perhaps, a pardonable bias towards those elements whose roots run deep in Geneva.

The breadth of the concept is a tribute to the planners who defended the Reform principles against a degree of opposition. Overlooking Calvin's clear disapproval of the cult of the personality and the hallowing of images, a few of his followers insisted that the Reformer deserved a memorial more tangible than his words and work.

The long-standing issue arose again in 1864 as the 300th anniversary of Calvin's death approached. Only after much discussion did the pro-statue faction agree to combining a memorial gesture with a civic need. The tribute of 1864 was thus the "Salle de la Réformation", a multi-purpose hall that served for more than a century for conferences, theatricals, drills, expositions and, in 1920, the First General Assembly of the League of Nations.

By the early 1900s Calvin's memorialists were again restless as they saw his contemporaries, Luther and Zwingli, recognized with monuments and even the possibly-heretical Servet remembered with his own boulder on Rue Beauséjour (page 95).

Rather than wait for 1914, the 350th anniversary of Calvin's death, the battle was joined for the year 1909, the 400th anniversary of Calvin's birth. The debate over the appropriate concept concluded with the formation of the "Association for the International Monument to the Reformation", mandated to appeal to Protestant communities around the world.

In consonance with the agreed theme the Association set a competition for a design of "... an international memorial with a minimum of allegory showing men of action who spread the faith..."

> The Association chose the designs of a firm of architects from the neighboring town of Lausanne and began seeking a site on which to build. Partisans of every nook and cranny in Geneva produced justification for locating the monument in their corner of town. Coincidentally, the municipal engineers remarked that the masonry of the heavy Wall of the Reformers which overhangs the Bastions was deteriorating dangerously. Extensive, expensive reconstruction was imperative.

When the Association debated the final location for the monument, the æsthetics of the sunny park, the propinquity of Calvin's Académie — revived as the University of Geneva — and the utility of a new reinforcing wall weighted the decision in favor of the Bastions.

The Association and the town of Geneva — the biggest contributor — banked the needed funds just in time to lay the cornerstone on Calvin's 400th birthday, 10 July 1909.

> Of the many greetings and congratulations received, only one was from a head of state. Kaiser Wilhelm II, in his cable of felicitations, noted that, of the ten eminent Protestants depicted on the monument, three were among his ancestors.
>
> The outbreak of World War I diverted many of the skilled craftsmen from work on the monument into military service. The construction went on, however, in a spirit of world brotherhood. Geneva's hospitality to refugees and to prisoners of war brought forth a supply of Italian and other non-Swiss itinerant and interned stone-cutters, almost none of them Protestant but almost all happy to help. The memorial was finished on schedule for its dedication in 1917.

The long ensemble is united by the retaining wall with its motto of the Reformation — Post Tenebras Lux — "After the darkness comes the light".

Against the wall is the central sculpture of four commanding men of the church. These Genevese principals are in turn flanked by six smaller statues and eight bas-relief panels. Each of the eight panels and eight of the ten statues relate to specific nations in accordance with historical events and sources of contributions to the memorial. For the best idea of the flow of events the eight pictorial panels should be looked at in their chronological order.

First, note that Calvin and Bèze, the central pair of figures, are not involved in any of the events shown on the panels.

The other eight historical figures have links with panels and nations which should be considered in the following sequence:

(Event 1) Panel 4: 1534: Geneva's first Reformed baptism.
Statue D: Farel, representing the Swiss interest.

(Event 2) Panel 5: 1560: Preaching the Reform in Edinburgh.
Statue G: Knox, representing the Scottish interest.

(Event 3) Panel 2:1581: The unification of Holland.
Statue B: William the Silent, representing the interest of the Dutch community.

(Event 4) Panel 3: 1598: Henry IV signs the Edict of Nantes.
Statue C: Coligny, representing the French interest.

(Event 5) Panel 8: 1606: The Treaty of Vienna.
Statue J: Bocsky, representing the Austro-Hungarian participation in the work.

(Event 6) Panel 6: 1620: Pilgrims aboard the "Mayflower".
Statue H: Williams, representing the American interest.

(Event 7) Panel 1: 1685: Refugees from France's "Revocation" being welcomed to new homes in Prussia.
Statue A: Frederick William, representing the contributions from German sources.

(Event 8) Panel 7: 1689: William and Mary accept the terms of the Parliamentary Bill of Rights.
Statue I: Cromwell, representing the English interest.

The original plans for the monument call for its completion on some distant day with haut-relief panels of Cranmer of England and Olivetan of the Canton of Vaud plus the addition of unspecified memorials to the earliest recognized Protestants, John Wiclif and John Hus (page 73).

Three coats of arms are set in the mosaics in the pavement in front of the central figures.

The heraldic bear of the City of Bern represents Farel, the eagle and key of the Geneva seal are for Calvin and Bèze, and John Knox stands behind the belligerent lion of Edinburgh.

The Reformation Monument

This wall of quartz and granite was planned to commemorate in clear, universal terms events and men influential in the Reform movement. In furtherance of such an approach to better understanding the upper section of the illustration identifies each of the eight bas-relief panels by a number. The text on page 107 sets out the order in which to view these scenes to follow the story of 150 years of Protestant activities.

Capital letters identify the ten statues on the Monument, arranged in the lower photographs in their chronological order.

D. **Guillaume Farel (1489-1565):** French priest converted to Protantism: preached in Bern, persuaded Geneva to accept the Reform and Calvin to organize and administer the new movement (panel 4).

G. **John Knox (1506-1572):** Scottish priest and social reformer: led refugees from British persecution to haven in Geneva; founded The Church of Scotland, the only Presbyterian state church established by law (panel 5).

E. **Jean Calvin (1509-1564):** French lawyer: fugitive from persecution; stayed in Geneva to codify the Reform, organize the theocracy, set up schools to spread and preserve his form of Protestantism.

C. **Gaspard de Coligny (1517-1572):** French Admiral converted to Reform: Protestant victor in third War of Religion; his beheading by French Regent Catherine de Medicis set off Saint Bartholomew's Day Massacre of thousands of Huguenots (panel 3).

F. **Théodore de Bèze (1519-1605):** French poet: Rector of Calvin's schools; successor to Calvin as leader of movement; consolidator of Reformed Church in Europe.

B. **William I, (the Silent) (1533-1584):** Diplomat and Dutch statesman: Led revolt of Northern principalities of the Rhine delta against Catholic Spain; united them into Protestant Holland (panel 2).

J. **Stephan Bocskay (1556-1606):** Transylvanian prince: Allied his Balkan compatriots with Turks (note scimitar in belt) to defeat the Catholic Hapsburgs and win religious freedom for his land (panel 8).

I. **Oliver Cromwell (1599-1658):** English soldier and governor: Defeated Charles II and Royalists; ruled as Lord Protector of the Commonwealth; reconciled factions of Puritanism (panel 7).

H. **Roger Williams (1604-1685):** American clergyman: Migrated from England as Puritan; opposed Massachusetts oligarchy; defended rights of Indians; founded new colony of Providence (panel 6).

A. **Frederick, the Great Elector (1620-1688):** German ruler: Consolidated Prussia and organized its government; issued his Edict of Potsdam ordaining religious tolerance; encouraged Protestant immigration (panel 1).

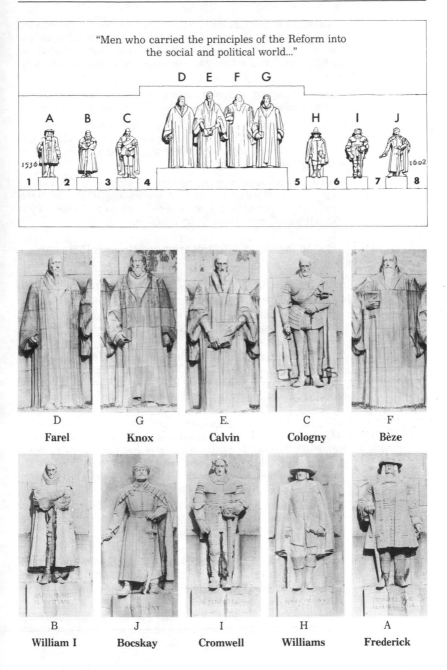

"Men who carried the principles of the Reform into the social and political world..."

D   E   F   G

A   B   C   H   I   J

1536   1602
1   2   3   4   5   6   7   8

D	G	E.	C	F
Farel	Knox	Calvin	Cologny	Bèze

B	J	I	H	A
William I	Bocskay	Cromwell	Williams	Frederick

Because the monument celebrates all the faiths of the Reformation and not just the creed of Calvin, the designers added at the ends of the steps a block engraved "Luther" and one marked "Zwingli" to recognize two other major religious leaders who influenced Switzerland.

Luther's enduring sect was strong in the northern cantons of Switzerland more than a decade before Calvin's arrival in Geneva.

Zwingli in Zurich was a preacher of comparable stature who is less well known today because, as of his death at the age of 47 (in battle as an army chaplain), he had not yet prepared a code, school, or organization to carry on his work.

Leaving the Monument by the path near Luther's block you pass a bust of Edmond Boissier, a botanist specializing in Oriental herbs. This student of Candolle wrote a six-volume work on his subject and left his collection to the Botanical Garden.

The parkside facade of the **University of Geneva [52]** is ahead to your right.

Originally established in 1559 as Calvin's Académie (page 45) this higher institute concentrated on the advanced study of the Bible and of Protestant theology as it shared the premises in the Old Town now fully occupied by the Collège.

The autonomy of the Académie was unchallenged for two centuries during which it rose above the town's parochial and political spats. In 1794 however, the anti-elitist leaders of the last of the "Petite Révolution" threatened to interfere with the traditional independence of its faculty.

Sir François d'Ivernois, an intellectual who had fled Geneva for England in the last two outbreaks of "Les Troubles" proposed to America's Thomas Jefferson some dozen of his friends from the staff of the Académie who would teach in the United States if the new republic were to open a national university. Jefferson's recommendation to President Washington went unanswered.

The Académie's autonomy survived unscathed both the revolutions in Geneva and — through the ingenuity of the Société Economique (page 82) — the occupation by the French.

In the mid-1800s, however, James Fazy's government ended the Société Economique and involved itself with the Académie's conservative staff. Discharges and serious disagreement between "town and gown" reduced the quality of both the faculty and the curriculum.

Even after the replacement of the Fazy government, the intellectual prestige of the Académie continued to fade until Fazy's successor, Antoine Carteret, acted to revive the school.

In a major move in 1872 Carteret ordered the new building in the Bastions and added a sixth Faculty — Medicine — to raise the Académie to University status.

The prestige of the designation "University" combined with the improved facilities and cooperation to attract once again a faculty of distinction. As prescribed by Calvin from the earliest days of the Académie the teaching staff included the best talents and minds of Geneva supplemented by a generous measure of foreign scholars. Among the earliest instructors was the French Protestant Joseph Scaliger, described as "... a well of erudition, one of the wisest men of his time..."

In 1901 the University employed as its Professor of Chemistry the scientist Chaim Weizmann. In the course of his five years in Geneva Weizmann married one of his students, Vera Chatzman. In Weizmann's political work in the advancement of Zionism, his wife was one of his closest collaborators. When in 1948 their efforts culminated in the creation of the revived nation of Israel, Professor Chaim Weizmann was elected its first president.

The University awarded its first honorary degree in 1909 on the occasion of the 350th anniversary of the Académie. The distinction went to a naturalized Swiss who had recently resigned from the Bern Patent Office — Albert Einstein.

The University you see here is a much expanded version of the two-story, rectangular original commissioned by Carteret. Shortly after its completion Geneva received a windfall of funds from the enormous estate of the Duke of Brunswick (page 116).

Geneva paid out of the Brunswick bequest a variety of civic improvements including the two wings added to the University.

The wing to your left is the Bibliothèque Universitaire — the University Library — and to the right was, until 1967, the Museum of Natural History.

The east wing contains the town collection of books, references, and manuscripts begun in 1543 by François Bonivard (page 52) with a few precious tomes, expanded by 1960 to 500,000 items, and grown by 1980 to more than 900,000 volumes.

The library's ground floor offers in the Salle Ami Lullin a rich sampling of Geneva memorabilia, readily appreciable on even a short visit. Displayed on the walls of two of the three rooms are portraits of persons prominent in Geneva history.

— the first room features temporary exhibits on subjects of special interest to Geneva;

— the second room displays manuscripts, early editions of Genevese texts, and a collection of historic Bibles;

— the third room is the museum of Jean-Jacques Rousseau, with various portraits, manuscripts, and personal items.

The west wing, to your right, has been classroom space since 1967, when Geneva transferred the natural history collection to its new Muséum de Genève at Place Guyénot.

Strolling around to the right of the west wing you pass through a small Alpine garden to a side entrance of the park leading to **Rue de Candolle.**

The modern restaurant across the street is on the **site [53]** of the **Café Landolt**, the brasserie preferred in years gone by professors such as Weizmann, students like Ferenc Molnar who wrote the popular play *Liliom*, performers like Maurice Chevalier, and political refugees including Bakunin, Léon Trotsky, and Lenin.

Lenin arrived in Geneva in 1900 and spent nine of his next seventeen years in its libraries and a variety of living quarters. Aided by his wife Nadia Kroupskaia, Lenin read, wrote, planned a revolution for Russia and the world, met his compatriots regularly at the Landolt, and mollified the persistently inquisitive Geneva police.

The Landolt played a large part in the legend of Lenin. When the original landmark pub was scheduled for demolition in 1969, the Soviet news agency Tass sent a full crew to Geneva to make for the national archives a pictorial record of Lenin's favorite bistro.

Turning away from the Rue de Candolle and walking on the path to your left, you see in the park the **statue [54]** of **"David Defeating Goliath"** by an apprentice of James Pradier (page 104), Jean Chaponnière of Geneva.

Chaponnière made two versions of this work, the first with David draped in a bearskin. When a rival twitted the young sculptor on his inability to model flesh, Chaponnière reworked the piece to this less-draped version and with it won the Gold Medal at the Paris Exposition of 1837.

While "David Defeating Goliath" is considered one of the finest works of sculpture in Geneva, Chaponnière's best-known work is still the panel on Paris' "Arc de Triomphe" depicting "Kléber Taking Alexandria".

Continuing past the statue toward the Old Town you see ahead the Bastion's **municipal bandstand [55].** This oasis offers both a covered and an open air terrace suitable for sipping and reading and, on certain evenings in summer, free entertainment.

On the site of the bandstand stood, in defiance of popular dis-
approbation, the first and second of Geneva's theaters.

While Calvin expressed no disapproval of moral, character-building
performances and Bèze actually wrote a successful drama — *The
Sacrifice of Abraham* — later pillars of the Reformed Church
frowned on theater in any form.

Performances were few and objections thereby limited until the
mid-1700s when Voltaire arrived and produced his own plays privately at "Les Délices" (page 77) with Genevese amateurs filling out
his cast requirements.

The controversy arose when Rousseau, himself a well-compensated
playwright and composer, perversely warned Geneva against all
"spectacles" and the moral menace posed by the contaminating
presence of actors.

In spite of Rousseau's opposition in principle, his writings were indi-
rectly instrumental in bringing theater to Geneva. When the Town
Council condemned Rousseau's works and precipitated the third
outbreak of the "Petite Révolution" it had eventually to call in
French troops to maintain order. The urbane officers of the temporary garrison assessed the local ration of lectures and religious services and then ordered the town to provide a bit more exhilarating
diversion.

In 1766 Geneva grudgingly built its first theater. Located near
the horse market outside the town walls and officially named
the "Théâtre Rosimond" after its Lyonnais director, the house
was more disdainfully referred to as the "Grange des Etrangers", the Foreigners' Barn.

A hundred and forty-four performances after its opening the showplace caught fire — Voltaire slyly insinuated that Rousseau encouraged an act of arson — and burned to the ground when the pious
women of Geneva refused to join the bucket brigade to save this
"place of depravity".

One fire, however, was not enough to close the case for theater in
Geneva. In 1782 the fourth and most disruptive of the episodes of
the "Petite Révolution" brought 12,000 soldiers from France, Bern,
and Sardinia, first to besiege, then to occupy Geneva. Once again
the officers of the foreign troops called on the Town Council for
entertainment.

In erecting its second theater Geneva used the same site but
less combustible materials and opened the stone-and-mortar,
940-seat "Théâtre de Neuve" on 18 October 1773 with a performance of Marivaux' *Le Jeu de l'Amour et du Hasard*.

The courtly leading roles were played by two French professionals, Fabre d'Eglantine and Collot d'Herbois. Fabre d'Eglantine was not only an actor but also a playwright and poet and — a decade later — an active participant in the French Revolution. The most notable contribution of the poet Fabre d'Eglantine to the Revolution was his confection for its calendar of the descriptive names such as Brumaire (fog), Thermidor (heat), Fructidor (fruit), etc., for each of its months.

According to the poet Lamartine, the French Revolution, like the Roman god Saturn, devoured its own children. In 1794 Fabre d'Eglantine went to the guillotine on orders of the Committee on Public Safety.

That Committee's most blood-thirsty member was Fabre d'Eglantine's fellow-actor-turned-politician, Jean Collot d'Herbois. He condemned guillotining only because it was too time-consuming; he recommended simply blowing up the prisons.

The Revolution in its turn consumed Collot d'Herbois. Condemned to Devil's Island, he died there of fever in 1796.

In the 1794 "Troubles" Geneva had its own revolutionaries who first annexed the theater as their "cercle" or clubhouse and later converted it into a factory for spinning thread. With the French occupation in 1798 another garrison settled in and encouraged Geneva theater to resume its erratic career.

Empress Josephine, deposed by Napoleon in 1810 (page 163), came to Geneva and enjoyed at the Théâtre Neuve a command performance of Grétry's (page 90) opera *Richard the Lion-Hearted.*

Napoleon's sister Pauline, the Princesse Borghese of Tuscany, was in the audience in 1812 to watch the performance of François Talma, the most acclaimed actor of his day and her traveling companion of the moment.

The talented Talma earned the admiration of not only the Princess, but also her imperial brother. Napoleon I studied intently the stage comportment of the majestic Talma to learn the posture, gestures, and diction appropriate to the exalted rank that the Corsican conqueror had assumed.

With the "Restauration de la République" Geneva grew more tolerant of the theater as it presented a mélange of Italian opera, ballet, drama, vaudeville, French opéra-comique, and even circuses.

Among the more notable performers was Carlotta Grisi, the legendary Italian ballerina who danced at the Théâtre Neuve the fable, *Giselle,* as adapted for her by the adoring poet and novelist Théophile Gautier.

After conquering every capital of Europe with her art, Grisi at 34 abruptly quit the theater to bear and raise in Geneva her daughter sired in Saint Petersburg by Prince Radziwill. Grisi's home for the fifty years of her retirement was a villa near "Les Délices" (page 77) on the cliff of Saint Jean overlooking the Rhone. Through the five decades of Grisi's residence her neighbors knew her simply as the "little grey lady" with no inkling of the drama and glamor of her professional career.

For much of her retirement Grisi was pursued but never caught by the urbane Paris critic, Gautier.

Gautier made many visits to Geneva and knew the canton well. From his observations he produced another local literary landmark when he used the Château de Dardagny as the "Château de la Misère" in his picaresque classic *Capitaine Fracasse.*

In his active amatory career Théophile Gautier fathered 23 children, two of them with Carlotta Grisi's sister Ernesta.

To tutor their eldest child, Judith, Gautier hired a mandarin to develop her intellectual gifts. A challenging beauty, Judith became notorious at the age of 18 for the stormy passion that she aroused in 56-year-old Richard Wagner and at 22 for her liaison with 70-year-old Victor Hugo before going on to mere celebrity for her talents as an actress, Orientalist, critic, and author.

From the bandstand and the site of the memorable old theater proceed now to the high gates leading from the park out to the open square.

◆ The Driven arriving from page 86 are welcomed to the **Place Neuve** side of the high iron gates through which The Walkers emerge from the Parc des Bastions.

◆ Those among The Driven who at this point can leave their buses, cars, or other wheeled transport for a visit afoot to the Reformation Monument turn back to page 105 for comments on this Geneva attraction.

◆ The ornamental entry to the park at which The Driven and The Walkers meet consists of five wrought-iron gates and fencing set in eight stone columns.

Atop each of the two columns flanking the ironwork is a large cast-bronze eagle with a ducal crown to remind one and all that the funds of the Duke of Brunswick paid for these ceremonial portals.

Geneva inherited the vast fortune of Charles II, the purported Duke of Brunswick — he had long contested his deposition by popular revolution in 1830 — almost by accident. The wealthy, eccentric ex-monarch of the rich Duchy of Braunschweig in Northern Germany had fled to Geneva from Paris in 1870 as a refugee from the Franco-Prussian War.

Partially in gratitude for the town's hospitality and largely to frustrate the many relatives and lesser claimants in pursuit of his millions, Charles II as an interim measure wrote in his own hand a secret will in which he bequeathed his vast fortune to Geneva.

◆ When in 1873 Charles Este-Guelph suddenly dropped dead, Geneva heard for the first time that the town was the heir to his estate estimated by the financially punctilious, deposed Duke of Brunswick at SFr 160,000,000 in gold at a time when the average income of a family in Geneva was SFr 1,000 per year.

To collect its inheritance Geneva had to carry out various specifications of the succinct will, among them the embalming of the body. As Protestant Geneva never practiced this procedure it requested from Italy instructions on how to preserve human remains. While awaiting the reply the town immersed the corpse of the abstinent late Charles II in a bathtub filled with alcoholic spirit — reportedly Swiss kirsch — placed a rock on the stomach of the cadaver to assure total coverage, and kept its benefactor in storage in the greenhouse of the Bastions Park.

Once embalmed in accordance with the Italian prescriptions, the body of Charles II was the centerpiece of a royal funeral by which it was laid to provisional repose in a sarcophagus well clear of the ground (he had suffered from claustrophobia) in the cemetery of Plainpalais. Six years later the body was moved to the monumental tomb (page 141) twenty feet above the terrace in the Right Bank's Parc des Alpes.

◆ After liquidating such assets as were immediately at hand and negotiating settlement of disputed claims, Geneva collected some SFr 24,000,000.

The first funds were spent on the Duke's funeral, his monument, legal fees for litigation that extended over four decades, and the retirement of the municipal debt of more than SFr 7,000,000.

The remainder was used for the University Library and Museum, these gates, the Municipal Office in the Old Town, the Grand Théâ-

tre in the Place Neuve, four schools, a few canvasses for the art collection, a SFr 1,000,000 standby fund, and the improvement of the
streets, parks, promenades, and slaughterhouse.

◆ Opposite the gates of the Bastions in the middle of
Place Neuve is a pond, fountains in the warm season
and, since 1887, the equestrian **statue [56]** of **General
Dufour**, soldier, engineer, statesman — the quintess-
ential Genevese.

> His statue stands close to the site of the Porte Neuve, once one of
> the main gates into Geneva. The entry was actually an arched por-
> tal passing under a two-story customs-house that controlled a port-
> cullis and a drawbridge across a broad moat. The disused guards-
> room on the upper floor served Dufour as his office until the demoli-
> tion of the fortifications in 1854.
>
> Guillaume-Henri Dufour was born in Constance because his family
> had migrated from Geneva during the fourth outbreak of the "Petite
> Révolution". From the time Dufour was 10 most of Europe was
> under French domination. He, accordingly, became a soldier in Bo-
> naparte's army.
>
> When the Napoleonic Wars ended and Geneva became a canton of
> the Confédération Helvétique, Dufour returned to his new home-
> land with its commitment to armed neutrality. Continuing as a pro-
> fessional soldier in Switzerland he planned a new militia, esta-
> blished the military academy at Thun, and modernized the out-
> moded fortifications.

Later employed as Geneva's chief engineer in an era of expansion and change, Dufour rebuilt its quays and ports, constructed bridges, improved the water supply and the drainage
system, demolished the old fortifications and redesigned outmoded structures, and directed the installation of railroad service, while teaching at the University courses in hydraulics,
geodesy, and geometry.

> As the military leader of Switzerland in 1847, Dufour prevented the
> secession of the seven cantons of the Sonderbund. In 1855, when an
> aggressive Prussia threatened to intervene in a Swiss internal con-
> flict in Neuchâtel, Dufour marched an army of 30,000 Federal troops
> to the banks of the Rhine to face down an equal force of Prussian
> soldiers. Asked later what he would have done if the Prussians had
> turned up with 60,000 men, Dufour replied, "We might have had to
> shoot twice".
>
> Dufour supervised thirty years of surveys and drafts that produced
> the still-valid maps of the rugged Swiss terrain. These handsome
> "Cartes Dufour" won gold medals at the Paris Exposition of 1867.

At age 76 Dufour was a member of the "Committee of Five" for the planning of the Red Cross (page 101). He presided over the international meetings approving both the First and the Second Geneva Conventions, and was the dominant figure on almost every official occasion until his death at age 88.

Among the many effusive obituaries, one cited Guillaume-Henri Dufour as a man whose "... fairness was equalled only by his lack of ambition".

◆ For The Driven planning another turn about Place Neuve for a closer look, the following description continues in the flow-of-traffic or counter-clockwise direction.

◆ First to the right is the Greek-columned **Musée Rath [57]**, the Rath Museum, opened in 1825 as the first public art museum in Switzerland.

The Rath family consisted of brother Simon, who served in the Tsar's army opposing Napoleon in Russia , and his two sisters, students in the art classes at the Calabri of the technique of painting miniatures.

As a Lieutenant General in the Russian army Simon Rath had acquired at the age of 40 a collection of art and a substantial fortune on which he retired to Geneva and bought a farm for the family.

On Simon's death at the age of 44 his sisters sold the farm and gave half the proceeds to Geneva to build, as a memorial to their brother, this gallery for his collection of paintings and sculptures and below it high-ceilinged studio space for the old School of Drawing and for the Society of the Arts.

In 1910 the Museum of Art and History consolidated the Rath Collection with other art works. The Musée Rath became in World War I the working space where the International Committee of the Red Cross kept its records of prisoners of war and sorted and distributed their mail.

The marble plaque on the pediment of the Rath Museum commemorates the wartime service of the ICRC. Much of the effectiveness of the ICRC in World War I was attributed to the leadership of Gustave Ador. In 1919 he was elected to the presidency of the Swiss Confederation, the only Genevese ever to hold the post.

Geneva was gratified by Ador's rise to the highest office in the land even though the post is almost purely ceremonial. Out of the nearly two hundred representatives in the Swiss Federal Diet — its Parliament or Congress — seven are chosen to be Federal Councilors. One out of these seven is in turn voted by his peers to serve as President for a one-year term to preside at their meetings, lay cornerstones, plant memorial trees, award prizes, and greet celebrated guests.

Many of the egalitarian Swiss take a perverse pride in their inability to name either the incumbent or any recent President of the Confoederatio Helvetica.

◆ Next to the Musée Rath is the **Grand Théâtre [58]** whose facade resembles the grandiose Paris Opera but in miniature.

By the 1850s Geneva's population and its taste for richer musical fare were growing while the age and the restricted capacity of the Théâtre Neuve frustrated any expansion. Geneva joined another Continental trend and contemplated owning its own opera house like those being built in Brussels, London, Vienna, and Paris except, perhaps, a bit less ornate.

The location of any new theater would be, it was assumed, that of its predecessors, visible from the river along the avenue of the Corraterie and unifying the thoroughfare's varied architecture. As planning developed, the town realized that such a new showplace would cover a greater surface and that its setting in the Bastions would involve chopping down certain trees. Forthwith the planners resited the theater to its present locale despite constricted space, an unstable base over a recently-filled moat, and the lack of an approach vista. In Geneva, trees come first.

Architect J. Elysée Goss designed the theater as a scaled-down model of the new Paris Opera, even though Garnier's masterpiece, commissioned by Napoleon III expressly to depict the glory of his imperial realm, had been described as resembling "...an overloaded sideboard".

Goss' rendering of his showplace startled Geneva. The town had been thinking along more Spartan lines and had no resources to pay for so imposing a structure. Goss' dream was, however, turned into reality, financed by the unforeseen legacy from the Duke of Brunswick and on 4 October 1879 Geneva inaugurated its pseudo-Renaissance Grand Théâtre with a gala performance of Rossini's *William Tell*.

In ensuing seasons Hugo de Senger (page 59), the force behind the Grand Théâtre, produced more ambitious operas and promoted in Geneva a taste for symphonic music. Among the composers who have conducted their own work at the Grand Théâtre are Tschaikowsky, Saint-Saëns, Massenet, Delibes, and Stravinski.

The musical season has occasionally been supplemented by presentations of spoken drama and comedy. Sarah Bernhardt played here on several occasions and there was once even a colossal production of *Around the World In Eighty Days* with a cast of a hundred plus elephants, a steam boat, and a full-sized locomotive on stage.

The most devastating drama took place in-house in 1951. For the final act of Richard Wagner's *La Walkyrie* in which the Fire God Loki isolates Brunhilde in a circle of flames, the stage manager resorted to new technology to make the scene more vivid. In place of the usual magnesium flash powder he substituted an oxygen bomb of advanced design.

His flame thrower did indeed produce for the dress rehearsal of 1 May 1951 an awe-inspiring, ten-foot tongue of fire. The resulting blaze, however, not only kept unworthy suitors away from Brunhilde but, within a few hours, incinerated the entire stage and auditorium.

At the time of this conflagration the Grand Théâtre was already more than seventy years old and the section that burned down was the part of the house most in need of modernization.

When the Grand Théâtre reopened in 1963 its classic facade and foyer remained intact but behind them were 1,488 seats of superior design, a spectacular ceiling and curtain by Jacek Strykenski, and a technically advanced stage.

The terrace and marquee of the Café Lyrique in the lower corner of Place Neuve occupy the site of Geneva's pioneer power plant.

In 1883 engineer Théodore Turrettini (page 132) ran lines from the new generating station to provide electric lighting for the Grand Théâtre. The spotlights, switches, and dimmers made possible by electric controls produced effects that took the breath of audiences accustomed to candles, lanterns, or gas jets burning throughout the performance.

The innovation of extinguishing the house lights, which had long provided equal illumination to stage and auditorium, revolutionized theater-going as the attention of fashionable audiences was at last concentrated more on the paid performers than on one another.

◆ The Italianate building towards which General Dufour seems to be directing his attention is the **Conservatoire de Musique [59],** the Music Conservatory, built in 1856 to expand the smaller school organized in 1825 in the rooms of the Casino (page 70).

The Bartholoni family, the rich, music-loving sponsors of the earlier conservatory, were encouraged by its success to build this Florentine counterpart of their personal villa on the edge of the lake (page 157).

◆ Turning once again in the direction of the Old Town you see in perspective above the Bastion wall the windowed facades of the Louis XV mansions of the Rue des Granges behind their stone-railed terraces in a model of architectural harmony.

The Walkers move now towards the wall of the Old Town and cross the "zebra" stripes at the Rue de la Croix Rouge to the arm of sidewalk opposite. Look on the wall for the stone plaque with its diagram of Porte Neuve and its fortifications as they were in 1602, the year of Geneva's "Escalade" victory.

> During the decades of the Wars of Religion Duke Charles Emmanuel I of Savoy, the son-in-law of the fanatically anti-Protestant Philip II of Spain, had harassed Geneva with economic blockade, political sanctions, and the pillage of outlying villages.
>
> By the first years of the 1600s, however, Geneva had extended its defences and stocked its larders well enough to feel secure from any assault. Then, on the longest night of 1602, 11/12 December (by the old Caesarian calendar), Duke Charles sent 6,000 troops to cross the River Arve and capture Geneva.

While the main force of men from Savoy and Spain waited in the dark on the plain south of these walls, two hundred commandos filled the town moat with faggots and set up their scaling ladders. The Savoyard advance party silently clambored over the ramparts intent on opening the gates from the inside to let in their brothers-in-arms.

> As the Savoyards crept through the streets towards the gatehouse they chanced upon a lone Genevese sentry. His startled cries were heard by the citizen on the night watch high in the Cathedral tower. The great church bells began to toll.
>
> At the sound of the bells the gatekeeper of Porte Neuve, Isaac Mercier, dropped the portcullis (the "herse" mentioned on the plaque) to seal off the main access up the ramp to your right.
>
> From a gunport in the projecting bastion a cannon fired a load of chain laterally that carried away the scaling ladders of the Savoyards.

The assault team was trapped in the Old Town, by then swarming with aroused citizens. Some of the commandos were killed in the streets, others in dropping from the walls. Those who survived the long fall retreated into their own army.

The main body of Spanish troops — mistaking the clamor for a rout of the Genevese — advanced and slaughtered their allies as they collided in the dark.

> The town, exhilarated by the victory, immediately improvised a court to try its sixty-three prisoners. The captives reinforced their pleas for mercy with offers of ransom equal to the man's weight in silver, all to no avail.
>
> On 12 December 1602 the Genevese condemned, hanged and then beheaded the invaders, flung the bodies into the river, and ranged the heads in a line along the top of these ramparts.

Walkers continue now across the Rampe de la Treille to reach the semi-circular plot on which stands yet a third memorial (pages 45 and 102) to Henri Dunant.

◆ This somewhat cramped setting for the heavy **bust [60]** of **Henri Dunant** was a choice site among the several in Geneva used for official tortures and executions.

> As recently as two centuries ago, the torture, corporal punishment, and execution of the condemned were popular spectacles in most European towns. Geneva was no exception.
>
> Geneva, however, had no expectation of ever seeing such spectacles of public disgrace with a cast including the long-dominant elite of the "Ancien Régime". Nonetheless in the final "Petite Terreur" of the "Petite Révolution" seven members of Geneva's oligarchy stood before a Revolutionary Tribunal and — astonished to hear themselves called "aristos" — were condemned to death as "...enemies of the people".
>
> Lacking a firing squad willing to carry out their sentence, the revolutionaries recruited from among the foreign workers idling in the bistros a band of amateur executioners. Some of the sentenced "Messieurs-du-Haut" won reprieves but the revolutionaries, determined to apply seven sentences, lined up a mixed group for the inept squad to shoot and at length execute against the wall known thereafter as the "Montagne de Plomb", the Lead Mountain.

Executions as punishment continued into the mid-1800s but with decreasing frequency as judges responded to the campaigns of men like Jean-Jacques Sellon (page 86) and Henri Dunant. The latter, a bitter opponent of legal killings and particularly shocked by a badly bungled hanging in 1862, appealed to Victor Hugo for support. An eloquent reply from France's dedicated foe of capital punishment persuaded Geneva's Council to pass in 1871 a law abolishing the death penalty.

Although by 1980 Dunant's role in the Red Cross had been recognized by two memorials in Geneva, a group of citizens remained dissatisfied with the quality of the monuments and raised SFr 14,000 for this bronze bust.

The town assigned the private tribute to this spot in the Place Neuve where, its sponsors contend, it is difficult to see let alone to contemplate. From the standpoint of symbolism, however, the presence of a Dunant monument watching over the site of the executions which he helped abolish does seem sound.

In addition Dunant would be gratified by the description of his historic role on this third dedication where, elevated from "promoteur" (page 45) and "initiateur" (page 102), he is named "Fondateur" of the Red Cross, a distinction to which he in his latter years laid vigorous claim.

◆ Leaving Place Neuve, all enter the street called the **Corraterie,** an odd term contracted from a long Latin phrase meaning "The Neighborhood for the Running of Horses".

This section of Geneva was once associated with a variety of equine activities — their trading, their training, their racing and, eventually, the treating of horse's hides.

◆ The point at which the Savoyard commandos crossed the moat and scaled the walls in the attack of 1602 is marked by the **Escalade Plaque [61],** set high in the wall on your right, just beyond the stone fountain.

The Escalade is not, of course, ranked with Marathon, Tours, Waterloo, or Stalingrad as a battle that decided the fate of nations, but the course of Protestantism depended on its outcome.

Geneva's triumph served not only to keep Calvinism alive at its source and to reconcile for a while the town's hitherto disparate community but also to encourage the leaders of the expanding Protestant world — Henri IV of France, Elizabeth I of England, the German princes, and the newly-united Dutch states — to lavish on the town their grateful praise and substantial political and financial backing.

The segment of the town wall carrying the Escalade plaque is a remainder of the second phase of the fortifications, those built around the base of Geneva's hill well beyond the first set of walls which simply ringed its summit.

Bishop Guillaume of Marcossay ordered the extended walls built in 1360 to defend the commerce of the lower town against the bands of desperate marauders who roamed the Continent in the impoverished 1300s.

Of the 22 tall watchtowers built into the long wall, only the "Tour Thelusson" survived for more than five centuries. Then, in 1902, despite strenuous popular objections the "Thelusson" was demolished and replaced with its approximate replica at 7 Corraterie.

◆ The door of 7 Corraterie has as its keystone a carved head, a "mascaron", representing Mère Royaume, the vigorous mother of sixteen children who earned instant immortality in the Escalade by dropping a heavy stewpot out of her kitchen window on to a Savoyard head.

Royaume's stewpot or "marmite", cast in chocolate, is the ubiquitous symbol of the Escalade celebration, an occasion for parades, costume, and — for children only — masks (page 225).

The highlight of the annual holiday is the torchlight parade through the darkened streets on the Sunday evening nearest 11 December. The leading citizens in folkloric costumes thread their way to assemble in the Cour Saint-Pierre around a towering bonfire to hear a reading of the 1602 victory proclamation and the 124th Psalm.

The outcome of Mère Royaume's momentous pot drop is portrayed in the "mascaron" of the startled Savoyard at the end of the line above 5 Corraterie.

Across the Corraterie from the Escalade wall is an impressive variety of quality shops, shoulder-to-shoulder under the unifying facade designed by General Dufour in 1825.

◆ The Driven follow the traffic flow along the striped lanes of the Corraterie beyond the next traffic signal where they turn a wide right into Place Bel-Air.

Walkers turn right at the next corner into the **Rue de la Confédération**, the street formerly called the Rue des Allemands, the Street of the Germans.

The name originated in the 1300s when traders from northern cantons concentrated their stalls in this area near the bridge. The name remained until 1914 when passions rose over World War I and Geneva showed where its sentiments lay by renaming the street for the homeland.

At the foot of the steep **Rue de la Cité** is the **Fontaine de l'Escalade [62]**, executed in 1857 by Johan Leeb of Munich, the sculptor of Lola Montez' "Boy with Crocodile" (page 57).

The plaque on the street side depicts the Escalade encounter in great detail. The uphill side shows Théodore de Bèze celebrating the joyous victory in Reformed style in the Cathedral with a reading of the 124th Psalm and the ordering of a day of fasting.

◆ **The six thoroughfares leading to the bridge over the Rhone have for centuries made its approach the most animated crossroad in Geneva.**

The ancient shrine of "Our Lady of the Bridge of the Rhone" served travelers here until the 1300s when foreign bankers replaced it with their richly ornamented "Chapel of the Florentines".

When the Reformers of Geneva permitted the increasing numbers of Germans to open their first Lutheran house of worship in the early 1700s (page 60), it was located, predictably, on the Rue des Allemands.

Looking up the steep slope of the Rue de la Cité, note on the left a Genevese "dôme", a tall wooden upright extending to support the building's top floor.

This curious architectural form developed with the arrival of the refugees in the Reformation. When Geneva was unable to lodge newcomers by expanding beyond the limits of the town walls, rooms were added atop existing houses and out and over the street. At one time Geneva had hundreds of such "dômes" creating a chain of arcades sheltering the open shopping counters of the street markets below.

For an impression of the "dôme" effect, continue along Rue de la Confédération a few more meters to see against the Old Town hill a stylized reconstruction of three "dômes" and contrast them with the one in the rue de la Cité, the only authentic relic of this unique form.

The disappearance of the practical and picturesque arcades was another change lamented by Victor Hugo in his report of his visit in 1839.

Turning away from the Rue de la Cité, cross the street into Rue de la Monnaie, Mint Street.

When Geneva declared itself a Republic in 1536 it began minting its own coinage in a "Monnaie" in the Cour Saint-Pierre. In 1543 Geneva moved its "Monnaie", the Mint, into this market area.

In this short street you pass the heavy steel sculpture, readily identifiable as "The Great Friendship", to continue into the Place Bel-Air.

◆ The area at **Place Bel-Air** is the nucleus from which Geneva grew. The plaza was the approach from the hilltop town to the river bridge that gave Geneva its reason to exist.

> The bridge could be built in ancient times because nature — long before the tribesmen settled at the lake edge more than 5,000 years ago (page 35) — provided two hard-rock islands a few meters apart in the middle of the Rhone here at the end of the lake.
>
> Some primitive engineer used the island as his central pylon to build a bridge from shore to shore. This crossing was the only point in the 800-kilometer (500-mile) length of the river where travelers could traverse without risk to their goods.
>
> Once the bridge was in place, the pylon grew into an island, crowded with stalls and dwellings until they overflowed on to its approaches. Such densely packed wooden market stands, taverns, and inns were highly vulnerable to the great fires that regularly swept though the town.

A conflagration in January 1670 devastated both the over-crowded island and this adjacent square. The clearing of the debris let the people see clearly, for the first time in centuries, the river and surroundings. The unfamiliar salubrity suggested the name "Fresh Air Plaza", Place Bel-Air.

> The wholesome name of Place Bel-Air did not deter the site from being the one preferred for Geneva's public punishments. Here the remains of the flayings, drawings, quarterings, and beheadings could be quickly tidied up with the help of the convenient river to flush away such leftovers as were deemed of too little interest for extended display on surrounding posts and hoardings.
>
> Natural deaths in Place Bel-Air were rare. Among the exceptions was that of the brilliant English physicist, Sir Humphry Davy, who contributed so broadly to theoretical chemistry and electricity but is best remembered for his Davy lamp, the light that made safe the digging of coal from deep mines of great capacity and thus fueled the Age of Steam.
>
> On 29 May 1829 Davy dropped dead of an apoplectic stroke in Place Bel-Air. He is buried in Plainpalais Cemetery.

A two-day civil war between the townspeople and the militia of Geneva in 1846 centered in Place Bel-Air.

When the town's conservative government of that year refused to vote in the Federal Diet against the secession of the seven cantons of the Sonderbund from the Swiss Confederation (page 37), four hundred incensed citizens took up arms. From the industrial quarter of the Right Bank the insurgents fought three thousand disciplined militiaman for 48 hours with a running attack, sniping from windows and doorways.

On 7 October 1846 the street fighters broke through the lines of troops at Place Bel-Air and swept into power their liberal leader, James Fazy (page 59).

Charles Dickens arrived for his first visit to Geneva in that same October 1846. In his week's sojourn Dickens was impressed both with the town's new government and with its citizen's rapid resumption of calm and order. Dickens added to the list of literary references to Geneva when in *David Copperfield* he has his hero, traveling to forget the death of Little Dora, spend his winter here.

◆ The Driven passing through Place Bel-Air now follow the traffic lanes to their left across the barely perceptible Pont de l'Ile to the **Ile**, the Island.

Walkers crossing the Pont de l'Ile may see to their left, about a hundred meters downstream, a largish white structure at the end of the Ile. Once the municipal slaughterhouse and central food supply depot, the building is still called **Les Halles de l'Ile [63]**, the Island Market, but is actually an all-purpose cultural center.

In addition to its galleries, exhibits, studios, and craft shops, Les Halles offers for sipping or dining a sidewalk café, a bistro, a formal restaurant, and an outdoor terrace, prettily situated just above the river.

Although the Island began as a primitive trading and commercial center, the Romans' annexation in 120 B.C. made this a key point in the imperial line of defences.

Julius Caesar arrived in 58 B.C. to block the bridge in a military operation, perhaps to protect Roman property but certainly to enhance his standing in the First Triumvirate of Rome.

Caesar's version of his exploits as translated from the Latin of the plaque described on page 129 reads approximately:

"Geneva is the farthest town of the Allobrigians and the closest to the territory of the Helvetians. A bridge connects the town to the Helvetians. When it was told to Caesar that the Helvetians intended to come into our provinces he hurried to leave Rome, proceeded by forced marches to TransAlpine Gaul, and reached Geneva. He there had the bridge of the town cut away."

Caesar's report ignores the point of view of 360,000 Helvetians. In 58 B.C. this peaceable Celtic tribe was in the process of migrating from its broad valley north of Lake Geneva to Aquitaine in southwest France to escape the continuous harassment of Germanic tribes pressing south from the Rhineland.

By his blocking of the Geneva crossing and his army's subsequent slaughter in the unequal battle of Bibracte, Caesar drove the Helvetians back to their struggles on the plain between the Jura mountains and the Alps.

Such Helvetians as survived their ordeal were annexed by the Romans and, in 71 A.D., were promoted to the status of a Roman colony. Their name endures in the term "Confoederatio Helvetica" — Switzerland's official designation in Latin and the source of the "CH" initials that identify Swiss-registered vehicles.

◆ Approaching the Island from the Place Bel-Air note on the edge of the building on the left-hand street the vertical sign **Tourist Office [64].**

Access to this storefront facility is on the Rue des Moulins, marked by a large blue "**i**" on a white background, the international symbol for "Information".

Geneva's "Office du Tourisme" is also its "Intérêts de Genève", a multilingual, free, well-documented service sponsored by the town's hotel and restaurant owners.

◆ The clock tower on the right-hand street is the **Tour de l'Ile [65],** the oft-reconstructed lookout point of the castle built in 1219 for the Bishop Aymon of Grandson.

Aymon's citadel sprawled across both of the original islands, uniting them permanently. The bishop-princes had governed Geneva for centuries from the Evêché (page 67) on the summit of the hill. The Château de l'Ile gave them a water-level strongpoint from which to control the river crossing and combat the inroads of the encroaching Counts of Savoy and Geneva (page 8).

In 1290 the army of the Count of Savoy besieged the castle on the Island for fourteen weeks before it capitulated.

During Geneva's trade expansion of the 1300s, however, the Island proved to be of less importance as a military redoubt than as a commercial center. The bishops' château, eroded by frequent fires and overrun by shops and stalls, disintegrated until there remained only the tower, carefully preserved as relic and landmark.

The ornamental clock atop the tower is flanked on its right by the seal of Geneva and on the left by the seal of Grandson, the town on Lake Neuchâtel where Bishop Aymon was born.

◆ The statue at the foot of the tower is that of Philibert Berthelier, the Huguenot leader decapitated here in 1519.

Berthelier collaborated with Besançon Hugues (page 101) and François Bonivard (page 52) in the early 1500s to ally Geneva with the Swiss rather than submit to the House of Savoy.

John the Bastard, Geneva's Savoyard bishop-prince and the sworn enemy of the Huguenots, after many efforts contrived to capture the proud Berthelier and have him tortured and beheaded here on the Ile.

When Geneva prepared this monument to its martyred hero the town did not overlook Berthelier's pet and mascot — the furry "belette" that lived in his master's pocket.

Looking closely at the stone pedestal, you can see the likeness of the weasel carved in its right side.

The half-dozen lines in Latin engraved on the stone plaque on the tower and facing the street are from Book 1, Chapter 7 of Julius Caesar's *Commentaries on the Gallic Wars* and are translated on page 127. Caesar's text is the earliest written reference to Geneva and the first words in the town's recorded history.

While the Island from its earliest times was a profitable market place, the swift-running river beside it was also an asset, useful for the disposal of debris and for cold-water laundering. Eventually the Genevese learned to channel the stream to turn wheels geared to grindstones for grain and to tools for working metals.

By the 1700s the Old Town needed water for its many new mansions, theretofore subsisting on wells, water wagons, and catchwater. For this supply Geneva contracted with a Frenchman, Joseph Abeille, who had designed for Louis XIV the "hydraulic machine" pumping water to the fountains of the King's retreat at Marly-le-Roi.

In 1708 Abeille installed on the Island a high waterwheel driving crankarms into pumpchambers that delivered a modest ration of the Rhone to six fountains on Geneva's hilltop. Unfortunately, the drinking water's pollution index — whether from the debris in the river or from the 500 meters (a quarter of a mile) of lead pipe in the delivery system — was high enough to upset the stomachs of the unhabituated consumer.

When no one actually died of the ill effects the citizens set aside their suspicions of the Catholic Abeille and his rumored Popish plot to poison innocent Protestants.

Six makers of modern Geneva

1740

1799

H.B. de SAUSSURE

Horace-Bénédict de Saussure, explorer, scientist, and writer, delighted in mountains not only for adventure but also as subjects for study. To advance his research he experimented in physics, geology, and meteorology, inventing new instruments to meet his needs. A practiced Alpinist, Saussure led the scientific expedition that in 1787 made the second climb of Mont Blanc. His eloquent report of the exploit awakened wide interest in tourism, mountaineering, and his home town of Geneva (page 83).

Charles Pictet-de-Rochemont, statesman and diplomat, retired from the French Army in 1783 to a life of literature, gentleman farming, and the breeding of Merino sheep. Called forth at 61 to represent the Republic of Geneva at the post-Napoleonic peace talks of 1814, he arranged through the Great Powers to have Geneva join the Swiss Confederation. Thereafter, as head of the Swiss delegation, he persuaded the treaty-makers to recognize the "universal neutrality" of Switzerland (page 98).

1755

1824

C. PICTET de ROCHEMONT

1778

1841

A-.P. de CANDOLLE

Augustin-Pyramus de Candolle, botanist, left Geneva to study, write, and teach in Paris and Montpellier. Returning to Geneva at 44, Candolle became a force in politics, science, the arts, education, and society, enhancing the international renown of Geneva's culture and thought. Candolle's research into and reclassification of plant families and the Botanical Garden he planted in the Bastions placed Geneva in the forefront of the academic centers of botany (page 70).

Guillaume-Henri Dufour, soldier, engineer, and statesman, retired from the French Army to return to his family's roots in Geneva. Over several decades Dufour engineered the demolition and rebuilding that expanded and transformed Geneva into a modern metropolis. In Swiss affairs Dufour led the victorious Federal troops in the civil War of the Sonderbund in 1847 and, in international activities, was, in 1864, among the five original founders of the Red Cross (page 117).

1787   1875

GENERAL DUFOUR

1794   1878

JAMES FAZY

James Fazy led the liberal government that swept into power in Geneva after two centuries of conservative oligarchy. Fazy's Constitution of 1847 changed Geneva from an agglomeration of tall houses crowded within an outdated fortress to an urban center of parks and avenues linking the town to its countryside. Fazy's meteoric rise and fall in politics, followed by disastrous undertakings in private banking, reduced him to the poverty in which he died at the age of 84 (page 137).

Théodore Turrettini, engineer and scion of one of Geneva's oldest families, advanced local industry with the provision of improved hydraulic power and then with the new electrical energy. While deeply involved in Geneva's development and civic affairs, Turrettini added to the town's prestige abroad with his technical counsel to the projects of many nations and to the international venture to harness the power of Niagara Falls (page 132).

1845   1916

THEODORE TURRETTINI

◆ The Driven, as they cross the second segment of the Pont de l'Ile, bear into the right lane for the turn and a glance left downstream at the **Pont de la Coulouvrenière [66]** whose graceful design was inspired by the Pont de l'Alma in Paris.

> This most aesthetic of Geneva's bridges was built to widen the access to the Left Bank's Plainpalais drill-ground where the summer-long Swiss National Exposition took place in 1896.

The sweeping concrete quay between the bridges and in front of the Hôtel du Rhône is the **Quai Turrettini,** named for the designer and builder of the Coulouvrenière Bridge, an engineer and statesman of many achievements, Théodore Turrettini.

> As an engineer Turrettini concentrated less on such civil engineering projects and more on hydraulics and electricity. He designed new hydro-turbines to drive the town's pumps, the watchmakers' tools, and the lathes and milling machines of the Société Genevoise d'Instruments de Physique, the prestigious maker of precision instruments, a company he headed at the age of 24.
>
> As his reputation grew internationally, Turrettini in 1876 designed and made the freezing machinery for London's — and the world's — first all-season ice-skating rink and in 1880 visited the United States to meet Thomas Edison and to study his electric lighting system.
>
> By 1888 Turrettini was already a consultant to many governments for their hydro-electric development and high-voltage transmissions when he was invited to join the International Commission planning electrical power generation at Niagara Falls. He was offered and refused the post of head of the "Cataract Construction Company".
>
> In addition to providing Geneva with its hydraulic installations, the safety valve that produced the original "Jet d'Eau", the lighting for the Grand Théâtre, and the Coulouvrenière bridge, Turrettini directed a vigorous but futile effort to promote a Jura tunnel for a direct Paris-Geneva rail link (page 184), served as an officer in the Swiss artillery and, although spurning all political party affiliations, was elected to both of Geneva's Councils and to the Federal Diet.

Alongside the Quai Turrettini is a landing for an excursion boat offering a relaxing two-hour ride down the Rhone as far as the artificial lake behind the dam at the hydro-electric power station. At this point the boat turns back while the Rhone continues eastward into France through the Jura Mountains at the water gap called the "Fort de l'Ecluse", the Fort at the Lock — as in a canal or river.

Although this gap is one of Europe's more important strategic points in military terms, the Fort de l'Ecluse is known to art lovers as the subject of a watercolor by Joseph M. W. Turner, the "Shakespeare of British Painting" whose work includes many impressions of Swiss scenes and backgrounds, sketched during his frequent visits to this area.

◆ The Driven turn to the right to continue beside the river on the **Quai des Bergues**, indisputably on the Right Bank, while continuing the "Left Bank Tour".

Walkers at the end of the bridge make a short excursion into the Saint-Gervais quarter. For centuries this was a tiny village, isolated beyond the customs barriers of the Island and alien to Geneva.

By the early 1400s however, Geneva was prospering but cramped behind the walls erected by Bishop Marcossay around the base of its hill (page 124). One natural direction for expansion beyond the walls was towards Saint Gervais. Geneva eventually absorbed the area and developed it as a model of early urban planning. A strict code written in 1424 regulated the size of each ground plot, the shapes of roofs, stairs, and windows, and the heights of the buildings as they ranged from the Pont de l'Ile up the slope of the **Rue de Coutance.**

The name "Coutance" is the Genevese patois version of the name assigned by Jean de Brogny to commemorate the Council of Constance over which that bishop-prince had presided from 1414 to 1418 (page 73).

Two blocks up the hill you see above the entry of "La Placette" department store its three-story-high **facade [67]** designed by the contemporary and popular Swiss artist, Hans Erni, to depict a legendary scene between **Isaac Rousseau and his son** Jean-Jacques.

The twelve detailed books of *Confessions* of Rousseau devote only a few lines to his father Isaac, an intelligent but unstable jack-of-many-trades, who spoiled his younger son, taught him to read and to respect literature, and then disappeared from his life.

Isaac did, however, make a deep impression on Jean-Jacques when he counseled the seven-year old, "Jean-Jacques, aime ton pays..." — "love thy country".

Erni's design is appropriate here because it was in Saint Gervais that Rousseau lived during the years of his apprenticeships, first as a clerk and then as an engraver.

Saint Gervais was always the poorer quarter of Geneva, the inexpensive neighborhood where refugees and newcomers settled on their first arrival.

> Among the families immigrating in the 1600s was one whose name Fawzi signified "victorious" in their native Arabic. The factory they founded for the weaving and printing of textiles grew into an important Genevese industry and the financial base for their descendant, James Fazy.

Returning down the Rue Coutance one long block from "La Placette", turn left into the narrow **Rue des Etuves**, Bathhouse Street, a vestige of an older Geneva.

> It was at 13 Rue des Etuves that Rousseau was working as an engraver's apprentice when in March 1728 he returned from a country stroll to find the town gates locked and so simply wandered off to a new existence.

At the end of the Rue des Etuves turn right across the Place Chevelu to the river at the **Pont de la Machine,** the Bridge of the Machinery.

◆ The bridge combines a walkway across the Rhone with the control gates and sluices that govern the discharge of Lake Geneva into the river and, in the other direction, the lake level all along its 500-kilometer (300-mile) shoreline.

> On days in the warm season when the sluices are open and the waters are cascading through, kayakers use the torrent for their sport. They paddle their fragile craft upstream close to the quay and then veer into the middle for a short shoot-the-chutes ride into the current.
>
> In the cold season, on a Sunday near Christmas Day (page 225), this bridge is the finish line for the 130-meter (150-yard) swimming race in 5° C (40° F) water for the "Coupe de Noël" in which hundreds of masochists from all over Switzerland clamor to participate.

From the bridge a long block of smart shops and boutiques along the Quai extends to the Place des Bergues.

> The name "bergues" is a fragment of the name of Johann Kleberger, a financier from Nuremberg. The rich and cultured Kleberger is remembered today by one syllable of his patronym surviving in Geneva and his portrait in the Vienna Museum of Art painted by the eminent Albrecht Dürer in 1526 in the unusual form of a medallion.

In the 1520s when Kleberger owned the farm that extended the length of this bank of the Rhone, he was known to his neighbors as "the good German".

◆ At the **Place des Bergues [68]** the bronze sculpture "La Flamboyante", The Flaming Object, by Antoine Poncet, stands among welcoming benches for The Walkers, arranged around the bricked-over mall where the Rue William Tell meets the Rue Winkelried.

William Tell is the symbol of Swiss independence as expressed in the legend of the late 1200s in which he refused to bow to the cap of the Hapsburg's Gessler and was sentenced to shoot an apple off his son's head. His successful shot, his threat to Gessler with the second arrow, his escape and killing of Gessler are all related to the Swiss alliance of 1291 and the revolt of "der Schwytzers" against the rule of the Hapsburgs.

Arnold Winkelried was the hero of the Battle of Sempach in 1386. When the Swiss infantry phalanx was deadlocked against the tightly-serried front of the Austrians of the Hapsburgs, Winkelried in the forward rank gathered the enemy lanceheads to his chest and fell on them, thus immobilizing the Austrian weapons and opening the way for a great Swiss victory.

The textbooks report that Winkelried died shouting "Look after my wife and children". The popular schoolboy rendering claims that Winkelried was actually yelling, "Quel est le salaud qui m'a poussé?" — "Which one of you s.o.b.'s pushed me?"

The Russian novelist, Feodor Mikhailovich Dostoevsky, when registering the death of his infant daughter Sophie in May 1868, gave as his address a boarding house in the Rue William Tell.

Dostoevsky first visited Geneva in 1862 on a trip through Germany to Spain that he undertook to elude his difficult family in Russia and to accompany Appolinaria Suslova. This great love of his life was, however, so enamored of a Spanish matador that throughout her travels with the novelist she kept him at arm's length.

Until this tour with Suslova, Dostoevsky, a pathological gambler, had kept his impulses under control. Released from the constraints of family and homeland he embarked in 1862 on an eight-year career of ruinous plunging. After his losses on a circuit of the German casinos Dostoevsky gambled in Geneva's "Cercle des Etrangers", a private club in the mansion of James Fazy who had sublet a salon to a professional operator (page 138).

When Dostoevsky lost his last centime he was reduced to begging from Appolinaria. She pawned her ring for their train fare back to Moscow.

The novelist drew upon his costly experiences for the book he wrote in haste to get back in funds — *The Gambler*, dictated in 1866 to his 18-year-old secretary, Anna Snitkina.

In February 1867 the 46-year-old Dostoevsky married young Anna. After another unprofitable tour of the casinos of northern Europe the couple came to Geneva (page 187). Settled in for a protracted stay, Dostoevsky gambled, wrote part of *The Idiot*, and observed closely the colony of Russian revolutionaries who provided material for his 1872 *The Possessed*.

Jubilant at the birth of their daughter, Dostoevsky coddled the delicate infant through its fewer than three months' existence. A few days after Sophie's burial in the Plainpalais Cemetery, her parents moved away from the scene of their family tragedy, first to Vevey, then on into Italy.

◆ At the end of the Quai is the Hôtel des Bergues, opened in May 1834 as the first hotel to be built on the Right Bank.

In spite of its initial advantage as the only hotel within Geneva's walls offering a view of Mont Blanc, the Bergues stood within the confines of the gloomy town ramparts, remote from the busier Left Bank and its success remained limited until the 1850s. Then the demolition of the fortifications on the Right Bank and the advent of the railroad service encouraged a new clientele, including such celebrated guests as Lola Montez, Eugène Süe, George Henry Lewes, and George Eliot.

When, in 1920, the League of Nations established its offices on the Right Bank, hotel business on this side of the water increased. To meet the demand the Bergues added another floor.

◆ At the crossroad at the Mont-Blanc Bridge all are now returned to the Left Bank Start point and headed towards the **Quai du Mont-Blanc**, the start of "Geneva, Right Bank".

For those afoot and ready for repose and refreshment, a little exploration of this Start Point vicinity could turn up no fewer than a dozen cafés, restaurants, terraces, fast food emporia, tea rooms, snackbars, and the garden on Rousseau's island, all within a two-hundred-meter radius.

Geneva Right Bank

◆ The **Start** for the visit to the Right Bank of Geneva is by the **Pont du Mont-Blanc**, Mont Blanc Bridge, diagonally across from the Hôtel des Bergues, at the corner nearest the boat landing.

Proceed along the **Quai du Mont-Blanc** on the tree-lined boulevard that Geneva built in the 1850s after the town's demolition of its thick walls.

> In the 1600s Geneva built heavy defences around this section of its Right Bank. The fortress wall began downstream, at the river island, circled the ridge of the hill, and ended here in a salient out over the lake at the entrance to the harbor.
>
> All threat of invasion by land or by lake had long since passed when James Fazy, installed as head of the government by bullets then ballots in 1847 (page 127), ordered the fortifications removed and the long-congested inner town opened to expansion.
>
> Fazy's forceful personality and his audacity in changing Geneva more radically than any leader since Jean Calvin won him a strong popular following. His appreciative partisans in his government awarded Fazy for personal use two plots of the newly-recovered Geneva terrain, one on each side of the lake.

The town property granted to James Fazy on the Right Bank is now occupied by the "Arab Bank (Swiss)".

This building of the 1970s is the antithesis of the Victorian palace ordered by Fazy and elaborately furnished to house his paintings — including a Rembrandt, a Titian, and a Van Dyck — and to entertain such distinguished guests as Lola Montez (page 56), Marie de Solms Bonaparte (page 65), and Richard Wagner (page 182).

> Fazy's tenure of the cantonal leadership was revolutionary but short as his dictatorial ways alienated voters and his projects proved overambitious. Within a decade of his spectacular victory his political image was badly tarnished, his party was out of power, and his personal finances desperately low.
>
> Even out of office Fazy remained a Genevese celebrity. When in 1867 the "Congress for Peace and Freedom" attracted to its highly promoted meeting in Geneva such prestigious delegates as Victor Hugo, John Stuart Mill, and Giuseppe Garibaldi, Fazy received them all at his mansion.

Garibaldi was the hero of the decade, venerated for his daring in liberating occupied principalities to form a united Italy. As Fazy's guest Garibaldi appeared on the balcony overlooking this Quai to accept the ringing cheers of the crowd. Assuming that he was addressing an assemblage of Calvinists, the Italian revolutionary began his impromptu speech with, "The Papacy, that pestilential institution..."

The crowd fell deathly silent. Seconds later a riot broke out between the Protestant bystanders and the hundreds of Catholic Italians gathered to greet their erstwhile hero. The bewildered Garibaldi, turning to his friend Fazy, inquired, "Did I go too far?"

Fazy, excluded from political life, went into private banking, financing such ventures as a variety theater and a projected interocean canal through the Central American isthmus.

As his investments miscarried Fazy sought interim funds by subletting part of his outsized mansion to a professional gambler.

The entrepreneur converted the salons of Fazy's home into the "Cercle des Etrangers", a notorious gambling club, purportedly "private" but with little pretence of exclusivity.

Forced to the wall, Fazy sold first his mansion's contents and then the building. On his death at age of 84 he was buried at the town's expense.

The days of Fazyist grandeur lived on when in 1902 this town house became Geneva's "Hôtel de Russie", a paragon of gingerbread splendor, particularly distinguished by its wide entry steps guarded by a pair of marble sphinxes.

When Geneva demolished the hotel in the 1960s it auctioned off the marble figures for Sfr 3,100 to a "camping" — a trailer camp — at Avenches.

A few years later a dramatic feature was needed to decorate the entrance of the new underground mall at Cornavin Station (page 187). Geneva then recalled with nostalgia the long-familiar marbles and took off in hot pursuit.

Fazy's sphinxes, repurchased for Sfr 8,000 and set on new pedestals at the head of the pedestrian mall, once more keep their enigmatic watch over the Rue du Mont-Blanc.

The embarkation pier of Geneva's fleet of passenger cruisers is on the lake side of the **Quai du Mont-Blanc**.

The choice of round-trip excursions ranges from two-hour airings to all-day cruises. Special events afloat include lunch-hour outings and dancing evenings on board. The scheduled service provides pleasant transport to the harbor towns in Switzerland and France along the 500 kilometers (300 miles) of shoreline.

For thousands of years boats have plied Lake Geneva, propelled by wind or oar. The shift to mechanical propulsion began about 1820 when news of the steamboat invented by Robert Fulton circulated in Geneva. A stagecoach operator, nervous about such competition, sought to save his stable and clientele with a ship of unique design.

He ordered construction of a four-horsepower vessel, powered literally by four horses plodding in a circle around the upper deck to turn a vertical winch geared to paddle-wheels.

The craft was ingenious and inexpensive to ride. It was also noisy, odoriferous, and slow. The arrival in 1823 of a steam paddle-wheeler, ordered by Edward Church, an enterprising American consul in France, retired Geneva's one-design ship to ferry service within a few days. In memoriam, Geneva's poet-laureate Petit-Senn wrote:

> The Snail of the Lake, it's existence is done.
> It used to go slowly; now it won't even run.

The first steamboat on Lake Geneva, the *William Tell*, was 23 meters (75 feet) long and carried 200 passengers at 13 kilometers/hour (7 knots). In 1824 the bigger, faster *Winkelried* was launched in competition. Both ships were soon eclipsed by a floating palace, 37 meters (125 feet) long, carrying 500 passengers at 17.5 Km/hr. (9.5 knots) — the *Léman*.

◆ At the Hôtel de la Paix, at the next corner, Ulysses S. Grant, retired in 1877 after his eight-year term as President of the United States, installed himself and his family for their visit to Geneva.

Grant was touring Europe as a private citizen, unencumbered by bullet-proof vest or Secret Service escort. By a notice in the local press the ex-President announced that on 27 July 1877, between 7:30 p.m. and 10 p.m., he would be happy to receive anyone who cared to meet him. Seated in the lobby of the hotel, Grant greeted hundreds of Genevese from all walks of life and walked away unscathed.

The building line of the hotel along the **Rue des Alpes** coincides with the line where the town wall formerly bordered on "Le Fossé Vert", the Green Ditch, a stagnant moat until filled with the debris of the demolitions in the 1850s.

Two brass plaques, neither in plain view, are attached to the lake side of the railings of the quay, approximately opposite the Rue des Alpes. The first marker along The Walkers' route is a metal rectangle about the size of a telephone book, the other a larger, flat, semi-circular tablet.

The **half-moon-shaped plaque [69]** is an **"orientation guide"**, etched with lines from its center to a series of profiles of mountains engraved along its outer edge. The full-sized counterparts of these mountains are located by projecting with your eyes from the radians out to the summits to the east.

Mont Blanc, the highest point in Europe, is along the shiniest radian, a trace polished by thousands of fingers in search of this leading attraction.

Its perpetually snowy peak is, however, 70 kilometers (45 miles) away and visible only on some 60 days of the year. When the "bise" blowing from the Swiss glaciers to the north cools Geneva and sweeps away the intervening haze, you can see the summit described as resembling "...Napoleon in bed, wearing his hat and with the sheets pulled up under his nose..." — a frivolous image but Geneva's traditional way of pointing out Mont Blanc to visitors.

To anticipate a question frequently asked, the prominent "mountain-shaped" mountain rising symmetrically in center stage is "Le Môle" — 25 kilometers from Geneva and about a third the height of Mont Blanc.

Moving back along the railing several meters to your right, to the **rectangular plaque [69],** you learn that it marks the spot where **Elizabeth I of Austria** was assassinated in 1898.

◆ The most sensational and shocking crime of the 1890s was the senseless stabbing here of Empress Elizabeth of Austria, the ill-starred "Sissi" of history and literature.

In the years before this visit to Geneva the beautiful Elizabeth of the House of Baden had suffered a series of family tragedies. Her beloved cousin, Ludwig II of Bavaria, was drowned in a shallow stream in 1886. Her son, Archduke Rudolph, died mysteriously with his love, Maria Vetsera, in a hunting lodge at Mayerling in 1889. And in 1897 her sister was among the three hundred women burned to death in the "Charity Bazaar" fire in Paris.

Almost from the outset of her marriage at 17 to mutton-chopped Franz-Jozeph of Austria, Elizabeth had shunned the protocol of the stuffy court, preferring to read, exercise strenuously, cultivate flowers, and, when not secluded in her marble palace on the island of Corfu, to travel.

On 10 September 1898 Elizabeth was in Geneva on her further travels, undertaken as a distraction from painful memories. After lunching with Baronne Rothschild the Empress crossed from the Hôtel Beau Rivage to board the lakeboat *Genève* to return to Territet.

Out of the crowd at the quayside stepped a deranged workman who suddenly stabbed her with an improvised dagger and fled up the Rue des Alpes. While three citizens seized her assailant, Elizabeth was carried back to the hotel. Two hours later she was dead.

> The murderer, Luigi Luccheni, was a self-styled anarchist who proclaimed at his trial his conviction that "... all who eat must work..." It was his mission to eliminate the unproductive. He confessed that he had not had the slightest notion of the identity of the Empress but had judged at a glance that she was "... sufficiently aristocratic to deserve death...".
>
> The court sentenced Luccheni to solitary confinement for life, Geneva having in 1871 abolished capital punishment (page 122). Over the ensuing years editorials deplored the convict's "...pleasant, well-cared-for existence in a prison with all modern improvements..." where Luccheni harassed his jailers with unremitting demands, threats, and tirades, then, in October 1910, hanged himself in his cell.
>
> When Geneva returned Elizabeth's remains to Vienna, the imperial procession to Cornavin railroad station passed en route the Basilica of Notre Dame (page 185). Emperor Franz Josef later installed in Geneva's Catholic church a chapel and stained-glass window in Elizabeth's name.
>
> The other memorial to Elizabeth in Geneva is the small brass rectangle on the quayside railing.

The simplicity of the marker for the Empress contrasts dramatically with the opulence of that of her cousin, the Duke of Brunswick, commemorated in the catafalque across the street.

For a closer inspection of the pretentious Brunswick Monument, The Walkers cross the roadway at the "zebra" and traffic signal, controlled by a pushbutton on the lamppost.

◆ The **Brunswick Monument [70]** is both a memorial to the ducal family of northern Germany, the Brauschweigs or Brunswicks, and the tomb of Charles Este-Guelphe, once Duke Charles II.

Este-Guelphe financed this ornate edifice out of his considerable fortune which he bequeathed to the town of Geneva (page 116).

The Duke of Brunswick, the title to which Charles clung even though formally deposed for ineptitude and corruption in 1830, was an unusual man. He was a gifted linguist, an accomplished horseman, a formidable litigator, a knowledgeable musician, a chess master, an astute investor, a gem expert, and a proficient calligrapher.

He was widely read in law, history, and theology and, in his personal conduct, was abstinent, piously Protestant, and intemperately fond of animals.

By way of contrast Charles was so paranoid that he had his Palais Beaujon in Paris fitted with an iron-lined bedroom, secret exits, and an armor-plated food delivery service.

For added protection and a touch of show he kept at hand a pack of vicious hounds, a posse of six-foot-tall lackeys, and, as his personal bodyguard, a Nubian giant towering over the ducal master who stood a full 158 centimeters (5'3") in his elevator shoes.

In addition to his paranoia Charles suffered from necrophobia, claustrophobia, and psychosomatica. He searched constantly for cures for his gout, dyspepsia, residual cholera, migraines (for which he had his head shaved daily and wore one of his 35 wigs), and seasickness (which he avoided in 1850 by crossing the English Channel in a hot-air balloon).

Quite aware of his quirks, Charles himself remarked that if he were "... not so very rich he would long since have been locked up as a madman".

Charles' bequest to Geneva was no act of madness but a combination of generosity, of an intent to frustrate greedy claimants, and of his confidence that the town would carry out his wishes faithfully.

And Geneva did indeed follow his will. The town provided a five-doctor autopsy, embalming, a state funeral, and — after six years of artistic crafting — this prominently placed monument.

The style follows that of a work of art of the 1320s which Charles at age 19 had admired at first sight, the tomb of Consignorio of the Scaligieri family of Verona.

Among the monument's wealth of detail are eight scenes from the history of the Brunswicks, sculpted in haut-relief in the sides of Charles' marble coffin. The story begins with the panel that faces the lake depicting the wedding of Albert Azzo II to Cunegonde of Guelones to start the family of Este-Guelphe and ends with the panel showing the death of Charles' father, the "Black Duke" at Quatre-Bras in 1815.

In insistent affirmation of his rank, Charles ordered his tomb topped by his equestrian statue, a prerogative reserved for royal sovereigns.

The sum total of the memorial's parts added up to a precarious concentration of iron and marble installed over the recently-filled moat, Le Fossé Vert. With the instability further increased by the horse and rider offering, high above the center of gravity, a broad flank to Geneva's potent "bise", the town engineers counseled their friends to refrain from sneezing anywhere in the monument's vicinity.

More practical precautions were taken when the technicians reduced the gross tonnage and lowered the balance point by transplanting sculptor Auguste Cain's bronze statue of Charles and beast to the solid pedestal to the right.

◆ The Hôtel Beau Rivage on the Place des Alpes was opened in 1865 by the Mayers, a family whose linear descendents continue very much in charge.

Memorabilia of such guests as Charles II of Brunswick, Empress Elizabeth, the founders of Czechoslovakia, and Sarah Bernhardt are displayed in a small museum, open to the public, to the left off the lobby.

Two Golden Books of signatures separate the royalty from the merely celebrated and include between them the autographs of monarchs, potentates, statesmen, diplomats, artists, and performers. Douglas Fairbanks, Sr. immortalized himself not only by his signature but by his scaling the columns in the lobby to reach his floor without recourse to the elevator.

The elevator of the Beau Rivage, installed in 1873, was said to be the first in Switzerland. This facility was among those that decided the Brunswick contingent to move here after a tiff with the management of the Hôtel Métropole. Charles found his suites in this Right Bank hotel so comfortable that from January 1873, grown fat and feeble, he never left the second floor. He did all his business in bed, arising only at 5 p.m. for a two-hour session with his cosmetician followed by an evening of chess. It was in the middle of his game at 10.30 p.m. on 18 August 1873 that Charles died here of a heart attack.

Among the museum's displays is the hotel's register for 10 September 1898 — the date of the assassination of Elizabeth — along with a box of photos, letters, and flowers, and a piece of lace and a scarf stained with the blood of the Empress of Austria.

When the Austro-Hungarian Empire ended with its capitulation to the Allies on 29 October 1918, the new nation of Czechoslovakia rose up from its ashes. Meanwhile, Edward Benes and Stephen Osusky, an American Slovak, were in Geneva drafting a democratic constitution to give the incipient state its form.

The Brunswick Monument

When Charles Este-Guelph, the deposed Duke of Brunswick, left his vast fortune to Geneva (page 116) his will specified in Clause 4 that the town was to "...erect a mausoleum situated in a prominent and dignified locale, executed according to the design provided, using the best artists of the era working in bronze and marble without regard to cost".

The "...design provided..." was that of the tomb of Consignorio of the Scaligieri family standing in a crowded square in the heart of Verona. This Brunswick version is 20 % larger than the Italian original and enjoys a "...prominent and dignified locale..." in the well-tended Parc des Alpes [70].

The centerpiece, the sarcophogus, is decorated with eight haut-reliefs. Each panel depicts an event in Este-Guelph history, starting at the head end with the marriage of the progenitors in 1040 and showing at the foot the drowning of Prince Leopold in a rescue attempt on the Oder River in 1785. The six side panels picture events in the lives of the six Brunswick figures standing guard around the tomb, beginning to the left:

> **Ernest the Confessor (1497-1546),** hearing the Lutheran Melanchthon read the *Creed of Augsburg* to Holy Roman Emperor Charles V; 1530.
>
> **Henry the Lion (1129-1195),** on his pilgrimage to the Holy Land, meeting Amaury, King of Jerusalem; 1172.
>
> **Charles I (1735-1806),** Prussian Field Marshal, shot in the eye, dying at the Battle of Augsburg (Jena); 1806.
>
> **Frederick (1771-1815),** the "Black Duke" of the Death's Head Hussars, dying on a stretcher at the Battle of Quatre Bras; 1815.
>
> **Otto the Boy (1217-1252),** receiving title to the duchy of Brunswick from Holy Roman Emperor Frederick II; 1235.
>
> **August the Younger (1579-1666),** philosopher, in his 180,000-volume library, accepting the homage of his fellow savants; 1635.

Non-family guardians of the sarcophogus are the angels praying at each of its corners, the six virtues in niches above the arches, and the six shield bearers in smaller towers, the full cast supported by twelve crosses, seven ducal crowns, two lions at the apex of the tower, two more at the entry steps, another curled at the feet of the marble effigy, and the *tout ensemble* bracketed by a pair of vigilant griffins. Also present are seventeen assorted heads and a skull peering from niches and, in season, a resident flock of pigeons.

The remains of Charles II rest secure, presumably, in his unsealed coffin set as he wished − some say − with his stiffly Protestant back

Ernest

Frederick

Henry

Otto

Charles I

August

turned against Rome. Others contend that he had planned eternal contemplation of the lake and mountains but that his sarcophogus was turned about by mistake. For whichever reason, Charles may spend the ages scrutinizing the world headquarters of the General Surveillance Society at the far end of the park.

In November 1918 a delegation of Czechs, Slovaks, Moravians, and Bohemians met here in their Constitutional Convention that refined and agreed upon the document by which they created Czechoslovakia. The salon in the Beau Rivage in which the country was born is named after that convention's and Czechoslovakia's first president, Thomas Masaryk.

A few meters farther along the Quai du Mont-Blanc and across the street, you see a municipal **bandstand [71]** (pages 36 and 112), another setting for free entertainment during the warm season.

◆ On the next street, the Rue Alfred Vincent, is the church registered in the official archives as the Protestant "Chapelle Emmanuel" but far more familiarly known as the **American Church [72].**

Its structure is a chapel of rugged stone, as unassuming and stolid as Ulysses S. Grant, the ex-President who laid its cornerstone on 27 July 1877.

Nearly eight decades elapsed before the second presidential visit. In 1954 Geneva played host to a Summit Meeting of Eden of Great Britain, Bulganin of the Soviet Union, Faure of France, and America's Dwight Eisenhower. On 17 July 1954 the U.S. President dropped by with his family and staff to attend Sunday services.

The congregation of the American Church — about two-thirds United States citizens — maintains the Protestant ritual, Sunday School, coffee hour, and social activities in a style that reproduces faithfully in Geneva the atmosphere typical of such communities in America.

As of the 1870s the American colony in Geneva numbered about 200 adherents of various Protestant sects. Seeking an alternative to the Anglican services at the English Church (page 188), the Americans formed an ecumenical "Union Church" overseen by its "three patriarchs" — Naylor, Barbey-Lorillard, and Bates.

The land grants made to temples of all faiths under James Fazy (page 54) were no longer available when the American congregation planned its own premises so a campaign to buy the ground and erect the church was managed by Henry Barbey-Lorillard and James T. Bates.

James T. Bates had served in the Union Army in America's Civil War, mustering out at age 21 as a full colonel.

While visiting his sister who was studying piano in Europe, Bates met and married Amélie Chenevrière of Geneva and settled in her home town as a banker and leader of the American community.

In addition to his activities in finance and local society, Bates acquired in Geneva two English-language newspapers which he consolidated into *The Continent & Swiss Times.*

Although Bates' journal enjoyed enough success to inspire James Gordon Bennett to launch his *Paris Herald,* the astute banker-publisher replaced his English-language paper with the French-language *Tribune de Genève,* still the highest-circulation journal among Geneva's four dailies.

Bates also founded here the first American bank in Switzerland, named "The Union Bank of Geneva" in recollection of his former military affiliations. His UBG was bought up in 1920 as an affiliate of the Union Bank of Switzerland, the UBS.

◆ The **American Library [72]** is on the next street, the Rue Monthoux, on the ground floor of the parish house behind the American Church.

The English-language library with its selection of 20,000 works of literature, reference, children's books, and periodicals is open to all at the hours listed on the sign on its door.

Geneva's fine free public library system, the "Bibliothèques Municipales", has six branches around the town with titles available in English as well as in German, Italian and, of course, French.

◆ The modern block of a building next along the Quai du Mont-Blanc is the latest edition of the **Grand Casino [73],** sharing its premises with the Hôtel Hilton.

This lakeside site originally belonged to the local hospital. In 1873, François Durel, a Lyonais casino operator, bought the land and built here his Kursaal in the opulent Second Empire style of the Paris rail terminal, the Gare d'Orsay.

At Durel's Grand Casino, the successor to the ill-reputed "Cercle des Etrangers" in Fazy's mansion, gamblers could play every game known to Hoyle and the house prospered accordingly.

The Casino managed to turn a profit even when Geneva in 1912 passed a law banning the popular game of baccarat. When, however, in 1920 Switzerland voted by referendum to prohibit all gambling, the Casino changed character completely. Without rich gaming revenues to subsidize its ballroom, vaudeville theater, restaurant, and tea terrace the Casino was doomed to lose money and was therefore of no interest as a commercial venture.

Geneva recognized the value of these facilities to tourism and took over the property as a civic enterprise.

Fiscal prudence forced Geneva to develop a more viable formula. In 1972 the town demolished the quaint old pleasure dome and erected at this prime location all of the facilities of the original Casino with the addition of a hotel, underground garage, health club and pool, private nightclub, and public discotheque.

Of the many new features, those most readily accessible to The Walkers are the two-story mall of deluxe shops and, on the level above, the public terrace for a clear view of the lake and mountains from its café and restaurant.

The Grand Casino's share of the building includes the shops, conference rooms, several eating places, the garage and, also undergound, the 1,500-seat theater.

Next to the Grand Casino's showplace on the lower level is the municipally-tolerated gambling hell, made possible by a slight flexing of the 1920 law as a concession to the demands of tourism.

To permit a flutter of action without the nuisance of bankrupt suicides cluttering up the waterfront, the betting is restricted to a modest ceiling and the only game in town is "boule" — an activity remotely resembling roulette except that the numbers are fewer, the bets smaller, and the odds so appalling that the players are engaged less in gambling than in lightly-anesthetized charity.

Indeed, the beneficiaries of most of the tables' winnings are Genevese charities and social services. A law requiring that a "place of music" exist next to any gambling room accounts for the presence of the adjoining discotheque.

The hotel portion of the Grand Casino was inaugurated in October 1980 as the "Noga Hilton". The first word is no Japanese prefix to the Hilton corporate identification but an anagram of the last name of Nessim Gaon, who arrived in Geneva as an immigrant from the Sudan in 1946 and has since prospered in peanut oil trading and real estate investment. Monsieur Gaon financed the hotel for which the Hilton organization provides the name, its promotion, and administration.

The opening of the Noga Hilton Hotel was preceded by the ceremonial immersion in the murky Lake Geneva of all the cooking-, serving-, and table-ware "... for their purification before being used in connection with the Superior Spirit, Man".

The Genevese, well aware of the pollution index of their lake and justifiably apprehensive, were assured by the management that any such spiritual decontamination of the eating apparatus was followed by secular sanitization with several runs through the hotel's high-temperature sterilizer.

Walkers proceed from the Grand Casino to the "zebra" pedestrian crossing at Rue Barton to return to the broad lakeside promenade.

◆ Where the quayside boulevard curves left, you see to your right a jetty built up from boulders removed from the old fortifications in 1856.

The thick breakwater protects Geneva's inner harbor and provides the base for the **Bains des Pâquis**, the Pâquis Baths.

By paving over the breakwater and adding changing-rooms, a snack-bar, and protected pool areas, Geneva created its least expensive public sun-and-swim-basin located near the point where the lake water flows fastest.

Fast-moving water means clearer water and a lower concentration of the contamination that has in recent years touched even Lake Geneva.

The quality of Geneva water was a century ago the finest in Europe — so coveted that Paris discussed supplying the fresh-water needs of the French capital by constructing from this lake an aqueduct 500 kilometers (300 miles) long.

The temperature of the lake water tends to a summer average of 18°C (65°F). Winter temperatures are unmentionable but visitors to Geneva are fascinated to see at this beach on even the coldest days hardy fanatics of all ages taking a frigid plunge — some in training for the icy river race, the Coupe de Noël (page 225), others out of sheerest perversity.

◆ At the bend in the line here the name changes from the Quai du Mont-Blanc to the **Quai Wilson.** The building on your right with the broad, glassed-in terrace is the headquarters of the World Alliances of the YMCA and the YWCA.

The stroller on the well-tended promenade of the Quai Wilson is faced with a choice of distractions. There are, first, other strollers to study, then on the lake side the view, the waterfowl, and the water skiers in all seasons. Ashore there are resplendent beds of flowers in spring and summer and, across the avenue, the architectural anomalies of the disparate apartment houses built between 1890 and 1930.

◆ The all-windowed hotel at the next street is the Hôtel Président, a major link in the worldwide chain managed by Swissair.

The national airline took over the property from a struggling private enterprise, begun in the 1960s and financed (according to rumor) by Emperor Haile Selassie of Ethiopia.

◆ Behind the Hôtel Président is the **Palais Wilson [74]**, at one time the Hôtel National, built in 1875 as an opulent watering-place and requisitioned in 1920 as the office of the secretariat of the League of Nations.

Set against the stone railings atop the retaining wall of the Palais park are **two plaques [75]**, one for **Woodrow Wilson**, the other for the **League of Nations**.

The first and older marker recognizes President Wilson as the founder of the League of Nations.

In 1916 Wilson ran for re-election as President of the United States on a record of "He kept America out of war" and the promise of his "Fourteen Point Plan" for the arbitration of all future disputes. In conceiving a League of Nations, Wilson presumed that the United States would play a leading role. He therefore assigned to the U.S. President specific controls and decisions.

When the victorious Allies incorporated Wilson's lofty concept in their Treaty of Versailles, the League of Nations existed in principle.

The second plaque refers to the League of Nations' act of 29 April 1919 that translated the principle into an early tangible by naming Geneva as the seat of the new world body.

The plaque is further embellished with half-a-dozen lines of hardly relevant *Méditations* on a romanticized Geneva as imagined in 1841 by Alphonse Lamartine, a poet, politician and, briefly, President of France (page 61).

The selection of the seat of the League of Nations had not been as simple as these few lines might imply. The cities of Paris and Brussels — among others — campaigned vigorously for the distinction of being the capital of so august a body.

Geneva was, however, the personal choice of Calvinist Wilson and he used his powers under Article 7 of his Covenant of the League of Nations to push through its appointment as headquarters.

Wilson's proclamation did not close the issue. Under his rules the President of the United States was also empowered to summon the first meetings of both the League's four-member upper Council and of its all-inclusive General Assembly.

Wilson did indeed convene the higher Council. On the occasions of its several meetings the Council urged a first meeting of the broader General Assembly, preferably in Brussels in a last-ditch effort to hold open the Belgian candidacy for secretariat headquarters.

Wilson, secretly ambitious for a triumphal first session in Washington, persistently postponed the General Assembly while he returned to America to press for Congressional approval of the Treaty of Versailles.

The United States Senate never did agree to ratification of the Treaty and America took no part in the League of Nations. Without a peace treaty the United States remained on armistice terms with Germany until 1921 when the Congress unilaterally declared that World War I was over.

Meanwhile, Switzerland wished to retain Geneva's tenuous claim to the headquarters post yet wondered whether the League could stay if the host country were not a member of the organization. By national referendum in May 1920, the Swiss people agreed to join the League by a margin of $11^1/_2$ cantons in favor to $10^1/_2$ opposed.

With Swiss national approval added to Wilson's nomination, Geneva seemed assured of its role as the headquarters of the League unless the Council interfered.

Wilson's last official act in League affairs was in defence of his personal convictions. Using his self-assigned powers, he overrode the Council's suggestions and convoked the First General Assembly to meet in Geneva.

The auspicious inaugural meeting of the League of Nations opened in Geneva's unpretentious Salle de la Réformation (page 105) on 12 November 1920.

To administer the Assembly meeting, the League's tiny secretariat moved from its provisional base in London to Geneva's Hôtel Victoria near the Salle de la Réformation on the Left Bank while the town prepared the Hôtel National, gratefully renamed Palais Wilson, as more permanent office quarters.

Geneva then confronted the task of managing an international network from this commercial outpost, economically depressed in 1920 with few office premises, no main-line rail service, telegraph facilities only at the central postoffice, and a single long-distance telephone line, connected with Paris.

Geneva adjusted and survived and the League secretariat grew. It expanded from the Palais Wilson into the adjacent Maison des Congrès and other temporary structures that endured for decades after the headquarters left Palais Wilson for the still unfinished Palais des Nations in February 1936.

Barely visible beside the overgrown entrance to the Maison des Congrès on the Quai du Mont-Blanc is a war-surplus cannon transformed into one of the most arresting pieces of **sculpture [76]** in Geneva by virtue of the welded addition of an elongated barrel twisted into a huge overhand knot (page 190). The work is titled **"Frieden" — "Peace"** in German.

◆ Along the retaining wall near the next street corner is a **granite monument [77]** with a bas-relief profile of **Count René de Chateaubriand,** a resident in this Pâquis neighborhood in 1808 and again in 1831-32.

> Chateaubriand was a widely traveled, floridly romantic author, prominent in literature for his novel *René* about his youth in Brittany, and for *Atala*, drawn from his long sojourn in America.
>
> Chateaubriand, as an ardent Catholic and monarchist, was distinguished for his defences of "Altar and Throne" and, as an eloquent persuader, renowned both for his effective diplomacy and his assiduous philandering.
>
> Tiny, pock-marked, and bald at the age of 40, the notorious seducer in 1808 captivated the most classic of beauties of Staël's salon of Coppet, Juliette Récamier. Their blazing affair recessed when Chateaubriand joined the post-Napoleonic governments of the Bourbon kings to serve first as an ambassador and later as Foreign Minister.
>
> After the July Revolution of 1830 overturned the last of the ultra-Royalist Bourbons, Chateaubriand was exiled from France and returned, miserably poor, with his long-suffering wife to Geneva and his Juliette.

◆ At the end of the Quai Wilson The Driven start up the slope of the **Avenue de France.**

The Walkers along the lake shore pass the sculpture by Heinz Schwarz, "Young Man and Horse". The large bronze work stands just about where the French master, Camille Corot, set up his easel in 1859 to paint "Le Quai de Pâquis".

> Corot's canvas of Geneva's Old Town and Salève hangs in the gallery of the Museum of Art and History reserved for his works. An artist with ample private means and a Swiss mother, Corot enjoyed frequent visits to his relatives in Fribourg and his friends in Geneva.

As a young man Corot painted scrupulously academic set pieces
and mediocre nudes before relaxing into his quick and natural style
that anticipated the techniques of the Impressionists.

Seldom bothering to complete a work down to its last finicky detail,
Corot was prolific in output and easy to imitate. So readily was his
style counterfeited that one contemporary critic remarked that
Corot had "...probably produced about 3,000 paintings, of which
10,000 are on display in the United States".

◆ The Driven on the Avenue de France bear into the
right lane for a turn at the traffic signal into **Rue de
Lausanne.**

◆ Aligned along its next 700 meters (half a mile) are
the entrances to five contiguous lakeside properties.

A century ago these five terrains belonged respectively to the families Plantamour, Moynier, Bartholoni, Barton, and La Rochefou-
cauld.

◆ In the 1920s the League of Nations endeavored to
assemble three of the estates into a single lakeside
setting for its not-yet-designed Palais des Nations.

Strollers stay along the lakeside, taking the path past a copse
of giant trees and an ancient carriage house to the villa **Mon
Repos [78].**

This house at the lakeside was in 1762 the scene of the episode
described in Jacques Casanova's *Mémoires* of his third visit to Geneva as among the most erotic of the Venetian libertine's adventures
— an evening in this villa lent by Casanova's (and Voltaire's)
banker, Robert Tronchin, who managed the property for its owner,
Jean-Louis Labat.

Casanova describes in loving detail his summer supper and post-
prandial romp with Hélène and Hedwige, two charming and uninhi-
bited Genevese Demoiselles-du-Haut, around the garden and in the
small pool — still extant — a hundred meters behind the house.

◆ **Mon Repos [78]** at 114/116 Rue de Lausanne was
bought in the 1800s from its owner Labat by a family
of scientists, the Plantamours. Among their close
friends was Hans Christian Andersen, the Danish
writer of children's tales, who stayed at "Mon Repos"
on his frequent visits to Geneva betwen 1833 and
1873.

Philippe Plantamour bequeathed to Geneva the "Mon Repos" estate and Sfr 300,000 for its maintenance. The town used the villa for its Ethnographic Museum from 1901 to 1939 when it moved the much-expanded collection to an unused schoolhouse.

"Mon Repos" also served as an experimental center for broadcasting. From here on 28 January 1954 Geneva opened an era of reduced repose with its transmission of the first television signal across the lake to a receiver and screen in Palais Eynard (page 100)

"Mon Repos" meanwhile has been decontaminated from any taint of Casanova's wanton use of the premises by its dedication to a diametrically contrasting character. It is today the "Institut Henri Dunant".

◆ A few meters along the Rue de Lausanne are two unadorned buildings crowding the sidewalk. A plaque on the farther end notes the presence here of the famed "Hôtel d'Angleterre".

◆ The inn numbered among its guests the Emperor Joseph II in 1777 and, in 1798, Napoleon Bonaparte (page 46).

In 1808 the hotel was the scene of the honeymoon of writer Benjamin Constant and his Charlotte, enlivened by the violent intrusion of his former mistress, Germaine de Staël.

The "Angleterre" was also host to such royal exiles as France's Empress Josephine in 1810 (page 163) and Empress Marie-Louise in 1814 (page 163) as well as to voluntary exiles from England in 1816, the poets Shelley and Byron and their companions.

The impecunious Shelley, accompanied by Mary Wollstonecroft and their son and under the guidance of Claire Claremont (page 32), came in May 1816 and took rooms in the hotel attic to await the arrival of George Lord Byron.

Ten days later the Milord appeared in his improved version of Napoleon's finest carriage, fully furnished with bed and writing desk and, as accessories, his physician and a pair of friendly girls.

Miss Claremont introduced the poets who, finding the company agreeable, decided to pass the summer exploring Lake Geneva. Byron's banker, Charles Hentsch, rented for him the "Villa Diodati" across the lake. The Shelley household settled close enough for Claire to launch her amorous attack on the blasé Byron from their "Campagne Montalègre". And the name Allegra resurfaced in January 1817 as the one Claire bestowed on Byron's daughter to whom she had just given birth.

During the summer of 1816 Byron had written copiously (page 89), Shelley very little, and Mary enough to complete a draft of her

Frankenstein (page 31). Restless by the end of August, the two contingents went their separate ways.

In 1822 they met in Lerici for a few days just before Shelley drowned in a sailing accident off the Mediterranean port.

The widowed Mary Shelley returned to England. There she lived quietly, rejecting as suitors the American actor and songwriter John Howard Payne and the essayist Washington Irving as she edited Shelley's writing and raised her son Percy.

In 1840 Mary Wollstonecroft-Shelley made a sentimental journey back to Italy and, en route home, stopped by for a last tender look at Geneva.

◆ The second gate, 120/122 Rue de Lausanne, was the main entry to the Hôtel d'Angleterre for the century of its existence.

When the hotel closed in 1842 one Barthelmy Paccard bought the property and replaced the buildings with the present mansion as a gift to his daughter on the occasion of her marriage to Gustave Moynier (page 94).

◆ In 1863 the proprietor of the new **Villa Moynier** **[79]** became the president of the International Committee of the Red Cross and made his home the headquarters of the new organization.

Moynier was a prosperous lawyer and head of Geneva's "Society of Public Utility" when he perceived in Dunant's *Souvenir of Solferino* a challenging cause for his civic society.

Taking charge of the project for providing aid on battlefields, Moynier developed the details with the great efficiency that led to the formation of the ICRC and his election as its president.

Moynier organized the approval of the Geneva Conventions and, within a span of ten years, initiated national committees in twenty-six countries. From this Villa Moynier and for the next half century he managed the ICRC as his private fief, much to the distress of the over-shadowed Henri Dunant.

Since the ICRC was called on only in times of battle, Moynier used the occasional lulls in violence to serve as Consul General in Geneva for the Congo, to campaign for the abolition of slavery and the encouragement of temperance, and to found an Institute of International Law.

Adding to the long list of his commendable works, all executed with humorless zeal, he established at the University Library the "Salle Moynier" for periodicals and promoted an ambitious "Week of Religion" in 1910, the year of his death at 84.

◆ "Villa Moynier" continued as the headquarters of the ICRC even during World War I when most of the Committee's increased workload was shifted to the Musée Rath (page 118).

◆ In 1926 the family sold the property to the League of Nations. After the change in the plans for the siting of the Palais des Nations, the League leased the "Villa Moynier" to the town of Geneva for the continuing use of the ICRC.

> The ICRC remained in residence until after World War II at which time its much enlarged staff moved up the hill to a former hotel across from the Palais des Nations (page 178). The Villa Moynier became in 1946 the Center for European Studies directed by the philosopher and writer, Denis de Rougemont.

Walkers continue on the lakeside to the tea terrace and restaurant of the Perle du Lac.

◆ Any of The Driven with enough time for a short visit to the edge of the lake can turn in at the third portal, 128 Rue de Lausanne, through the iron gate headed **"Perle du Lac" [80]**.

◆ At this parking area you are within the former Bartholoni estate made up of the Italianate residence to your left and, down by the lake, the villa's outbuildings, now the tea terrace and restaurant.

> François Bartholoni, a Genevese from a Florentine family, had made his fortune as a banker in Paris by the age of 24.
>
> Very much enjoying his prosperity, Bartholoni bought a working farm here with the intention of creating an architectural showplace. He began by tracing winding paths in the ploughed fields and planting scattered trees to form an English-style garden.
>
> While removing the farm-house, Bartholoni retained its three service buildings at the lake edge where they remain in use today.
>
> The carriage house and stable in their Swiss-châlet style are now the offices and the kitchen of the restaurant. The ancient hothouse still grows flowers. And the "Orangerie", no longer warming tender citrus trees, is pampering connoisseurs of fine cooking.

In 1923 the Bartholoni family, in less prosperous straits, sold the three older structures to the founder of the Rolex Watch Company, Rodolphe Wilsdorf. When English-born Madame Wilsdorf exclaimed over their new property. "Why, this is the pearl of the lake!" she spontaneously dubbed the châlet group with its present name.

> The **Villa Bartholoni [81]** stands on the rise above the "Perle du Lac". With its Tuscany design including a flat roof, the house was in 1828 unusual in a land where most buildings had high-peaked roofs with fast-draining pitches to disperse accumulations of snow.
>
> As to the interior, architect Félix Callet designed the villa less for day-to-day comfort than for impressive entertaining. Wide double doors link the dining-room, salon, and billiards room into one airy space with lofty ornamented ceilings, Pompeiian-style frescos, and parquet floors of six varying woods.
>
> So pleased with his villa was Bartholoni that, on increasing his fortune with railroad building (page 183) in addition to his banking, he endowed Geneva with a Conservatory of Music (page 120), built in this same style.

◆ The League of Nations, in its second real-estate transaction, bought the buildings and grounds from the families of Bartholoni and Wilsdorf. And, as in the case of the Moynier grounds, the League eventually leased the property back to Geneva.

When Raymond de Saussure in 1953 sought a locale for a temporary display of the "History of Science", Geneva made its leased villa available. As tends to occur with things temporary, the exhibit remained in place for decades with its original array of ancient medical and dental equipment, precision instruments, and a steam tricycle.

> Among the optical instruments exhibited were microscopes for botanical and medical research and early telescopes used by Genevese observers of celestial phenomena, distant mountains and — according to Shelley's account written in 1821 — the peregrinations of Claire Claremont shuttling between the family farmhouse and Lord Byron's mansion (page 154).

Walkers leaving the Bartholoni house take the path leading away from Geneva along the crest to the lakeside. The next house on your left is the plainly pink Barton-Peel mansion, renovated and enlarged with the addition of an extra story.

◆ The Driven may note, a few meters beyond the wide gate of the "Perle du Lac", the nearly hidden entrance to 132 Rue de Lausanne. The sign on one of its portals announces the **International Institute of Higher Studies [82]**, the plaque on the other upright reads "Parc Barton".

◆ This estate, the fourth of the five adjoining lake properties, was sold by Philippe Dunant-Gallatin to the English family Peel in 1858.

> The grounds and the villa built in the 1830s were bought by the third Sir Robert Peel, son of the second Sir Robert Peel, twice Prime Minister of England. The nickname of the second Sir Robert is still familiar in London where he organized the Metropolitan Police whose constables continue to be called "Peelers" or "bobbies".
>
> The highly placed second Sir Robert sent his son forth at age 24 as the British Minister to Switzerland. After service through the Sonderbund crisis and a passionate interlude with Lola Montez (page 163), the third Sir Robert turned to civic affairs in Geneva (page 188), married lovely Emily Hay, daughter of the Marquis of Tweedsdale, and settled his family on this country estate.

The eldest child of the Peel-Hay union was Victoria Alexandra who at 21 married 37-year-old Daniel Barton.

Barton, in Geneva as an apprentice banker to learn how to manage his huge fortune, devoted more of his energies to his fleet of yachts and the town's musical life as the vice president of the Geneva symphony orchestra and sponsor of a seagoing musical aggregation, the "Harmonie Nautique".

> Rendered slightly more serious by marriage, Barton accepted the agreeable assignment of British Consul General in Geneva and, to cover such diplomatic demands, in 1892 bought from the then-impecunious Sir Robert this family villa and park which Lady Emily had named "Lammermoor" after her family's Tweedsdale estate in Scotland.
>
> Barton's concern about the maintenance of the skills of his waterborne orchestra outside of the boating season led him to build as its winter quarters the elaborate 1,800-seat Victoria Hall.
>
> The auditorium opened in 1894 as Geneva's largest concert house. The town acclaimed its first-rate acoustical qualities and gave almost equal attention to its piquant facade. Embellished by the sta-

tue of "Harmonie" — a voluptuous, full-frontal nude — Victoria Hall turned drab Rue Général Dufour into the favorite promenade of Geneva's bucks and blades.

The harbor on The Walkers' right was the home port of the Barton-Peel private fleet of steam yachts: the *Peri* and the *Aida* named for favored operas and the *Saint Frusquin,* as a self-deprecating private joke, nearly untranslatable but meaning approximately "superfluous".

> After the death of Daniel Barton in 1907, his childless widow expanded her travels and maintained an ambitious social program for such celebrated guests as passed through Geneva.
>
> When the League of Nations settled here in 1920 Lady Barton-Peel blossomed. She commandeered and lionized its Secretary General, Sir Eric Drummond, and with him drew into her circle the new organization's delegates and diplomats with all the authority of the name they ultimately accorded her, "The Queen of Geneva".
>
> The affinity of Lady Barton-Peel for the loftier strata of the world organization left its administrators reassured as to her cooperation at such time as they were ready to ask her to relinquish "Villa Lammermoor" to complete the ground plan for the projected Palais des Nations.

Once the League had the two adjacent properties in hand, its representatives took the formal step of approaching the dowager on the subject of the sale or perhaps even the gift of her estate. The Lady's exceedingly firm "No!" blew away all plans and prospects for a lakeside Palais.

> The League, the owner by then of 7 hectares (16 acres) of lake property too small to use, appealed to the town for a solution.
>
> The legal minds of Geneva worked out a complicated but ingenious exchange. The town leased from the League these lakeside holdings and, in return, leased to the League, on a 99-year contract, real estate on the Pregny hill to which Geneva held a restricted title and could not, under terms of its donor's will, ever sell.
>
> The League adjusted its building plans and Lady Barton-Peel reigned unperturbed in her political salon by the lake.

On Lady Barton-Peel's death in 1935 the estate passed neither to the League nor to Geneva but to the Swiss nation. By her will her ashes were strewn over the grounds of "Villa Lammermoor" which the government must never sell nor subdivide nor change by so much as cutting down a tree.

◆ The Swiss Property Foundation for International Organizations, the SPFIO — manages the property and today leases it to the International Institute of Higher Studies, founded by William Rappard in 1927.

> William Rappard was binational — American by reason of his birth in New York and Swiss through his parents' Genevese citizenship. Educated internationally as a lawyer and political economist, Rappard taught at Harvard University before returning as a professor to the University of Geneva in 1913 to remain firmly rooted in Geneva thereafter while retaining strong American ties.

> By 1917 the United States' embargo on the sale of food to neutrals in World War I had left Switzerland with a severe shortage of grain. It was Rappard who persuaded America's President Wilson to change the rules and supply the needed cereals. Beginning with these friendly negotiations, Rappard became an important intermediary between Wilson and the Swiss government for the League of Nations project.

> Rappard had been working for several years in the International Labour Office when he recognized the need for greater expertise in international affairs. With his scholarly connections the professor in 1926 obtained a generous grant from the Rockefeller Foundation with which to organize his "Institut des Hautes Etudes Internationales" to train graduate students.

> The Institute was based at 5 Promenade du Pin — now the Library of Art and Archaeology (page 51) — until 1938 when the SPFIO assigned to it the enlarged "Villa Lammermoor". The training has continued and the facilities have expanded, subsidized since 1952 by a Swiss foundation and the governments of Geneva and Switzerland.

Continuing along the lake towards the rectangular structure, the "Centre Rappard", The Walkers see on their left a waist-high bronze ball. Examined closely, it turns out to represent humanity tightly intertwined in the **sculpture [83] "Earth"**.

> Mankind again, in a less compressed but more depressed state, is depicted in "Human Effort", the 1935 work of James Vibert, leader of the between-the-Wars school of Geneva sculpture.

At the lake edge just beyond the Centre a path at right angles offers The Walkers a choice:

a) to continue along the lake path to reach a pedestrian tunnel under the Route de Lausanne to the Botanical Garden and then pick up this trail on page 163; or,

b) to turn left on the path towards the Centre Rappard for a closer view and then to cross the Route de Lausanne at the traffic signal.

This text proceeds on the assumption that The Walker takes the path to the left to the Centre Rappard.

◆ The Driven, on the down slope of the Rue de Lausanne, bear into the left lane for a turn near the entrance of the grey building on the right, the headquarters of the International Labour Office, the ILO, until 1974 when it became the **Centre Rappard [84].**

When the Treaty of Versailles created the intergovernmental League of Nations, it set up separately the ILO "... to reinforce peace through social justice..." in a forum where delegates of governments, employers, and workers could negotiate on equal terms.

The estate on which this independent entity was settled had belonged to the family La Rochefoucauld-Montesquieu-Fézensac until 1898. It had passed through other hands by 1919 when the Swiss government requisitioned it for this building which the ILO completed in 1925. In 1970, the ILO, by then a specialized agency of the United Nations, turned the premises back to the Swiss Property Foundation for International Organizations and moved to far larger quarters near the crest of the Pregny hill (page 180).

The Swiss Foundation then leased the premises to be shared by the General Agreement on Tariff and Trade, GATT, and by UNHCR, the United Nations High Commission for Refugees. In 1974 the Foundation recognized the Swiss internationalist's accomplishments by changing the name to "Centre Rappard".

In the earlier days of international organizations diplomatic custom prompted member governments to offer gifts of native art and crafts to decorate their meeting place.

◆ The wrought-iron triple gates guarding the entry to this estate were presented by King Carol II of Rumania. As a playboy prince Carol scandalized society in the late 1920s by abandoning his family and abdicating his right to the crown in order to live in exile with "...commoner Magda Lupescu".

Following the death of Rumania's King Ferdinand, his grandson, 6-year-old Michael, was enthroned until 1930 and the return of the young king's unrepentant father.

In 1940 King Carol II passed the crown back to Michael and left for Portugal one month before the troops of Nazi Germany annexed Rumania.

Michael, twice a king, was deposed a second time in November 1947, overruled by Communist pressure. The exiled monarch migrated to Geneva to begin a new career as plain Michel Leroi, employee of an investment bank.

Walkers rounding the Centre Rappard will find near the building's entrance a gift of the Italian government, a mosaic fountain overseen by a statue of Neptune.

The Swiss government presented the two statues beside the entrance, from left to right, "Peace" and "Justice". Neither, according to the cynical wisecrack, has been seen inside the building.

Of Carol's three high portals, the middle gate is unusual in that it is fitted with three locks. For each lock there is a heavy golden key — one for government, one for employers, one for labor. Symbolically this means that any approach to a meeting of the tripartite International Labour Office required the concerted action of each of its three elements to open the way.

◆ The Driven swing left around the traffic island on which stands the granite statue of "Labour", consisting of four contrasting racial types, whose workclothes are identified with basic occupations in the fields, in the factories, under the earth, and on the sea.

◆ The Driven, as they ascend the **Avenue de la Paix,** have on their right the **Jardin Botanique [85],** the Botanical Garden.

The flora transplanted here from the Bastions in 1902 are now only one aspect of a complex which includes a library, tea terrace, laboratories, three greenhouses, a rock garden, aviaries, and a deer park.

Walkers leaving the Centre Rappard through its high gates go to the right to cross with care and the traffic signal the high-speed **Route de Lausanne.**

Continue into the Botanical Garden to go along whichever garden path tempts you but bear ever farther away from the town direction until you reach the broad lawn.

The Walkers who, on page 160, selected the "Underpass Option" emerge from the tunnel at the bottom of the lawn of the garden.

The villa [86] at the head of the lawn is "Le Chêne", The Oak, formerly a country house of the family Duval (page 50).

The villa, now the staff offices of the Garden, stands between the Deer Park to the right with its animals, waterfowl, and cages of exotic birds and, on the town side, the aviary housing a colorful, chirpy collection of smaller specimens.

Behind the villa are the botanical laboratories and library; near the aviary is a flagstone terrace with a refreshment stand.

The path back towards the Avenue de la Paix leads past the series of greenhouses for tropical, Mediterranean, and arctic plants and the rock garden with Alpine blooms and a waterfall.

The road away from town running alongside the Garden is "Le Chemin de l'Impératrice", the Empress' Way, named after Empress Josephine.

In 1810 Napoleon reluctantly annulled his childless marriage to Josephine and banished her from the Paris area. The Empress, reduced to the title of Duchess of Navarre, came to Geneva to join her daughter Hortense, the ex-Queen of Holland (page 59).

In November 1810 Josephine bought the nearby villa (not open for visits) and resided here for nearly a year before being allowed to return to her beloved Malmaison near Paris. On Josephine's death in 1814 her executors sold most of her assets, including this "Villa de l'Impératrice", to settle her debts.

Marie Louise of Austria succeeded Josephine as Napoleon's wife and empress until deposed by the Great Powers. With Napoleon dying in exile on Saint Helena and Marie Louise demoted to Princess of Parma, Metternich assigned to her as guardian, lover, and eventual husband the one-eyed Count Neipperg. In their exile from Paris they stayed in Geneva and in 1820 rented this house from its new owner.

Marie Louise and friend moved on shortly but she evidently retained a fondness for the "Villa de l'Impératrice" since in 1829 she rented it again, this time to share with her latest husband, Baron Werklein.

Another titled lessee, the Countess of Landsfeld, or − more familiarly — Lola Montez (page 56), in the summer of 1848 rented the "Villa de l'Impératrice" expecting to share it with King Ludwig I of Bavaria.

During her few months' sojourn in Geneva the Irish-Spanish dancer fascinated the townsfolk with her variety of lovers, her blackmailing by the villainous August Papon, and her full-scale zoo, purchased impetuously and en bloc from a passing circus.

Walkers strolling through the Garden, back towards the town and up the slope, emerge on the Avenue de la Paix near the bridge over the railroad.

◆ Crossing the short bridge over the main line of the railroad that connects Geneva to the rest of Switzerland, you see on the left the **workshops [87]** of the **Sécheron Company**, manufacturers of road transport and rolling stock — one of Geneva's few heavy industries.

The next street on your left is the present boundary of the "Varembé" property, a large country estate before its division into parcels of the International City.

The Rockefeller family gave lavish support to the international effort in Geneva between the World Wars with a series of gifts and grants. In 1942 John D. Rockefeller, Jr, bought the "Villa Rigot", the mansion house of the "Varembé" estate and donated it to the University of Geneva.

This Pregny neighborhood was as recently as 1946 a largely rural area with a few mansions each on its own generous acreage. In a couple of decades the expanding delegations, international organizations, and agencies have acquired most of the private estates.

Many of the villas have been razed to make room for modern office buildings in what Geneva recognizes as a distinct and distinctive "International City".

◆ Insofar as an International City can have a heart, the geographical heart here is the open and unadorned **Place des Nations [88]**.

The City is an urban agglomeration of organizations dedicated, in principle, to improved cooperation and coordination. Coordination is, however, notably absent from the City's architectural mixture. The individualistic style of each building is scarcely a model of urban planning and the eclectic result is sadly remote from the thoughtful project laid out by the town of Geneva for orderly development.

The buildings within view from the Place des Nations include the United Nations's specialized agencies of the World Intellectual Property Organization, WIPO (blue glass); the International Telecommunications Union, ITU as marked; and the World Meteorological Organization, WMO; as well as the offices for non-governmental organizations, the NGOs; and the town of Geneva's own International Conference Center.

The International City extends to your right up the hill to even bigger buildings. The new structures dominate the crest that Geneva calls the "Côteau des Altesses", the Hill of Their Highnesses, because almost all of the property owners here in the 1700s bore titles of rank.

Such allusions, not invariably respectful, to individuals privileged to live higher than others, spread to this Right Bank summit from Left Bank roots. The residents of Geneva's other prestigious hill were identified even earlier by the equivocal sobriquet, "Les Messieurs-du-Haut", The Gentlemen on High.

◆ At the Place des Nations you pass the side entrance of the **Palais des Nations [89],** a building ranked high among the contenders for the title of the "Biggest in Europe".

If the proportions of the Palais as you see them from this side hardly justify any such claim to grandeur, bear in mind that the white colonnades at the top of the drive mark the lateral entrance to a long narrow building.

Its architects designed the Palais to impress the viewer with its bulk and powerful sweep when seen straight on from the front. If the expansive facade of the Palais were set as originally planned at the edge of the lake and reflected in that shimmering surface, its creamy panorama would be visible through a wide angle and from great distance. Here, alas, it is not.

The League opened its architectural competition calling for a Palais poised at the lake edge and budgeted at Sfr 17,000,000 in 1926 when a dollar bought Sfr 5, a pound sterling Sfr 25. Of the 377 entries received, none was accepted.

For five years committees and General Assemblies pondered the assortment of plans. Meanwhile the staff increased and so did space requirements while the lakeside acreage assumed to be procurable unexpectedly diminished.

When in 1927 the Rockefeller family offered to pay for an extension to the international reference library, the League declared that with this wing the Palais required more land than was available by the lake. At that point Geneva salvaged the Palais project by leasing to the League a large segment of the Ariana Park that the town had recently inherited from Gustave Revilliod.

On 7 September 1929, just short of a decade after the planning began, Secretary General Eric Drummond laid the foundation stone for the Palais des Nations.

> By February 1936 the secretariat of the League had begun to move up from the Palais Wilson. Work on the new headquarters was completed in 1937 at a final cost of Sfr 34,000,000 plus the $2,000,000 contributed by the Rockefellers for the library by the mid-1930s when the dollar was worth Sfr 3, the pound Sfr 15.
>
> The dinner to inaugurate the Palais was offered by the President of the General Assembly. Providentially, the president for 1937 was the Aga Khan who paid the bill out of his own resources.
>
> The Aga magnanimously proclaimed an open house for anyone who cared to come. He had reason to regret his generosity only when the wholehearted response overwhelmed the supplies.
>
> The host himself went hungry at a time when the diet and the revenues of the Aga Khan were interdependent since his Ismaili Moslem followers accorded him an annual income equal to his weight in gold.

◆ The side entrance from the Place des Nations is intended for UN Secretariat staff and participants in meetings.

◆ Visits by interested onlookers, heads of state, popes, and schoolchildren begin at the front entrance up the **Avenue de la Paix** to your right.

◆ As you go up the Avenue de la Paix look on your right for the **Ariana Museum [90],** a domed Renaissance structure that was never completed but houses, nonetheless, an important collection of ceramics.

> The estate was named "Ariana" by Gustave Revilliod in honor of his mother, Ariane Revilliod-de la Rive. As of 1877 the family property ranged from this ledge of the Pregny hill down to the shore of the lake.
>
> The town's actual utilization of the terrain — first for the Botanical Garden, later for the Palais des Nations, not to mention transit by the Route de Lausanne — has raised legal questions and legalistic answers.
>
> In leasing the upper segment of the park to the League of Nations in 1928, the town did retain custody of two structures within the grounds: a 1600s Swiss mountain châlet, now a shed for the UN groundskeepers, and the Ariana Museum.

The town assigned the museum in 1934 to the management of the Museum of Art and History which concentrated in the "Ariana" its collection of porcelains, pottery, and earthenware. In 1954 "Ariana" became the headquarters for the International Academy of Ceramics.

Gustave Revilliod in 1869 took time off from his dilettante interest in publishing, scientific experiment, and civic affairs to represent the Swiss government at the opening of the Suez Canal. Fascinated by Egypt, Revilliod returned with a variety of objects of interest and then traveled farther abroad to expand his souvenirs into a collection that overflowed the family house in the Old Town (page 63).

To provide display space for his coins, pewters, jewelry, furnishings, and ceramics, and galleries for his paintings and sculptures, Revilliod in 1877 ordered this museum, intended to rival his collection as a work of art.

In 1887, exhausted by the effort and the expense, Revilliod stopped the construction, still far from complete. When Revilliod died a bachelor in 1890 he bequeathed to Geneva his house in the Old Town, his unfinished museum, SFr 1,000,000 for their upkeep, and this vast parkland.

In his will Revilliod was specific in his directives to the town. Geneva must never sell the park. It must keep the grounds ever open for the pleasure of the public. It must never tolerate on the property a "... cabaret, boarding house, inn, cemetery, or shooting gallery..." And the town must provide space and care within the park both for his tomb and for his free-ranging favorites, those symbols of reincarnation, his pet peacocks.

The Italianate theme of the museum's exterior continues inside where its Florentine dome is supported by black marble columns twisted in the style of Bernini's baldachin at Saint Peter's in Rome. Within this decorative foyer the architect planned a monumental stairway to link the upper gallery with the ornate entry doors.

With the stairway in place the grand vista from the upper gallery across the elegant foyer and through the double doors would have encompassed an incomparable sweep of lake and the Alps of Savoy.

Work on the staircase was never even begun. Had the stairs been built, however, any breathtaking view to distant summits would have shrunk as of 1937 to a look at the back wall of the Palais des Nations. Once the ground plan of the Palais had cut off the front terrace of the "Ariana", visitors to the museum entered through its back door.

The first impression of the foyer, columns, and dome was still stunning but quickly quenched as the visitor went through a service door to the back stairs, the only access thus far provided to reach the upper gallery.

Geneva closed the museum in 1980 while seeking funds for the extensive repairs needed for the roof and facade, the installation of more suitable stairs, a heating system, and elevator, and — most costly of all —∤ the construction of an underground vault as now required by Swiss Federal Code to preserve all art treasures against unspecified holocausts.

◆ Close to the Avenue de la Paix on your right is a structure of girders and brown glass. In conjunction with the adjacent villa this comprises the Swiss hotel training school and public restaurant called **"Vieux Bois" [91],** the Old Woods.

"Vieux Bois" is not a name attributable to any stand of "old woods" in the vicinity but to that of "Monsieur Vieux-Bois", the popular character in the "comic strip" created by Rodolphe Toeppfer (page 49).

When the family of father Adam Toeppfer was evicted from the Rue Farel in the Old Town (page 67), the cultivated owner of this villa, François Duval, invited them to move into a tenant farmhouse with studio on his property. The villa later served as the country residence for the large family engendered by the happy marriage of Duval to Rodolphe Toeppfer's younger sister Ninette.

Geneva acquired the villa in 1932 and opened next to the nascent Palais des Nations a commercial restaurant, "L'Auberge de Monsieur Vieux-Bois". Finding the facility of limited interest to the international clientele, the town turned it over to the Swiss trade-training program as a hotel school.

With its name trimmed to "Vieux-Bois", the restaurant is open for lunch only on weekdays to offer food selected, prepared, and served by trainees being schooled to manage hotels and restaurants, not only in Switzerland, but around the world.

◆ The main and **visitors' entrance [92]** to the **Palais des Nations**, is the gate at the foot of the square of lawn in front of "Vieux-Bois".

The United Nations encourages visits to its Geneva premises which include both the Palais des Nations and the Ariana Park in which it stands.

The UN Visitors' Service conducts tours of the Palais year-round, seven days a week. The accompanied visit takes just under an hour and ends with an invitation for you to stroll through Monsieur Revilliod's parkland at your leisure.

The tour lecture comes in a variety of languages on special request. The standard issue is in English, French, and German. Should you be fitting a Palais visit into a tight schedule, telephone the Palais at 34 60 11 after 8.30 a.m. and ask the multilingual operator for the Visitors' Service to learn the departure times of the tour in the language of your choice.

◆ The Driven, if planning to visit the Palais at this juncture, park on the Avenue de la Paix.

Buy entry tickets at the gate and, once inside the grounds, walk to the newer building, Door 39, marked "Visitors' Service".

◆ Such followers of this text as are not planning a walk through the Palais forthwith, may cull a notion of the tour's coverage in the next pages or can keep moving ahead by skipping to page 178.

Visitors to the United Nations should be aware of certain distinctions of purpose between the headquarters in New York and this office in Geneva.

The distinction exists because the United Nations Organization is very much a dual-purpose tool with a political edge and a technical side. Its political element is rooted in the headquarters of New York, partially out of deference to the neutrality of Switzerland. Much of the technical activity is in the more flexible premises of Geneva.

The political aspect of the UN involves the debate of accusations, defences, resolutions, and peace-keeping forces and is dealt with in the Manhattan building. In New York the higher-level, fifteen-member Security Council convenes as required by world events.

The all-nations General Assembly also meets in New York but in scheduled session for three months each Fall for the purpose of setting policy, a matter more political than technical.

The practical work with plague control, allocation of broadcast frequencies, refugee aid, uniform road signs, and thousands of other issues for coordinated action are assigned by the General Assembly to one among the 40-odd "Specialized Agencies", "Technical Organs", and "Commissions".

On the Right Bank you have already passed the headquarters of GATT, UNHCR, WIPO, ITU, and WMO. Ten other such UN subsidiaries are also in Geneva while four each are based in Rome and in Washington, three in Vienna, two in Nairobi, and one each in Bern, Paris, London, Montreal, and Tokyo. The Visitors' Bureau has excellent organizational charts for anyone interested in delving deeper into the details.

The Palais des Nations had as its first tenant, of course, the League of Nations. Although the League was by no means the first group to try to arbitrate national differences, it was the first to organize the effort in depth and combine a Great Power Council with a universal General Assembly to guide a permanent international secretariat settled in appropriate quarters.

At its outset in 1920 the League had the strong backing of the public, weary after a long war. The League's decisions, however, were backed by neither military nor economic force and thus were largely ineffectual and disappointing.

Throughout the 1920s meaningful negotiations on naval limitations, border disputes, war-debt funding, and arms reduction had to involve the United States, Soviet Russia, and Germany, none of them members of the League which was therefore excluded from work of real consequence.

As military confrontations increased in the 1930s, the weakness of the League was ever more apparent. Its inability to restrain violence in Manchuria in 1931, in Ethiopia in 1935, and later in Spain, Austria, and Czechoslovakia eroded its prestige until it dissolved entirely with the intervention of the Soviet Union in Finland as the League stood helplessly by. This 1940 meeting closed the Council and within a matter of weeks the League secretariat disbanded and dispersed.

As the League lay dormant during World War II, delegates of anti-Axis nations met at Dumbarton Oaks in 1944 to plan another world body. In June 1945 the Allies and their backers agreed in San Francisco on the principles of the United Nations charter.

By the time that a majority of these fifty-one "victor-nations" had ratified the agreement on 24 October 1945, the original "United Nations Day", the secretariat was already at work in improvised offices at Lake Success, New York.

The League, meanwhile, still existed and controlled substantial funds, documents, and property. After a six-year hiatus, the League Council reconvened in April 1946 to dissolve the organization and bequeath its assets to the United Nations.

Already committed to headquarters in the United States and busy with a thousand new challenges, the staff of the new organization saw its sudden legacy of a substantial piece of real estate in the non-member nation of Switzerland as another awkward item on a long agenda.

The United Nations' headquarters disposed provisionally of the issue with an announcement in August 1946 of the opening of a new working unit, warily nominated "The Office of the United Nations in Geneva".

> The Palais did not remain long in limbo. The premises filled quickly as specialized agencies for refugee settlement, relief, and rehabilitation launched programs to rebuild war-torn Europe.
>
> Other technical agencies also began their work in the Palais, outgrew the nursery, and moved to built-to-measure headquarters, each adding another structure to the booming International City.
>
> Thirty years after this second incarnation the international world accounted for the presence in Geneva of no fewer than 20,000 polylingual, multinational diplomats, experts, and their families, 90 % of them of nationalities other than Swiss.

Visitors preparing to tour the Palais des Nations may not realize to what degree such visits are an innovation.

> In the days of the League, visitors dropped by the offices and wandered about as they pleased. The United Nations at the outset was equally casual and had no inkling that its working areas in New York or in Geneva were in any way potential competition for the Empire State Building, Madame Tussaud's, or the Téléphérique of Mont Salève.
>
> The travel boom of the 1950s, however, coincided with the well-publicized United States' participation in the United Nations to generate a demand for a first-hand look at the famous premises. Caught a bit off guard by its popularity, the UN administration drafted as guides a few genial members of the maintenance staff, more at ease with the details of the Palais' hectares of carpeting and light-years of wiring than with its purpose, policies, and significance.

Well-briefed linguists have replaced the early technicians and today explain such intangibles as the history and the organization in the course of a stroll through the Palais to show the more specific features such as:

> In the new Building "E":
> — Its space-age auditorium;
>
> In the Palais:
> — One or two out of a half-dozen meetings rooms;
> — the marble gallery, the "Salle des Pas Perdus", the Hall of the Wasted Footsteps. The name is that of the long gallery of the Palais de Versailles where French citizens waited in the hope of

presenting their pleas personally to King Louis XIV. As they tarried for frustrating weeks, the petitioners named the huge waiting hall after their wasted walk from Paris — their "pas perdus";

— the paintings in the central gallery, respectively of "War", with the Four Horsemen of the Apocalypse motif, and of "Peace", with the Hand of God reaching down from a cloud;

— the General Assembly Hall for meetings of all nations of the League, used for large gatherings and addresses by celebrated visitors. The panels at each corner represent abstractly each of the four seasons — gifts of Japan;

— the Council Chamber, designed for meetings of the League's six "Great Powers", used for smaller, high-level meetings such as those on disarmament. On the chamber's walls and ceiling Spain's José-Maria Sert, an admirer of the regime of General Franco, depicted Peace and Freedom with the heroic figures and outsized cannon, gates, and chains in sepia and gold leaf.

The visit to the Council Chamber is the last on the conducted tour. Your guide may next lead you to Door 6 and point out three options:

1) to follow the guide to an exit near the Main Gate to return to your automobile or tour bus (Pick up the route again on page 174);

2) to leave through Door 6, turn left and walk to the Place des Nations to catch the public bus back to midtown (For instructions, see page 181);

3) to cross the lobby and the corridor to Door 23 in the direction of the lake for an unaccompanied stroll through Ariana Park.

Park visitors emerging through Door 23, walk to the left in a diagonal towards the two giant Cedars of Lebanon and across the ample lawn.

The total ground controlled by the United Nations in Geneva under lease and ownership is about 40 hectares (100 acres).

The purchase of adjacent estates began with the League administrators who were left uneasy by the collapse of their attempt to assemble property and were very much aware of the fixed term of the ground leases.

The United Nations has continued the purchasing program. As a result the UN controls — in addition to the 17 hectares originally taken under lease in Ariana Park — the 7 hectares (16 acres) owned and sublet to Geneva at the lake edge plus an additional 16 hectares (40 acres) owned in Pregny. None of this includes terrain acquired independently by the various UN specialized agencies and technical organs.

The United Nations territory, whether leased or owned, is not — according to the treaty with Switzerland — part of the Swiss nation but an autonomous enclave.

As an independent government the United Nations is free to make treaties, to accredit ambassadors (even if they happen to be non-grata in Switzerland), to employ its own security forces, print its own stamps, issue passports and, presumably, to mint its own money and to enter a team in the Olympic Games.

The possible violation of the United Nations territory by terrorists or vandals or seekers of sanctuary has been considered and provided for.

The UN security contingent cooperates with other forces of order who are prepared to intervene in accordance with the circumstances.

With the increase in violence in recent decades, the United Nations has increased its precautions. Today's augmented fencing, reinforced guard details — both uniformed and plain clothes — and challenges and document checks would have been unthinkable in the 1950s.

In the Ariana Park, however, public access continues as long as the wishes of donor Revilliod prevail. As you enjoy his hospitality, note that the farther you walk towards the lake, the better your perspective on the proportions and size of the Palais.

You may also be remarking from afar sculptures and monuments of varying degrees of significance.

The gilded **"Armillary Sphere" [93]** in the center of the pond of the Court of Honor is dedicated to Woodrow Wilson. The sphere is "armillary" by definition because it is made up of concentric rings. The sphere rotates constantly but imperceptibly in such a way that the heavenly constellations and signs of the zodiac welded to its surface mirror the position of the corresponding formation in the celestial sphere. The League bought this microcosm of the universe out of an unrestricted gift of $25,000 from America's Wilson Foundation.

An artwork composed of a pylon sheathed in titanium — the heat-resistant metal used to protect spacecraft — and a seemingly inflated astronaut is called the "Monument to the Conquest of Space", contributed in 1971 by the Soviet Union to commemorate its pioneer venture in this domain.

The tall, slab-iron profile of two full-length adults bracketing the open silhouette of a child is called "Family", donated in 1979, the "Year of the Child", by its sculptor, Edwina Sandys, a granddaughter of Winston Churchill.

The marble sarcophogus of Gustave Revillliod stands in Ariana Park as stipulated in the will of the donor. His tomb is in a copse in front of the Library Wing.

The **Rockefeller Library [94]** was the first and largest of many gifts to the League. This international research center holds more than a million volumes, 15,000,000 documents, and 15,000 periodicals on world affairs.

The Library also has a small museum displaying mementos of early peace movements, souvenirs and photographs of the League of Nations, a collection of peace prizes, and an album with renderings of some 150 of the design concepts proposed for the Palais des Nations.

To return to the Main Gate of the UN complex, walk around the newer "E" building and up beside the driveway.

Those who on page 172 chose "Option 1" meet the "Option 3" or park-visiting contingent on the path to the Main Gate.

From the Main Gate look back at the marble facade which gives so striking a first impression to the formal entrance to the Palais.

The fine stone-facing was the gift in 1934 of Italy under the regime of Benito Mussolini. While embellishing the League showplace with the marble of Carrara, the Fascist dictator was vitiating its purpose with his contemptuous defiance of its condemnation of his "... war in disregard of his nation's obligations..." — the 1935 invasion of Ethiopia.

Mussolini's flaunting of the League's resolution and his subsequent dismissal of the League's inquiry into his army's use of poison gas against spear-wielding tribesmen were major blows to the body's authority and prestige and marked the end of its useful life.

Three decades earlier Mussolini already had a criminal record in Switzerland where he had sought refuge while under sentence in Italy for desertion from military service. After the authorities of Lucerne, Bern, and Lausanne had each expelled him in turn, Geneva on 9 April 1904 ordered the deportation of one B. Mussolini on charges of falsifying his passport.

In addition to the conducted tour and park stroll, available to all, the Palais has a few features of limited but possible interest to those on official delegations or staff with full access to the building.

The following page is a diversion intended particularly for the several thousands of such denizens of the Palais while the saturated casual visitor skips on to page 178.

In the vicinity of Door 6, the domain of its highest Council in the League days, is a series of seven rooms:

— Room I, now marked C-108, is a meeting-room decorated with an oversized carpet, a gift from the Shah of Persia;

— in the room adjacent, described only as " .. once the Office of the Council President" is another noteworthy Oriental rug and a wooden conference table inlaid with an elaborate map of the world;

— the "Delegates' Lounge" is a preciously preserved example of 1937 "Art Deco", a gift of pre-war Czechoslovakia;

— Room II is a large reception room with Leleu mirrors and table and petit-point chair seats and backs;

— Room III has a Swiss fresco, "Concorde", shown as a sailing dinghy crewed by five languid ladies, indifferent to lines and tiller as they drift past a trio of swans;

— Room IV can no longer be located;

— Room V has metal bas-reliefs representing Medieval Europe, Classic Greece, Traditional Orient, and Skyscraper Moderne.

The series of meeting rooms continues around the marble Central Gallery near the General Assembly Hall:

— Room VI is a staff lounge with frescoes by Carl Hügin on its three walls:

To the north — exemplifying "Generosity" — St. Martin gives his cloak to a beggar, St. George slays his dragon, and the Good Shepherd is present.

To the south — depicting the "Victims of War" — the survivors mourn a dead soldier.

To the east — representing Swiss lore — the arrest of William Tell, the herdsmen swear the Oath of Grütli, and Saint Nicolas de Flue blesses.

— Room VII, decorated by the French with mirrors and lights in vases;

— Room VIII, decorated by the Danes with an inlaid fresco of the world according to a drawing from the 1600s;

— Room IX, decorated by South Africa with inlaid paneling described in official literature as "stinkwood";

— Room X, decorated by Latvia in 1938 with massive glass chandeliers, inlays, and painted frescoes of peasant scenes;

— Room XI, decorated by Holland with wall paneling of natural leather over macassar wood;

— Room XII, decorated by Italy with a broad fresco of the Palais in the process or chaos of construction.

The United Nations buildings

The United Nations Office at Geneva is housed **[92]** in the Palais des Nations — a stone and mortar neo-classical edifice designed by a committee of five architects in the 1920s and inaugurated in 1937 — supplemented by its adjoining "E" (for "East") Building, a metal-frame and glass-wall structure designed by a committee of another five architects in the 1960s and inaugurated in 1973.

Any balance between the two structures is in terms of relative length, bulk, and height without attempting harmonization of style, shape, or materials. The variety of designs conceivable for a world headquarters is infinite.

On the opposite page are four out of the 377 projects submitted for the original Palais, most of them in the academic tradition embellished with eye-catching features that might be gracing Geneva's skyline today.

Among the non-traditional entries was the highly innovative, low-profile project (below) of Swiss-born LeCorbusier, rejected on grounds that its rendering was in printer's rather than India ink.

And the Palais as it might have been

A *Celestial Instrument* design that combined the salient features of a pipe organ with the profile of a space-shuttle launch site might have suggested to the League new harmonies on a higher plane.

Hagia Sophia means in Greek *Holy Wisdom*, a quality devoutly to be wished in governing bodies. The original in Istanbul is further noted for its durability through fires, earth-quakes, and hard use by three religions and for its unusual overhead, sustained without visible support.

A *Grand Opera* motif conveys overtones of heavy drama, heavily subsidized. Any encouragement of prima donna temperaments, however, might risk reducing the performance to the level of *Opéra-Comique*.

A prototypical *Galactic Space Ship* of Sécheron, a full 40 years before rockets to the moon, might have set the League off into literal flights of fantasy.

* * *

Approximately 150 similarly spectacular concepts still on display in the UN Museum may suggest further and even more arch associations. See for yourself in the Rockefeller Library [94].

◆ Turning from page 169 or 176, the visitors departing through the Main Gate return to Swiss soil and see on the hill across the Avenue de la Paix the headquarters of the éntirely Swiss **International Committee for the Red Cross [95],** the ICRC, in what was formerly the resort Hotel Carlton.

> The general term "Red Cross" is a famous one but, in fact, there is no organization with that concise name.
>
> "Red Cross" as the popular designation for relief agencies is a mix of several elements:
>
> — the ICRC — the all-Swiss group — founded in 1863, working only in times of war to carry out the Geneva Conventions;
>
> — the National Societies — the British Red Cross, the Swiss Red Cross, the American Red Cross, and many others — founded at various dates after 1863 (page 155), each working according to its means and policies in peacetime relief in floods, fires and other disasters in addition to wartime help;
>
> — the League of Red Cross Societies — the Geneva-based coordinator of the National Societies — suggested by America's Clara Barton in 1884, founded in 1920 (page 77), centralizing the international activities;
>
> — the International Red Cross — the conference of the previous three entities, meeting once every four years for clearer understanding.

The distinctions are internal subtleties to the world at large, as long as it is assured the "Red Cross" is there to help. The Nobel Committee, on the other hand, has singled out the elements in awarding its Peace Prize, first in 1901 to Henri Dunant, then in 1917 and 1944 to the ICRC for its work in two World Wars, and in 1963 jointly to the ICRC and the League of Red Cross Societies.

> While the names of the Red Cross and Geneva are tightly linked, the blunt, secular cross form is long familiar here in other hues.
>
> For instance, a Gold Cross identified bankers in the 1300s (page 39) and the White Cross of Switzerland flew over Geneva after 1815 (page 16). In 1863, the Swiss flag emerged with its colors reversed as the Red Cross (page 102).
>
> In 1888 a Green Cross Society looked after young soldiers. In the 1890s Moynier (page 155) founded the Blue Cross temperance group. In the 1900s another Green Cross stood for women's rights. And today a Green Cross identifies pharmacies and a Gold Cross marks a Catholic anti-drug center.

While the principles of the Red Cross concept appealed to Moslems, they considered its symbol to be a Christian motif. In Islam, therefore, the national relief organizations work under the "Red Crescent", except in Persian Iran which insisted on the "Red Sun and Lion".

The basic blunt cross has, in fact, not the slightest religious intent or significance. As far as the emblem is concerned in Switzerland, even local bankers enjoy the joke that the Confederation's mark is not actually a cross but a "plus" sign.

◆ The Driven return down the **Avenue de la Paix** and turn right at the first street, the **Avenue Appia**, for a shuttle trip to see a few recent additions to the International City.

Walkers may enjoy an effortless look at these same building exteriors higher up on the Pregny hill by riding the public bus.

The red-orange Geneva buses arriving up the Avenue de la Paix turn to their left into the Avenue Appia. For your shuttle ride to view more buildings before returning to midtown Geneva, go to the bus-stop on the ICRC side of Avenue Appia — the "Arrêt Fixe - Appia" sign near the corner.

Public transport in Geneva is sold by the hour. You may board here, ride to the end of the line which is either at WHO two stops farther along or, on the alternate line, a 15-minute ride to Ferney-Voltaire, wait on board the bus for its turnaround, and ride back along the same route to the center of Geneva.

Walkers pressed for time may cross to the Soviet Delegation side of Avenue Appia and, at its "Arrêt Fixe" sign, board any bus, and pick up the thread again on page 181.

To pay for public transport (page 229) in Geneva, one buys a ticket before boarding. At each stop there is a red box — a coin-operated dispenser — to sell tickets as explained on the front of the machine in four languages including English.

No one will collect your ticket because it is valid for a full hour of transport on all buses and trams in the public system. The only check-up is by a team of inspectors who, on about one ride out of ten, will walk through the car and ask to see everyone's "Titre de Transport", the chit issued by the red box.

If you haven't managed to get a ticket, explain your problem frankly to the inspectors who are reasonable and generally understanding.

◆ The Driven — now including the bus-borne Walkers — proceed up the hill where you see on your right the **bronze statue [96]** of the Mexican patriot, **Miguel Hidalgo y Costilla**.

> Hidalgo y Costilla was the priest and intellectual who in 1810 incited the Indians of Mexico to revolt against the Spanish colonizers. The Creole leader was captured and shot but his War of Independence continued until Mexico was free from foreign rule.

◆ The monument is a gift of the government of Mexico to the **ILO,** begun in 1919 as the independent **International Labour Office** and, since 1946, the **International Labour Organization,** a specialized agency of the United Nations.

> The **building [97]** on your left, faced with 8,000 cast aluminum modules, became in 1974 the new headquarters of the ILO, moved from its overflowing, fifty-year-old building (page 161) to this structure with 13 conference chambers and accomodation for 2,000 staff.

◆ At the top of the slope to your left is the Intergovernmental Committee for Migration, an organization of restricted membership, independent of the UN and responsible for the resettlement, transportation, and training of refugees and migrants.

> To deal urgently with the displaced persons problem in 1947 the United Nations formed the short-lived International Refugee Organization. Member nations within the UN differed strongly on the issue of the freedom of personal movement so the IRO was liquidated and its functions divided.
>
> Since 1952 the United Nations' specialized agency of the High Commissioner for Refugees (page 161) provides care and legal protection and assimilation for refugees; the Intergovernmental Committee for Migration assists refugees and those individuals and families who enjoy freedom of choice and wish to migrate to other lands in search of new opportunities.

◆ The Driven must turn right at the hill-top and continue around the rectangular lawn in front of the **World Health Organization [98]**.

> WHO was founded by consolidating many health services and programs existing both under the League of Nations and independ-

ently. In its mission to protect health throughout the world, WHO has, since 1948, pursued more than 300 medical research projects and developed well over a thousand joint undertakings with national health services.

◆ The Driven return down Avenue Appia to its dead end at Avenue de la Paix, where the wall and the fence to the right guard the compound of the **USSR delegation [99]** to the United Nations.

Walkers, turning from page 179 after deciding to skip the uphill shuttle, take the bus stopping at this "Arrêt Fixe - Appia" and thus relax like the other Driven on the route back to midtown.

> Look to your right after the right turn into Avenue de la Paix to see the self-sufficient enclave with residences, schools, offices, and all facilities for survival within a single community under heavy security protection provided by the Soviet Union for its personnel and their families.
>
> In the center of the blocks of functional structures is an incongruous villa in the style of Geneva, circa 1860. This mansion was built near the country house of François and Ninette Duval-Toepffer for the second of their eight children, Etienne Duval-Toepffer-Marcet, a respected painter of landscapes.
>
> Etienne was named for his uncle, Etienne Dumont (page 58), the conscientious Genevese who left at the time of the fourth outbreak of the "Petite Révolution" to work first in London with Jeremy Bentham, then in Paris with Honoré Mirabeau, and later in Saint-Petersburg — sponsored by the Duval family — as pastor of the Reformed Church in the brilliant capital of Tsarist Russia.
>
> The country house of the Russophile Duval family was bought in the 1930s by the delegation to the League of Nations of the republic of Estonia. In the course of World War II the Soviet Union, while acquiring the territory of the nation bordering on the Baltic Sea, annexed the house and grounds of the Estonian delegation in Geneva as well.

◆ The Driven turn from the Avenue de la Paix to their right into the Place des Nations. At the next traffic signal, turn left into the broad plaza and bear right.

Walkers — arriving at Place des Nations from page 172 after choosing Option 2 at the end of the Palais tour — board a bus with a prepaid ticket (page 179) at the sheltered bus-stop.

With all participants for the moment in the Driven category, let those aboard the bus note that their destination is the stop **"Cornavin" [100]**.

◆ On the broad Place des Nations The Driven bear right as they approach the next traffic signals. They then follow the right-bearing lane into **Rue de Montbrillant.**

> About a hundred meters along Montbrillant on the right are the carillon and chapel of the Church of Saint Nicolas de Flue named for the Swiss soldier, hermit, and statesman who "preserved the union" in 1481 by persuading the contentious cantons to accept together the Covenant of Stans.

◆ Very close to this site in 1865 stood "Les Artichauts", The Artichokes, the villa leased by composer Richard Wagner with the intention of taking up residence in Geneva.

> Wagner fled Dresden in the Revolution of 1848 and lived in German Switzerland for several decades. In the 1850s the musician visited the Geneva area for several extended stays to have his chronic skin infection treated by a specialist recommended by his colleague, Franz Liszt (page 50).
>
> Liszt's second daughter, Cosima, in 1857 married Wagner's admirer and protégé, the conductor Hans von Bülow. Cosima was still married to von Bülow in December 1865 when she gave birth to Wagner's daughter Isolde. In that same month Wagner left Munich for Geneva where he leased a substantial mansion and, intending a long stay, undertook its decoration with no expense spared.
>
> Wagner, a man with a gift for complicating life, was relieved of one of his current concerns when he received word in January 1866 of the death of Minna, his wife. At "Les Artichauts", however, he was bedeviled by a series of upsets: a disconcerting chimney fire, the insistence of his Calvinist staff on two hours off every Sunday for services, the death of his favorite dog, and an argument with his landlord. Thus sorely beset, Wagner implored von Bülow to send his wife Cosima to straighten out the domestic disorder in Geneva.
>
> When Cosima arrived in March 1866 (page 50) she had Wagner break his lease and depart with her so abruptly that he left behind only a single souvenir of his presence, a marble marker on the grave of his dog, touchingly engraved "To my Pohl, R. W."
>
> Souvenir hunters or ghouls or vandals have long since purloined this last tangible evidence of the sojourn of Richard Wagner.

◆ Once past the traffic signal at Rue Vidollet you see on your left the "Colossus of Cornavin", planned from 1930 as the **Centre Postal [101],** to improve international communications with French Switzerland. As of its inauguration in 1984 the installation was the most highly automated in Europe.

> In reconciling the look of this five-story structure to the surrounding semi-industrial area, the architects made ample use of glass and metal to attain this effect of an oversized toaster-and-broiler set. Within the efficient complex is not only the giant post office but the telephone and telegraph exchange, the customs bureau, a rail siding, underground garage, and shopping mall.

◆ The Driven in cars continue straight ahead at the traffic signal at Rue du Fort-Barreau and follow the rest of the automobile traffic in a turn left under the railroad bridge to emerge into **Rue de Chantepoulet.**

The public-bus-borne Driven will be turned left into the bus-only underpass at the railroad station. As the bus goes through the short tunnel, proceed to any of its doors and push the signal button on the upright post. Without your push the automatic doors may not open at your **"Arrêt Fixe - Cornavin" [100]**.

> **Le Cornavin [102],** literally "The Horn of Wine" was the name of an inn located at the northern gate into Geneva. Travelers arriving on the road from France and its Jura mountains passed over a drawbridge and through the portal in the walls to find refreshment waiting at this wayside tavern.

The leveling of the walls and the filling of the moat in the 1850s left a clear path for the tracks of the first railroad into Geneva. When François Bartholoni (page 156) completed at Cornavin the terminal of a railroad branching off from his successful main line, Paris-Lyon-Marseilles, Geneva at last had rail access to Paris.

> The installation of railroad service into Geneva had been delayed for about a decade by conservative misgivings about the effect of such an intrusion on the town's geography and morals.
>
> Progressives of the Fazy stripe finally prevailed and, with the enterprise approved, General Dufour took over the technical details of station location, track routing, and even the ceremonies of the inaugural.

On 16 March 1858 Geneva turned out en masse to Gare Cornavin to greet the arrival of the locomotives "La Petite Genevoise" and "Les Sallenches", each hauling eight well-varnished wagons of elated passengers. To mark the occasion Geneva called forth artillery salutes, fireworks, a parade, bands, and dancing, all tempered by a generous overlay of religious ceremony.

The Swiss Confederation of loosely-allied cantons, each with its own customs barriers and tolls, was not conducive to easy transit and the country accordingly lagged behind the rest of Europe in railroad development.

When the Constitution of 1848 removed many such obstacles rail service grew rapidly in the northern area. The cities of Basle and Zurich took a long lead in establishing cross-Continent service while Geneva hesitated over admitting railroads at all.

The commercial leverage of the northern cities increased when their 1850s east-west line was tied in 1880 to the vital north-south route. This new axis through the Alps to Italy was opened by the completion of the Saint Gotthard Tunnel, an engineering miracle performed by Geneva's self-taught technician, Louis Favre.

Belatedly Geneva recognized its error in delaying rail service and fought to become a main-line stop by campaigning for a route from Paris to run through a tunnel in the Jura down into Geneva. From here this main line would continue east to the Simplon Tunnel and under the Alps into Italy.

After a long struggle a tunnel was indeed dug but, unfortunately for Geneva, it pierced the Jura some 60 kilometers (40 miles) north of the nearby Col de la Faucille. From the tunnel emerging at Vallorbe the new main line passed through Lausanne leaving Geneva served only by its awkward spur.

From the hard lesson of the railroad disappointment Geneva improved its forward planning. With the inception of commercial air service in the 1920s the town developed its Cointrin airport as a major European gateway.

Walk from the "Cornavin" bus stop to the first big entry portal of the railroad station. On your left as you enter is the down escalator leading to the underground garage and shopping mall.

In the mall, turn right for a stroll past the snack bars, flower shop, the security gadget shop managed by the Geneva police, and branches of two department stores.

As you approach the area where the mall opens up, turn towards its ramped entrance but turn right short of the opening to take the up escalator.

Beside the moving stairs are the ticket windows of the "Transports Publics Genevois", the TPG, the town's consolidated public transport system. Ask here for route maps, full schedules, and their pamphlet in English describing the fares, special rates, types of passes, days and times of each route — in short, everything you need to know about Geneva's computer-coordinated, subsidized, and altogether excellent street transport.

From the "up" escalator at street level under the glass roundhouse, walk ahead across the bus lanes at the "zebra" to approach the second largest of Geneva's churches.

◆ The Driven at the top of Rue Chantepoulet see on their left the **Basilique de Notre Dame [103],** the Basilica of Our Lady. Geneva's principal Roman Catholic church was built in the 1850s by the French Abbé, later Cardinal, Gustave Mermillod (page 88).

When freedom of religion and grants of land for houses of worship were ordained under Fazy's Constitution of 1847, the ambitious Abbé Mermillod was the first to apply.

A plot of Geneva land (page 54) that had just been cleared of the old fortifications, the "Royal Bastion", was allotted for his Catholic basilica.

The term "basilica" is usually an architectural reference to structures of the Romanesque or earlier epoch. Mermillod's church, however, is very much in the neo-Gothic style.

The initial designation of the church mattered little to Mermillod. He considered the terminology an interim affair pending its elevation to the status of "Cathedral" — the seat of the bishop — with himself in the chair.

While the last bishop to preside in Geneva was Pierre de la Baume who fled in 1532, the Catholic Church assigned the title of Bishop of Geneva to succeeding absentee ecclesiastics. The issue of the actual residence here of any Bishop of Geneva is still a very touchy one.

Mermillod's own advancement was, in any case, frustrated by the "Kulturkampf", the "War of Ideologies" (page 88) which divided the Catholic Church over Pius IX's dogma of the infallibility of the pope. Between the two factions Mermillod sided with the Vatican while in Geneva Antoine Carteret, head of the government of this church-state, decided in favor of the dissenters.

To this latter group, known as the "Old Catholics" Carteret assigned all Geneva's Catholic property including the Basilique. Mermillod went into exile in France.

Elevated to Cardinal, Mermillod directed from afar the political strategy that in 1907 resulted in the separation of state from church in Geneva. Once again permitted to own property here, the Roman Catholic Church repurchased the Basilique in 1912.

The Basilique is decorated with chapels, windows, and plaques commemorating Catholics prominent in Geneva. Among these are such pre-Reformation figures as Saint Clotilde, who left Geneva to marry Clovis and convert him and his Frankish Empire to Roman Christianity (page 62); Bishop Adhémar Fabri, the grantor of the "Franchises of 1387" to the citizens (page 9); and Cardinal Jean de Brogny, president of the Council of Constance to close the church's "Great Schism" (page 73).

Other memorials to later Catholics recall Saint François de Sales, named in 1602 as Bishop of Geneva — in absentia — to advance Rome's Counter-Reformation; and Elizabeth, Empress of Austria, assassinated on the Quai de Mont-Blanc in 1898 (page 140).

The stained-glass windows of the Basilique were recently remounted into removable frames to expedite storage in vaults in the event of any threat of violence to neutral but never unrealistic Switzerland.

The window dedicated to Saint Louis of Gonzaga is by Alexander Cingria, the designer of the mosaics in the Arsenal (page 92), while the adjacent abstract pattern in stained glass is the work of Théodore Strawinsky, a Geneva artist and the son of the musician, Igor Stravinski.

The Russian-born Igor Stravinski lived and composed near Geneva from 1914 to 1920. In later years he returned frequently to collaborate on the proper interpretation of his challenging scores by his preferred performers, Ernest Ansermet and the Orchestre de la Suisse Romande, the Orchestra of French Switzerland.

Walkers leave the Basilique by its front steps, going to their right to the traffic signal and "zebra" to cross in greater safety the Rue Cornavin, another straightaway for Geneva's Formula One automobilists.

◆ The Driven on the **Rue de Chantepoulet** select a middle lane and at the next traffic signal continue straight ahead down the slope.

The neighborhood is part of Saint Gervais (page 133), the original center of Geneva's watchmaking industry. 25 Rue de Chantepoulet, built in 1798 for watch-enameler Etienne Roux as the "Palace of Saint Gervais" was fitted on its top floor with the rooms and windows designed for the work of "La Fabrique".

"The Factory" was the production method that made Geneva watchmaking efficient and gave its watches a substantial advantage in price. Charles Cusin, a French fugitive from charges of horse -thievery, evolved in the late 1500s the system whereby each technician became a specialist on one part of a watch — gears, springs, case, etc. — to be assembled into a finished timepiece.

◆ The parish of Saint Gervais was confined for centuries within the high walls against which were crowded the shops of the Rue de Chantepoulet. At the street's lower limit the Rue des Ramparts began and continued along the wall to its end at the lake.

When the walls came down the Rue des Ramparts was extended across their former path in a straight line from the lake up the cleared slope to the new rail terminal.

Renamed the **Rue du Mont-Blanc**, the widened avenue is today headed by the pedestrian mall watched over by Fazy's marble sphinxes (page 138).

The merchants of the 1860s counted on the new thoroughfare from the station to channel arriving visitors towards the lake. The entrepreneurs accordingly set up along the street their shops, stalls, taverns, hotels, and boarding houses.

The lodgings here accomodated the passing salesmen and tourists and a continuing clientele of social exiles eluding their pasts, and political refugees organizing revolutions and drafting constitutions for brave new worlds.

Among those fleeing their personal problems was the Russian novelist Fyodor Mikhailovich Dostoevsky who arrived in August 1867 with his new wife (page 136) to await the birth of their first child.

When Dostoevsky duly registered the birth of baby Sophie on 22 February 1868, he gave the family's address as 16 Rue du Mont-Blanc, just beyond the Beaux-Arts-style post office.

◆ At the point where Rue de Chantepoulet merges into the **Rue du Mont-Blanc** you see to the left the **Hôtel des Postes [104],** the official name of Geneva's most ornate post office.

The building, described as "monumental" at its dedication in 1892, seemed too rich to pass for a prosaic post office. Some Genevese with a pretty sense of fantasy have therefore since identified it as their "Ministère de la Marine", i.e. — the Navy Department or Admiralty.

While the overall grandeur of the building evoked comment, even more attention was paid to the decor of the upper cornice where the figures of four semi-nude goddesses lounge irrelevantly against the corner clocks. So much disclosure of the female form in the name of art agitated some observers and titillated the more prurient oglers until, in 1896, their attention was diverted by the unveiling of the even sexier stone sprite, "Harmonie", on Victoria Hall (page 159).

◆ The glass building to your right at the foot of Chantepoulet provides another sample of irreverence in nomenclature. The Genevese identify this office structure as "La Verrue du Verre", the Glass Wart.

In the little park on the Rue du Mont-Blanc stands the Tudor-style **English Church [105].**

Less often used is the name, "The Church of the Holy Trinity", the registered identity of this Genevan element of the Gibraltar parish of the Anglican Church.

The Church of England originated with King Henry VIII for personal and political reasons having little in common with the motivations of such protesters as Luther and Calvin. The other early Protestant sects were, however, countenanced in Tudor England until the ascension to the throne in 1553 of Henry's zealously Catholic daughter, "Bloody Mary". Under her persecutions reformers like John Knox and Miles Coverdale fled from Great Britain to settle eventually in Geneva (page 66).

After the succession of Protestant Elizabeth I in 1558 the British refugees left Geneva and the English colony remained small until 1815. Following the fall of Napoleon, English travelers eagerly returned to the Continent and a colony of Anglican faithful settled in Geneva. To provide them with a place of worship, the town made available the chapel of the hospital in the Bourg-de-Four (page 61).

The Anglican congregation in Geneva was among the religious groups entitled to grants of land under the Constitution of 1847. Led by Sir Robert Peel, the British Minister to Switzerland (page 158), the Anglicans appealed for the usual 100 toises of ground (page 54). They received not only this plot from the clearing of the fortifications but a supplementary contribution of a third of the £4,000 cost of construction of their chapel.

A further contribution arrived shortly after the consecration of the church in 1854 in the form of the timepiece in the square stone tower, presented by Geneva's clockmakers — for three centuries the collaborators and competitors of their English counterparts.

◆ On your left at the next corner the insurance company "La Genevoise" occupies the **premises [106]** of one of Geneva's two erstwhile Hôtels Victoria.

In August 1864 the hotel numbered among its guests the German socialist, Ferdinand Lassalle, the most practical and humane among the three contemporary German philosophers of social reform: Karl Marx, Friedrich Engels, and Lassalle.

Working with Otto von Bismark on the unification of Germany under a parliamentary government, the rich, eloquent, politically astute Lassalle was the most likely prospect to be the first president of the new Germany.

Lassalle visited Geneva in 1864 in honorable pursuit of the beautiful but flighty Hélène Doenniges. In his room at the Hôtel Victoria Lassalle virtuously resisted the passionate opportunings of the frivolous redhead, already the fiancée of one Prince Yanko Racowitz.

To avenge Lassalle's rebuff, Hélène precipitated a duel between her two suitors. In the unequal confrontation Racowitz, an accomplished marksman, shot the pacifistic Lassalle in the stomach. Four days later "... the people's hope of Germany...» died in the corner room of the Hôtel Victoria.

The event is commemorated in George Meredith's novel *The Tragic Comedians* and, at the scene of the duel, by a monument that has become one of the shrines of Socialism.

◆ 3 Rue du Mont-Blanc on the right, now a multipurpose building marked "Overland Trust Banque", was built in the 1920s as Geneva's most modern "Hôtel des Délégations", planned especially to accomodate delegates, diplomats, and their meetings.

When interest in the League of Nations diminished and its meetings dwindled, the occupancy rate of all Geneva's hotels suffered. The Hotel des Délégations was turned into office space.

◆ A few meters along Rue du Mont-Blanc, both The Driven and the Walkers are back at the map point **Start.**

At this juncture you have very much earned the appreciation of Geneva for your efforts and interest in the town's story and sights and the thanks of your guide for your patience with this presentation.

If you care to comment, write your thoughts on the enclosed, pre-addressed, postpaid card. Your remarks will be both welcome and carefully noted.

Der Frieden Forget-Me-Knotted Cannon

R. Brandenberger of the Canton of Glarus twisted the barrel of a cannon into an over-hand knot and on it suspended a locomotive wheel to represent by its circular form "absolute perfection".

In October 1983 Brandenberger led a march to bring this work to Geneva in an appeal for the continuation of peace talks. The marchers left as a gift to Geneva this remind-er of their plea. The peace talks recessed, *sine die*, in November 1983.

The sculpture is called "Frieden" – German for "Peace" (map 76).

After the Tour Is Over

Daytime Diversions

A tour of Geneva to introduce one to the town might well lead to a closer acquaintance. Visitors with additional hours or days to spend in Geneva should look into its cultural resources, first-rate recreational facilities, and tantalizing choice of short trips to new horizons.

For hobbies and cultural pursuits

Of Geneva's thirty-odd museums, libraries, collections, galleries, and gardens, more than half are owned by the town and are free of entrance fees. For those that are not town property but privately owned and endowed, the admission charge is modest.

To guide you in two fashions — by place and by subject matter — two indices have been prepared.

The first lists Geneva's principal museums, gardens, galleries and other exhibits by their French name, followed by an English translation, a hint as to their contents, and an alphabetical coding.

The second list is arranged according to "subjects-of-possible-interest". Each topic — books, clocks, etc. — is keyed to the foregoing alphabetical list to point out in which exhibit to find the objects you might wish to see.

For any given exhibit the details of address, telephone number, opening days and hours, entry fees, public transport lines and stop to use, etc. may change. Research of the current state of such facts is left to consultation of the daily newspapers or of the other resources listed in "References" (page 251).

Places to visit

AG	Archives de Genève (map: 42)	Official records with documentation back to the 1300s
AL	American Library (map: 72)	English-language books and periodicals
BAA	Bibliothèque d'art et d'archéologie (map: 14)	Multilingual, specialized reference library
BB	Biblioteca Bodmeriana (prvt)	Manuscripts and rare editions
BPU	Bibliothèque publique et universitaire (map: 52)	Multilingual public library of University of Geneva
CB	Collection Baur (prvt; map: 16)	Oriental ceramics and art
CE	Cabinet des Estampes (map: 14)	Prints and engravings from collection of MAH
CJB	Conservatoire et Jardin botanique (map: 85)	Garden, reference library, greenhouses, deer park, aviary
CSP	Cathédrale de Saint-Pierre (map: 30)	Stone and wood carvings, organ recitals, tower view
ER	Eglise Russe (map: 17)	Byzantine church with icons
FZ	Fondation Zoubov (prvt; map: 38)	Furniture and paintings in 1700s town house, Louis XIV
IMV	Institut et Musée Voltaire	Voltaire's home; manuscripts
JA	Jardin Anglais	Quayside park, Left Bank
MA	Musée d'Ariana (map: 90)	International Academy of Ceramics
MAH	Musée d'art et d'histoire (map: 19)	Paintings, sculpture, furnished rooms, archaeology, armor, etc.
MBM	Musée Barbier-Muller (prvt)	Primitive art
ME	Musée d'ethnographie	Development of civilizations
MG	Muséum de Genève	Natural history exhibits
MHE	Musée de l'horlogerie et de l'émaillerie	Clocks, watches, enamels
MHS	Musée d'histoire des sciences (map: 81)	Old instruments, memorabilia of Saussure Mont-Blanc ascent
MIAM	Musée d'instruments anciens de musique (prvt; map: 18)	Antique and unusual musical instruments
MSE	Musée des Suisses à l'étranger (prvt)	Swiss who were famous in other countries, also military uniforms
MVG	Musée du Vieux Genève (map: 33)	Items from Geneva's history
PB	Parc des Bastions	Statuary, tree collection
PG	Parc des Granges	Flowers, lawn, trees, summer concerts

PN	Palais des Nations (prvt; map: 91)	Meeting halls and working premises and park
PP	Petit Palais (prvt; map: 15)	Modern art in 1860s town house
RL	Rockefeller Library (prvt)	Part of PN; memorabilia of peace movements and League of Nations
SL	Société de Lecture (prvt; map: 36)	Oldest private library in Geneva
SAL	Salle Ami Lullin (ground floor of BPU; map: 52)	Reformation and Geneva Bibles and documents; Rousseau museum

Eminent directors and curators manage Geneva's collections and maintain fine facilities for scholarly research above and beyond the exhibits.

Temporary exhibits supplementing 'the permanent displays are held by Geneva in the Musée Rath, the Athénée, the Halles de l'Ile, and the Palais Wilson.

Subjects covered in Geneva's collections

Archaeology: Prehistory, Roman, Greek, Middle East, Geneva   MAH
    — Reference library, books and slides   BAA

Armor: 1400-1700: Helmets, halberds, pistols, etc.   MAH

Artillery: 1700: Light field pieces, decorated   MAH
    — 1600: Cannon, Dresden and Geneva models   AG

Birds: Live: Swans and waterfowl (map: 2)   Ile Rousseau
    — Peacocks, cranes, egrets: Deer park of   CJB
    — Parakeets and smaller species: Aviary of   CJB
    Mounted: Exotic species, natural settings   MG

Books: Art and archaeology, 80,000 references   BAA
    Bibles: 1500s and later, rare items   SAL
    Botany: 120,000 books plus periodicals   CJB
    English language: 20,000 volumes   AL
    General references, multilingual: Over 1,000,000   BPU
    Geneva and Swiss references   SL
    International Affairs: 1mm books, 5mm documents   RL
    Rare editions, Bibles, manuscripts   BB

Botany: Gardens, greenhouses, library, etc.   CJB

Ceramics: Chinese (5 dynasties) and Japanese   CB
    Comprehensive collection   MA
    Middle East earthenware   MAH
    Nyon: 1790-1815: 20 minutes by train to Nyon Museum

Clocks: Timepieces from the hourglass to electronics	MHE
Floral clock, four meters high	JA
Water Clock	Parc de Malagnou
Mechanical figures on parade	Passage Malbuisson
Fantasy in scrap iron	Airport Lounge

| Coins: Middle Eastern, Roman, Russian, European | MAH |

Decorations and furnishings:	
Town house: Louis XIV, fully decorated	FZ
Town house: 1860s	PP
Country house: "Les Délices", 1720	IMV
Château de Coppet: 1780	10 minutes by train
Château de Penthes: 1810	MSE
Model Rooms: Guardroom with roundtable, 1400s	MAH
– Château reception and bedroom, 1500s	MAH
– Chapel with stained glass, 1500s	MAH
– Dining room with Roman frescos	MAH
– Reception room, walnut panelled	MAH
– Reception room, tapestried walls	MAH

Documents: Calvin's journals, "Franchises", registers	AG
– Reformation records, portraits	SAL
– Rousseau manuscripts	SAL
– International treaties, Nobel Prize	RL
– Voltaire letters, manuscripts, references	IMV
– Manuscripts of famous writers	BB

| Drawings and Engravings: Small specialized exhibit plus collection of 300,000 items to be seen on request | CE |

| Egyptology: Mummy, statuary, relics | MAH |
| – Papyri, statuary, cuneiform | BB |

| Executioners' tools: Broadswords, manacles, guillotine | MAH |

| Fish: Live: Small aquarium of tropical specimens | MG |
| Mounted: Rare and unusual species | MG |

Flowers: Indigenous, Alpine, Mediterranean, tropical	CJB
– Indigenous, at School of Horticulture	Lullier
– Roses, week in June and international concours	PG

| Icons: | ER |

| Medical instruments: 1700s surgical; 1800s dental | MHS |

| Microscopes and telescopes: 1600s into 1800s | MHS |

| Military uniforms: Swiss regiments | MSE |

Musical: Instruments: Primitive, other civilizations	ME
– Instruments: 1500s through 1800s	MIAM
– Manuscripts: Mozart, Beethoven, Stravinski, etc.	BB

| Oriental Art: Chinese ceramics, enamels, bronze, jade | CB |
| – Japanese lacquers, ivories, enamels | CB |

| Primitive Art: Rotating exhibit from large collection | MBM |
| – From other continents | ME |

Sculpture: Classic Greek through Moore and Tinguely	MAH
— More than 300 recent works	Geneva Parks
Silver tableware: Archaeological: 300-600 A.D.	MAH
— Geneva work, 1550 through 1750	MAH
Stamps: United Nations: Special issues	PN
Swiss: Special issues	Central Post Office
Trees: Indigenous and exotic imports	CJB
— Cataloged collection of 150 species	PB
Watches: History and samples of unusual models	MHE
Wood sculpture: Choir stalls, 1400s	CSP
— Street doors, 1600s	Old Town

Sports and pastimes

Among the half-a-hundred activities taking place in Geneva and involving exertion and/or competition there may be a sport you have not yet tried.

Your sojourn here could be the occasion for starting a new interest under the tutelage of one of the local expert instructors — fully tested and licensed — to give you a taste of water-skiing, rock climbing, hang-gliding, and other less conventional outlets for the energies.

Lists of clubs, organizers, sports fields, and associations change frequently. Sport, moreover, is one aspect of well-organized Geneva that is not yet centralized. No single source has all of the answers.

Three municipal sport offices know about town-owned and -operated facilities. Professional sport is managed by individual promoters. And many special activities have their own groups, instructors, and private clubs. So long as no coordinating point exists, the listings here are as comprehensive as any that you are likely to find.

The first list tabulates sources of information. These references, updated regularly, are identified here by an alphabetical coding.

The second list spells out the sports and pastimes. Each is keyed back to the alphabetical list from which you should be able to track down the current state of the action.

Sources of sport data

AT   *Annuaire Téléphonique*   The Geneva telephone book, issued annually.

CLE   *La Clé (The Key)*   French list of some 600 non-commercial services. Buy in bookstores or Tourist Office.

GE   *The Guide to the English-Speaking Community of Geneva.*   English list of resources by GELCOS group. Issued annually, free at American Library, hotels, etc.

JI   *Jeune Information*   Multilingual folder with tips for youth. Free from Tourist Office, Welcome Car at station, University.

LIG   *Living in Geneva*   English information book by American Women's Club. Buy there or from major bookstores.

PJ   *Les Pages Jaunes*   French "Yellow Pages", the classified telephone book, issued annually

United Nations staff and delegates to UN organizations have a choice of in-house sports clubs and activities coordinated by the various Staff Associations.

Participation sports

Aerobics		See Gymnase
Archery	AT	Arc-Club, Genève
	LIG	Leisure, General, Archery
Aviation	LIG	Leisure, General, Aviation
	PJ	Ecoles de pilotage
Badminton	AT	Clubs, Badminton
	GE	Sport, Badminton Club
	LIG	Leisure, General, Badminton
Baseball	LIG	Leisure, Children, Baseball
Basketball	CLE	Sports, Basket-ball
	PJ	Associations Sportives, Basket-ball
Bathing	AT	Plages
	LIG	Leisure, General, Swimming
Bicycling	CLE	Sports, Cyclisme
	JI	Locations (Rentals), Vélos
	LIG	Leisure, General, Bicycling
	PJ	Associations sportives, Union vélocipédique genevoise
Boating	JI	Locations, barques, pédalos, bateaux à moteur
	LIG	Leisure, General, Boating
		See also: Rowing, Sailing

Bowling	AT	Bowling
	GE	Sport, Women's Bowling
	LIG	Leisure, General, Bowling
Boxing	AT	Clubs, Pugilistique
Cricket	GE	Sport, Geneva, Cricket Club
	LIG	Leisure, General, Cricket
Croquet	GE	Sport, Croquet
	LIG	Leisure, General, Croquet
Curling	AT	Curling Club
	LIG	Leisure, General, Curling
Diving		See: − Hang-gliding
		− Underwater diving
Fencing	AT	Escrime
	LIG	Leisure, General, Fencing
Fishing	LIG	Leisure, General, Hunting
	PJ	Pêche, Articles de
Fitness		See Gymnase
Gliding	GE	Sport, Gliding, Soaring
Gymnase		(Workouts for fitness are given in salons called, inter alia, "gymnases".)
	AT	Gymnases (5 listings)
	AT	Fitness (5 listings)
	GE	Sport, Stayslim
Gymnastique		(Tumbling, flying rings, horizontal bars, etc., are "athlétisme" or "gymnastique". Today, the term gets confused with "gymnase")
	AT	Gymnastique (5 listings)
	CLE	Sports, Gymnastique
	PJ	Association sportive, gymnastique
Golf	LIG	Leisure, General, Golf
Handball	CLE	Sports, Handball
	PJ	Association sportive, handball
Hang-gliding	AT	Delta Club
	CLE	Sports, Vol Delta
	LIG	Leisure, General, Hang-gliding
Hiking	CLE	Sports, Randonnées
	LIG	Leisure, General, Hiking
Ice Skating	AT	Patinoire
	CLE	Sports, Patinage, Club
	LIG	Leisure, General, Skating
Jiu-jitsu	PJ	Sport, Instituts et écoles de Judo
Jogging	CLE	Sports, Jogging
	GE	Sport, World Runners
	LIG	Leisure, General, Jogging

Judo	AT	Clubs, Judo (6 listed)
	PJ	Sports, Instituts et écoles de (6 listed)
Karate	AT	Centres, Karaté & Full-Contact
	AT	Karaté-Club (6 listed)
	PJ	Sport, Instituts et écoles de
Motorboating	JI	Locations, Bateaux à Moteur
Pétanque	AT	Cercles, Bouliste
	CLE	Sports, Boules et Pétanque
Ping Pong		See Table Tennis
Riding	AT	Manèges
	CLE	Sports, Equitation
	LIG	Leisure, General, Riding
	PJ	Ecoles d'équitation et manèges
	PJ	Association sportive, sociétés hippique
Riflery		See Target-shooting
Rock-	CLE	Sports, Alpinisme - montagne
climbing	LIG	Leisure, General, Alpinism
	PJ	Association sportive, Clubs Alpins
Roller-	JI	Locations, Patins à roulette
skating		
Rowing	CLE	Sports, Voile − aviron
Rugby	GE	Sport, International Rugby
	LIG	Leisure, General, Rugby
Sailing	CLE	Sports, Voile
	PJ	Ecoles de sport nautique
Skiing	CLE	Sports, Ski
	LIG	Leisure, General, Skiing
Soccer	GE	Sport, Football
	LIG	Leisure, General, Soccer
	PJ	Association sportive, football
Squash	AT	Squash
	GE	Sport, Geneva Squash
	LIG	Leisure, General, Squash
	PJ	Clubs (Cercles)
	PJ	Tennis-Clubs et Squash
Swimming	AT	Piscines
	CLE	Sports, Natation
	LIG	Leisure, General, Swimming
Table Tennis	AT	Clubs, Rapid Genève, CTT
	AT	Clubs, Table Tennis
	CLE	Sports, Tennis − Tennis de Table
	GE	Sport, Geneva Squash Club
	LIG	Leisure, General, Table Tennis
Target-	CLE	Sports, Tir
shooting	LIG	Leisure, General, Riflery

Tennis	AT	Tennis (20 listings)
	CLE	Sports, Tennis
	LIG	Leisure, General, Tennis
	PJ	Tennis-Clubs et Squash
Underwater	AT	Centres, Sports Sous-marins
diving	CLE	Sports, Natation – plongée
	LIG	Leisure, General, Underwater diving
Volley Ball	CLE	Sports, Volley Ball
	LIG	Leisure, General, Volley ball
	PJ	Association sportive, volley-ball
Walking		See Hiking
Water skiing	CLE	Sports, Ski – ski nautique
	LIG	Leisure, General, Water skiing
Windsurfing	CLE	Sports, Voile – Vélisurf
	JI	Location, Planche à voile (4 listings)
	LIG	Leisure, General, Windsurfing
	PJ	Ecoles de sport nautique
Wrestling	AT	Club, Lutte Satus

Pastimes

Billiards	AT	Clubs, Billiards
	AT	Clubs, Genevois des Amateurs de Billiards
Bridge	AT	Cercle, Genève de Bridge
	AT	Clubs, Bridge (4 listings)
Checkers	AT	Clubs, Damiers Genevois
Chess	AT	Clubs, Echecs (2 listed)
Darts	GE	Sport, Darts
Gambling	AT	Grand Casino, Boule (page 147)

As a sort of supermarket of social and sports action there are the official "Centres de Loisirs" of Geneva and the commercial "Cultural Services" of the Migros and the Co-op chains offering a range of instruction and participation.

Spectator sport

Geneva abounds in amateur team competition, followed closely by the local press. Professional-level sport with full seasons and league championships are to be seen in:

Basketball: Swiss professional league, laced with American ringers;
Hockey: Swiss semi-professional league;
Soccer: Swiss professional league; Class A team: Servette.

Regularly-scheduled events in Geneva sport include

Horse jumping: CHIO, see page 219;

Marathon: see page 220;

Swimming: Coupe de Noël, see page 225;

Tennis: Cup Martini, see page 223.

In addition, competition in bicycling, golf, boxing, dressage, and other events are promoted on an "as available" schedule.

Tours, scenery, and sights nearby

Spectacular valleys, summits, glaciers, ranges, passes, and lakes — many of the natural wonders of the world — are near enough to Geneva for a visit — there and back — within the same day.

The free pamphlet *Excursions* from the Tourist Office is updated annually, lists a fine choice of short outings, and tells you which train, boat, or other conveyance will transport you where and how long the tour will take.

Bookings of package trips are made through travel agents or at the rail [102] or bus [105] stations. Rail buffs who enjoy planning their own itinerary will delight in the *Swiss Official Timetable* and the country's heavily-subsidized-and-worth-it network of railroads, postal buses, and lake boats, all clean, comfortable, fast, and reliable.

Those preferring to drive themselves should ask the car-rental agencies or auto clubs about routings, possible road closings, and anticipated "bouchons" — literally "corks", traffic jams that can be kilometers in length and cause hours of delay.

The *Excursions* brochure tells the transport to ride, the times of departure and return, and the fares.

The table below divides the trips into half-day or full-day outings. Once you have selected the tour that suits you best, revert to the all-handy *Excursions* leaflet for the rest of your planning.

Half-day outings

Town Tour: Within Geneva's town limits by bus and a short stroll in about 2 hours.

Old Town Tour: A walk around the Old Town guided by a 20-minute cassette, tape player, and map lent free by the Tourist Office, 1 hour.

Old Town Tours: Theme tours — Reformation, Romantic Period, etc. — afoot with guide, 2 hours.

Rhone River Cruise: To see cliffs and birdlife, downstream to the hydro-electric dam by powerboat, 2 hours.

Mont Salève: From the top of Geneva's mountain, a great view and perhaps a stroll along the ridge after a ride on bus 8 from Rive and 3 minutes of cable car, 2 hours.

Geneva Countryside: Visit the canton's "viticole" (wine producing) Right Bank, and "agricole" (truck farming) Left Bank, for a different aspect of Geneva, by bus with guide, 4 hours.

Jura Mountains: From the pine-covered crest to the northwest, see Geneva and the Savoy Alps after bus and chair-lift ascent, with guide, by bus, 4 hours.

Lake cruises: Buy your ticket at the landing and go:
  — to cross the harbor, use the "Mouette", 5 minutes.
  — to visit the parks and the main bathing beach, use a "Mouette", get off and on at way-stops if you like, 30 minutes.
  — to cruise along the lake edge non-stop and hear about châteaux, celebrities, small ports, you have a choice of several private craft, from 35 minutes to 2 hours.
  — to follow a similar course but debark at any landing that tempts you, take a unit of the "Mouette" fleet.
  — to cruise around this end of Lake Geneva on Swiss CGN big boat, 3 hours.
  — to lunch aboard a CGN boat and back by 14.00 (2 p.m.). A pleasant meal while cruising to nowhere, 1½ hours.
  — to cruise by starlight, dancing parties afloat in the evening aboard the CGN, 3 hours.

Air touring, a view of the Alps from 7-seater aircraft:
  — scan Geneva countryside, lake and town, 30 minutes.
  — a turn around Mont Blanc, Europe's highest peak, and back, 75 minutes.
  — a trip to the picture-book Matterhorn with landing on adjacent glacier, 75 minutes.
  — your choice of any two glaciers in adjacent Alps, landings and return, 75 minutes.

Full-day trips

Western Switzerland: See Gruyères castle, Gstaad, Interlaken, and capital at Bern by bus, 12 hours.

Montreux and Chillon: Along lake road east to the Swiss Riviera and the castle of Byron's "Prisoner of Chillon", by bus, 8½ hours.

Glacier of Diablerets: Views and lunch atop 10,000-foot peak by cable car and bus, 10 hours.

Mont Blanc: See Europe's highest from across the steep valley at Chamonix by bus and cable car, 10 hours.

Chillon and Mont Blanc: After lakeside bus ride, cross a high Alpine pass then take highest cable car in Europe to get a close-up of Mont Blanc, 10 hours.

Jungfrau: Switzerland's highest mountain is a great white wall that you can ride through, train and cog-rail, 13½ hours.

Matterhorn: Switzerland's trademark mountain by train and two cog-railways for view from across the valley, 13½ hours.

Schilthorn: A rotating restaurant and glorious viewpoint near the Jungfrau, train and cable car, 13½ hours.

Cruise, Lake Geneva: Big cruise boat touches all ports, and makes round trip in 12 hours. Return from east end of the lake by train and total outing takes 8 hours.

Italian Lake Visit: To see Lago Maggiore and another country, take the train to resort town of Stresa, short boat ride to storybook castle on Borromeo Isles, 13½ hours.

A day in the country

Country outings are a Geneva tradition. Long before the Genevese discovered the automobile and took to hurtling 700 kilometers in 5 hours to pass a day on a rock-strewn beach, families sallied forth by public transport to explore afoot the riches of their canton.

The charm of the nearby hamlets remains intact. Each boasts its own attractions by way of views of lake and mountain, of châteaux, chapels, and churches often dating from medieval times, and with abundant flowers and greenery in season. Most villages offer a choice of rural cafés – many with gardens – and in a range of styles from family-modest to some of the most vaunted restaurants in this region.

The most distant point in the Canton of Geneva can be reached from the town center by bus, train, or boat in 45 minutes.

When the weather is kind and a quiet stroll tempting, arm yourself with the *TPG Horaire* (Public Service timetable) and the map *Carte Nationale 270* or one of its upscale counterparts – the identical map with walking trails superimposed: either *Carte 270T* or the Touring Club Suisse *Cartes des Loisirs* – and try a few-hour foray:

– to Cartigny for its château, 1700s atmosphere, and views of the Rhone;

– to Dardagny by river boat to La Plaine and a bus or trudge through the vineyards of the Mandement to reach the chateau (page 115);

– to Satigny for its church and a walk through the woods of Malval;

– to Versoix to follow the banks of its stream to the town of Sauverny;

– to Jussy for its view of the valley to Mont-Blanc, its church, then the Château du Crest, and on to Lullier for its horticultural school and gardens;

– to Hermance for its walls and castle from 1296 offering medieval houses, a chapel, church, and galleries. Walk from the fishing port up the banks of the river flowing through the town from the Voiron Hills;

– to Bardonnex for its "chicane" (page 68) shape, flowers, and rolling farmland;

– to Cologny for its views of the lake and the Jura mountains, restaurants and – on Thursday afternoons only – the Bodmer Biblioteca, a collection of exceptional editions and manuscripts.

Evening Entertainment

◆ Evening activities in Geneva change with the seasons from the outdoor entertainments of the warm months to the indoor events in cooler times.

Summer fare: In the clement weather of the long evenings the basic exercise is a stroll along the quays under the strings of lights and neon signs while floodlights dramatize the trees, Cathedral, and Jet d'Eau. For the best overview take the cable car to the top of Mont Salève before dusk and watch the dramatic transformation scene from on high.

Entertainment, much of it free, is offered along the quays and within walking distance or short public transport rides in other parks and locales. Check the newspapers under "Concerts", "Spectacles", "Variétés", and "Théâtre" to learn what is playing where tonight.

Town Bandstands: Rock groups, glee clubs, accordion bands, native troupes, yodelers – anything is possible on the open stages.
On Right Bank: Quai du Mont-Blanc, map 71.
On Left Bank: Jardin Anglais, map 5.
Near University: Parc des Bastions, map 55.

Jardin Anglais: Unadvertised special of stunt rollerskaters in spontaneous competition.

Quai du Mont-Blanc: Two-hour "Dancing Cruise" of the lake embarks here, map 69.

Hôtel de Ville: Concerts by Orchestre de la Suisse Romande and by guest artists in courtyard of Town Hall, map 43.

Parc de la Grange: Theater, jazz concerts, New Orleans combos, poetry readings with music, ballet – all in open air.

Various settings in and near Geneva: Summer theater out of doors.

At a dozen central locations: Festival de la Bâtie of all the arts; youth oriented, all welcome, 15 days in September.

Skywards: Fireworks: 4th of July: American Independence Day.
– 1st of August: Swiss National Day.
– 1st weekend in August: Fêtes de Genève.

Other seasons: The first cool evenings open the longer season with the circus as its harbinger, followed closely by the first of the eight presentations of Geneva's big time, highly subsidized opera, the opening concert of the Orchestre de la Suisse

Romande, and an outburst of theater in English by three local companies and in French by Geneva's two professional repertory groups, supplemented by touring companies from Paris and local amateurs in experimental theater. Again, follow the daily newspapers.

Grand Théâtre: Evenings: 8 major operas, 2 ballets, special events, map 58.
  – Sunday morning: Chamber music concerts in foyer.

Victoria Hall: Concert season by Orchestre de la Suisse Romande and concerts by touring artists and ensembles.

Grand Casino: Touring theatrical companies from Paris in subscription season and special events by pop stars, gospel singers, national troupes and ballets from Africa and the Orient, rock favorites, and plays by touring troupes in French and, less frequently, English, map 73.

La Comédie; Théâtre de Carouge: Two theaters with repertory companies, well subsidized, in subscription series plus visiting companies.

Salle Communale, University, Uni II, and elsewhere: Lecture season with subscription series for travel talks. Also lectures on music, opera, sports, exploits, etc.

"Little Theater": Geneva's equivalent of "Off Broadway" with sound performers, less elaborate productions, a variety of settings:
  Caveau, Pitoëff, de Poche, Traverse, Patino, etc.

English Language: Settings vary with availability.
  Geneva Amateur Opera Club
  Geneva English-Speaking Drama Society
  Little Theater of Geneva: American plays

Casino Théâtre: Satire on local political and social scene, full-scale revue for six weeks each spring by local professionals, who refuse to quit.

Churches: Saint-Germain, Cathedral, Notre-Dame, Madeleine, offer chamber music, organ recitals, carillon concerts.

Plainpalais: Circuses, starting with 21 days of Knie Circus in August.

Vernets Sports Complex: Professional ice hockey, basketball, boxing, wrestling, horse show.

Stadia: Professional soccer season, Swiss "A League" team, Servette, at Les Charmilles: other leagues on other fields.

In Italy or France: High-stake gambling and casino entertainment.

The year-round staple: Films: Throughout the year films are showing at Geneva's twenty-odd regular movie houses plus its "cinémathèque"-style public cinema and several film clubs.

Films listed in the daily newspapers usually offer a choice among American, French, British, Swiss, Swedish, Italian and other nationalities of production. Films routinely projected in

Geneva would require a major effort to locate in even larger cities.

Feature film programs are often split with two or even more different movies shown on the same day. To make certain that you will see the film you want in the "version" you want, check the timing carefully.

Films shown in Geneva are either with French sound track or with their original language, this latter noted in listings as "version-originale", or "v-o" with "sub-titles" indicated by "s-t" and their language.

If you are planning a family outing, check in the listing the minimum age allowed. Box offices in Geneva hold strictly to the age limit and ask for proof. The top of the scale is marked "(18 ans)", for 18-year-olds-and-over only. The word "osé" means "daring" and is usually hard-core porn.

Starting times do vary and almost no house will admit you in the middle of the feature film. The house is cleared at the end of each showing.

Films: Current: Cinemas are listed in the daily newspapers
       Classic: "Voltaire" cinémathèque, several films each day.
             English-language Cinema Club, at "Voltaire".
             CERN Cinema Club at premises outside Geneva.
             University Cinema Club, at Salle Patino.
             United Nations special showings, UN projection room.

Year-round stay-at-home ressources: No law obliges you to leave your quarters and almost every hotel and sitting room is equipped with a radio to receive the fine non-commercial broadcasts around the clock by two Swiss French-language stations, by the French government's "Musique" and "Culture" transmissions, as well as a dial-full of free-lance nearby radio programs including one in English.

Television in Geneva offers a choice of three French government services with separate programming and three Swiss channels, one in French, one in German, and the third in Italian in case you are using these as your language schools. For some time the prospect of cable transmission and satellite hookups has promised additional channels.

The Inner Person

Food is served in Geneva in elegant dining rooms, hotel salons, bistros, railway buffets, steak houses, snack bars, tea rooms, pizza parlors, hamburger joints, fondue "carnotzets", and public establishments of other descriptions. Well over a thousand eating places are listed in Geneva's telephone directory under the omnibus term "Cafés".

For the purposes of *All About Geneva* the telephone book's four-figure gastronomical catalog is digested into this section on "Restaurants".

When does one eat?

The Continental approach to a day's nutrition consists of coffee and a munch of croissant or bread to break the night's fast, a robust meal at midday, and, in the average home in the evening, soup and salad with perhaps a helping of cheese.

To accomodate the noonday tradition most local businesses and many shops close up tight for two hours at midday allowing their staffs to dine either at home or in one of Geneva's myriad restaurants that depend on the working clientele for the bulk of their income.

Most eating emporia appeal to this trade with their Daily Special, the "plat du jour". Filling, nourishing, and reasonably priced, the "plat" is the backbone of the diet of many Genevese.

Predictably, the midday session at most restaurants is their most crowded time and, for the most popular spots, tables should be reserved in advance. For the average bistro, however, arrive just before 12.00 or after 13.20 to be sure of a table without waiting.

Evening meals in restaurants are usually social occasions. These rarer events start well into the evening hours. If you try the door at your restaurant before 19.00 (7 p.m.), you will probably catch the owner, cook, and working hands at a corner table, half-way through their own meal.

The conventional hour for dinner reservations is 20.00 (8 p.m.) with allowances made for arrivals up to 21.30 (9.30 p.m.). A few accomodating eating places will serve you a full dinner as late as midnight.

In consonance with the daily habits of the Genevese and their tendency to absent themselves over the weekend, most restaurants open for lunch six days a week, for dinner on five evenings with fewer dining choices therefore available on weekends. Sunday outings take more planning.

For seven-days-a-week-service count on the restaurants in the hotels and at the railroad station and the airport. Then there are the burgeoning fast-food places — they never give up.

And what should we eat?

The "plat du jour", the most frequently ordered dish, is usually chicken, beef stew, pork chop, brochette, or other straightforward comestible backed by two vegetables.

Should you want more than the single plate and feel easier when you are sure of the final total, look for a "menu" — a three-, four-, or even five-course meal offering a choice of dishes. Such fixed-price repasts are served in many places both at midday and in the evening. Locating the selection of "menus" may take inquiry or thumbing through "la carte", the often-elaborate food list referred to in America as "the menu". Here "le menu" is a usually generous selection at set price and thus less profitable for restaurateurs who, not unreasonably, prefer one to order "à la carte".

Whether choosing "à la carte" or by "le menu" you may like to try regional specialties. As a first course, look for "viande des Grisons" (fine slices of air-dried beef, smoked black) or "escargots" (chewy snails in garlic butter) or "ramequins" (hot cheese tartelettes).

For the main course most popular varieties of meat and fish are available, supplemented — for fanciers of in'nards — by calves' liver, sweetbreads, brains, veal kidneys, all of top quality and expertly prepared and seasoned.

If you prefer a salad as a main dish, a choice of combinations exists and servings are generous. Vegetables and fruits follow the seasons: mushrooms and asparagus featured in the spring, berries in the summer, melons in August. Many restaurants advertise in October and November "la chasse", the choice pickings from the hunting season for wild game.

Cheeses are present in hundreds of varieties — hard, soft, mild, high, yellow, white — from French, Italian, and Spanish as well as Swiss cows, goats, and sheep. The Swiss staples, of course, are Emmenthal, Gruyère and, in season, Vacherin.

Before you can say you have "eaten Swiss" you must have tried cheese as a main dish or full meal. The four popular forms are the "fondue" (cheese melted with white wine and sopped up from a communal hot pot with bread on forks), "raclette" (melting cheese scraped from a wheel of Bagnes, eaten with potatoes and pickles), "bifteck au fromage" (no meat but bread dipped in melted cheese and grilled to a crisp crust), and "croûte au fromage" (a slice of bread dripping with melted cheese).

Other Swiss specialties are a variety of hot sausages — "longeole", "schüblig", "cervelas ravigote" — and "rösti" (crusty, homefried potatoes).

As desserts or simply as mid-morning or afternoon bracers, top-heavy "coupes des glaces" or sundaes are very popular. Too complicated for words, these confections are ordered from albums of colored photographs depicting knee-buckling assemblages of sherbet, ice cream, syrups, fruits, whipped cream, liqueurs, and sprinkles, crowned by a tiny parasol or flag of your choice. By way of saner desserts, custards, floating islands, open tarts, and fresh fruit cups are also available.

Something to drink?

As the ritualized proposal of a preprandial drink has not yet overtaken Geneva, the average waiter here may not even ask if you would like "... an apéritif to start...". If however a liquid appetizer suits your fancy, you may be less frustrated if you stay with the local specialities such as the vermouthy drinks — sweet or bitter — whiskies, or "pastis", the yellow, licoricy hard stuff of most of Europe.

Only in the international bars are the basic mixed cocktails of the western hemisphere available and these may be small, expensive, and confected in odd proportions from unfamiliar ingredients.

If you skip the "apéro" but, at the moment of ordering your meal, name your choice of wine, the drink will arrive almost instanter to sustain you through the wait for the first food course.

Wine ordering in Europe need not be complicated and is made a ritual only in the upper brackets of oenology. Unless you are a practising connoisseur braced with extensive credit facilities, set aside any voluminous *Carte des Vins* and settle for the "vin ouvert" in carafes. These may be glass pitchers, flutes, or pewter pots in a selection of capacities of 2, 3, or 5 deciliters, a "deci" being about 3.5 ounces — a generous glassful.

The usual red, white and rosé wines come in Swiss, French, and Italian varieties. The basic red of Geneva is a *Gamay*. Up the scale is the *Dôle* from the Valais, still cheaper than the quality-controlled *Salvagnin* from nearby Vaud.

The white wine from the Geneva slopes is *Perlan*. From the same grape the Valais produces the more expensive *Fendant*. Rosé is ordered without further specifications and may very well be the kitchen's mix of the red and white table wines of the house. The true Swiss vin rosé, if you like to name names, is *L'Oeil-de-Perdrix*.

For your primer on wines available locally, ask for the free, 64-pages sales catalog (only in French) from the Grand Passage department store. It lists a good variety with descriptions, vintage recommendations, and prices.

Beer on most occasions is quite as socially acceptable as wine. The expensive beer imported to other lands from Switzerland is the domestic brand here so enjoy it locally, particularly when served on draft ("bière pression"). Its price is controlled by law so economy is no excuse for sobriety.

Renunciation of all alcohol is considered eccentric but the staff will be mollified if you order a bottle of "limonade" (all forms of soda pop) or "eau minérale", mineral water of either the flat ("plat") or bubbly ("gazeuse") family. Such temperance tipples are a bit more expensive than the price-controlled wine and beer despite efforts of the Swiss anti-alcohol lobby to eliminate the penalty paid for abstention. Milk *can* be ordered with your meal in many restaurants. Persuading the staff on any level that you wish coffee served to accompany your main course amounts to a major diplomatic achievement.

Coffee served after dinner will usually be of the small, high-voltage "expresso" or "ristretto" breed. You may also specify the defused variety called "décafféiné". If you would compromise with a thin, milky brew, ask for a "renversé".

Liqueurs cover the international gamut. The Swiss specialty is *kirsch*, a clear, scalding rinse of distilled cherries. A similar cleanser, derived from pears, is named *williamine*.

Where to go?

Only a problem of choice. The population of Geneva increased between 1960 and 1980 by 40 %; in those same two decades the number of "Cafés" listed in the telephone book increased 230 %.

And, in addition, the more-than-a-thousand eating places within the town telephone area are supplemented by uncounted hundreds in the neighboring countryside and in nearby France.

Most of the established restaurants have joined the hotels in forming a trade association. The owners' dues plus additional contributions from the town, canton, and individuals finance Geneva's Tourist Office. This useful service lists its several hundred members in the annual free publication *Restaurants*.

A copy of *Restaurants* may be tucked into your **All About Geneva.** If not, ask for this basic reference at the Tourist Office.

Restaurants is laid out according to several categories of prices from the top of the scale of elegance through the economical supermarket cafeterias. Included is enormous detail concerning location, opening days and hours, prices, specialties of the house, credit cards, parking, music, dogs, public transport, etc. No attempt is made to grade those subjective and elusive elements of atmosphere or cuisine.

Opinions on style and quality of cooking are tackled by such audacious judges as the compilers of *Michelin, Gault-Millau, Le Coup de la Fourchette, Les Carnets des Gourmets*, all of which include among their listings of many restaurants in a country or region, several pages on some of the restaurants of Geneva. Other references such as *A Guide to the Best Dining in Geneva* and *200 Places to Eat in Geneva* appear and vanish with irregularity and suggest many of the places listed in *Restaurants* plus a few unaffiliated choices.

Those restaurants that are awarded the most tantalizing ratings — holding out hopes of good food at affordable prices — may not be that easy for you to try. Their proprietors favor their year-round clientele who keep the choicer spots fully booked. Before venturing forth in pursuit of any hot tip, telephone to make sure of a table.

Long-term residents and quite a few offices and corporations compile and up-date their own lists of highly classified "finds". If you are in Geneva for more than a few days, someone will probably tout you on to their latest entry. Geneva is a town where the only thing that remains confidential for more than a week is the number of one's bank account.

A tentative toe in the gastronomic pool

No classified hideaways or undiscovered treasures are unveiled in the selections categorized herein. The names are all taken from the *Restaurant* brochure. Rearranged in sets of three, they are intended to help you sort out special locales, atmospheres, or eating times. Almost all are within a fifteen-minute stroll of the Tourist Office (map: 64).

And bear in mind the fact that Geneva's major hotels all have dining rooms or terraces offering views of mountains, gardens, parks, or the water. Hotel restaurants provide international selections in their cuisine. They will serve you seven days a week.

Therefore, in the following listing, no hotel restaurant is mentioned simply because the hotels respond to almost every culinary whim.

As to the places included, most have existed for many years. This is, however, no guarantee as to how long any restaurant in Geneva will continue as it is, where it is.

The markings beside each name, (*, **, ***) are *not* indications of the quality of the service, cuisine, or setting but the price rating according to the categories in *Restaurants*.

For the Expense-Account Caper
Le Béarn ***
L'Or du Rhône ***
Le Duc *** (sea-food)

A Table With Running Water
La Perle du Lac *** (by the lake)
Le Lacustre ** (harborside)
Halles de l'Ile ** (by the river)

Before the Show or After
Café Lyrique ** (until 24.00)
Brasserie Landolt ** (until 01.00)
L'Internationale * (until 01.00)

For a Different Setting
Edouard Premier ***
Saint Germain ***
Palais de Justice **

Where the (Geneva) Gang Goes
Le Sénat ***
Les Philosophes **
L'Hôtel-de-Ville *

To Meet In a Garden
Parc des Eaux-Vives ***(open Sunday)
Au Fin Bec ***
Vieux Bois ** (weekday lunch only)

Sunday in the City
Red Ox Steak-House ***
Le Siècle **
Le Commerce Au Molard *

For Your Swiss (Cheese) Dream Outing
Les Armures **(open until 24.00)
Café Valaisanne/Chalet Suisse ** (to 01.00)
Edelweiss ** (with show; to 24.00)

Late Night Nonsense

Tales of John Calvin and his joyless sumptuary laws have saddled Geneva with the reputation of an early-to-bed town.

For an industrious sub-metropolis of a few hundred thousand inhabitants, many of them reporting for work by 8 a.m., Geneva manages handily in the accomodation of noctambules with late night action out of proportion to its size. For anyone exhilarated by an evening of dinner or theater and in search of more entertainment, music, drink, and/or company, Geneva is prepared to provide.

Pubs, pianos, discos, and dancing

Should a quiet drink at daytime prices cover the need, the midtown open-air terraces beside the lake and the public squares in summer — or, in winter, the cafés — remain open until midnight and after.

If a pub-crawl, that sport for all ages, is your game, you can find clones of London's originals reproduced on the Left Bank in the likes of "Shorts", "The Duke of Wellington", and "Griffin's Pub" and on the opposite shore in such taverns as the "Brittania" and "The Pickwick".

By way of a little late night music, Geneva sounds off in the full range of decibels.

At the lower end of the scale are the bars of the larger hotels and a few other quiet spots tempering drink with tranquillizing piano accompaniment.

For hardened ears demanding a stronger beat, the tumult escalates sharply. The friendly roar of the sound systems seldom reaches street level, however, as Geneva law protects its "couche-tôt" (sleep-early) majority. Late spots featuring the higher amplifications are located in sound-containing cellars — "caves" or "sous-sols" — in the Old Town and its environs or in upstairs "dancings" in the deserted business district. In short, you must know where they are to find them.

The major outlets are listed in the newspapers under "Variétés"; the lesser known are found by instinct or a knowledgable guide.

Late music live in Geneva

For fans of contemporary sound in live performance Geneva is a rewarding center as a regular one- or two-night stand on the European circuit for touring jazz musicians and rock groups.

The super-super attractions perform before adoring masses at the Vernet sports complex or in soccer stadia. Mere superstars appear at the "Grand Casino" or the "Palais des Sports" while the most respected musicians come to the "New Morning" or the "Palladium".

Other live talent is heard in musically-inclined Geneva through its two associations of more than five hundred performing members. Most are amateurs of near-professional skill organized into half-a-hundred ensembles ranging from Glenn-Miller-style Big Bands through rock groups in all their permutations and on to Dixieland combos and modern jazz trios. As these long-rehearsed aggregations are champing to play at the drop of a downbeat, their live music is widely presented, particularly on weekends.

For more informal performances individual musicians meet in in jam sessions at the "Sud des Alpes" hall of the AMR for weekly late-evening get-togethers. Unregistered talent is invited to drop in and sit in on this unusual participation opportunity.

The shows, attractions, and clubs

A late night outing to include a show could be as anodyne as the Swiss dinner and, in mid-evening, a performance of yodeling, accordian, and alpenhorn — the steady diet at the rustic "Edelweiss".

A bit more spicy and pricey a gambit could involve the more elegant "Maxim's" with its late show and even a second round a couple of hours later. The "Moulin Rouge" presents two shows but at a bit earlier hour.

Visiting delegates and businessmen are expected to appreciate "girly" shows. Geneva accomodates with its oldest established arenas, the "Bataclan" with some 20, count'em, 20 peelers and the "Pussy Cat", billed as a spinoff of Paris' "Crazy Horse Saloon".

If boys making like girls are of interest, "La Garçonnière" in the Old Town offers a show with dignity enough for the broad-minded at hours approaching midnight and again later.

Insomniac natives gravitate to dancing and drinking in clubs such as the "Whisky à Gogo" and "La Tour" in the Old Town, usually flexible about admitting non-members. "Club 58" is also penetrable by presentable visitors. In addition to dinner and disco it occasionally adds a light cabaret turn or two.

"Régine's" and "Griffin's" are indeed clubs for paying members and their guests. Even a well-situated concierge will have a problem shoehorning new arrivals into these precincts.

The champagne bars and girls

The prices of drinks in Geneva nightspots are high since the local practice is to make one or two glasses last the entire evening. The highest prices of all are in the "Champagne Bars".

Such bars, usually small, open late in the day to match the schedules of unaccompanied males interested in making friends easily. "Bar Club" is a discreet sign for some establishments, others are anonymous, and still others advertise under such tantalizing names as the "Dixie Sexy", "Dolly's", and "The Blue Cat". Almost all are approached through peepholes in heavy blank doors backed by a barricade of weighty curtains. Not unusual in the blacked-out storefront window is an offer hand-printed on cardboard "Cherchons hôtesses" — Hostesses Wanted — testifying to a frequent turnover in personnel.

Bars have been know to close for a while at the suggestion of Geneva's constabulary. The police take a practical view towards women turning a quick franc but do object to management sharing too heavily in the promotion and proceeds of the operation.

Recognizing the industry as an inevitable element in any international city, Geneva adjusts accordingly and supervises for health and good conduct the beauties working the champagne bars or patrolling the streets of Pâquis.

The women themselves, by way of contrast, have taken their own interests in hand. Some are organized into the union or trade association *Aspasia,* named for the talented, intellectual mistress of Pericles of Athens. Through collective bargaining *Aspasia* has negotiated for its membership protection from uncontracted-for abuse, freedom from harassment, and social benefits in the realms of health, job retraining, and retirement.

However enlightened is Geneva's approach to ancient professions, clients are advised to exercise prudence when patronizing champagne bars. Prices are high and the atmosphere usually redolent of the Surabaya waterfront.

While mention has been made here of the Pâquis area with its sprightly reputation, other quarters of Geneva are not off limits. Drink-sharing ladies — paid by the cork — are likely to surface in quite a few public drinking spots as the night rolls on.

Prudence but naught to dread

Female visitors to Geneva may also consider a word of caution. After 23.00, unescorted ladies on tour will find life calmer in hotels bars or open terraces. And even there, protected by a fairly numerous public, they may find the international wolf pack well represented and relentlessly attentive.

All such counsel is for the avoidance of nuisances rather than of danger.

Geneva is an orderly town, proud and protective of its reputation for security and serenity. For restless youth, couples on tour and on the town, and even for adventurous singles, the choice for late night outings in Geneva offers a variety of possibilities in what is still one of the safest cities in the world.

If You Have The Time...

Annual Events in Geneva

What's going on here? This calendar of events scheduled to recur annually in Geneva serves two purposes: first, it explains the significance of the occasion; second it indicates what is to take place and approximately when.

"Approximately" because promoters change dates of expositions and competitions — dropping some, adding others — and because Nature is unpredictable in such events as "L'Eclosion" (the first budding), "La Vendange" (the grape harvest), and Easter (Sunday following vernal full moon).

For exact dates and times, consult the newspapers for events of the day, the local monthly magazines for the monthly listings. Advance programs of several months of forthcoming action are available free from the Tourist Office (*Manifestations*, two months), from the Ville de Genève yellow sheet (*Programme de la Saison*, three months) and from GELCOS (*What's On In Geneva*, in English, one or two months at a bite).

The definitions below spell out a few terms used to explain certain dates.

> **Public Holiday** is one on which schools, banks, town offices, shops and businesses all close down. On such days the trains and public transport run on Sunday schedules.
>
> **Pont** means literally "bridge". To Francophones it also means a 3- or 4-day weekend, usually created by adding an unofficial day off to public holidays. In Geneva look out for Easter, Ascension, Pentecôte, Jeûne Genevois, and often Christmas and New Year's Day.
>
> **Bi- and quadrenniel events** are held every two or four years. "Odd Years" are 1985, 1987, etc.; "even years" are 1986, 1988, 1990 and onwards.
>
> **Soldes** means "leftovers" and are the officially sanctioned and controlled clearance sales permitted twice a year. "Actions" are short-run price cuts to promote products. "Occasions" are presumably once-in-a-blue-moon bargains or at least a good deal. "Occasion" may also mean "second-hand" as in "previously-owned" automobiles. In Geneva, "la période des soldes" is a big deal.

January

- 1st — **Jour du Nouvel An,** New Year's Day: Public Holiday that tends to stretch into 2 January.

- 5th — **Nuit des Rois,** Twelfth Night: The night that the Magi arrived in Bethlehem, 1 A.D. Children wear costumes and gilt crowns and overeat on a special cake-of-the-season.

- 6th — **Epiphany:** Both the Christian celebration of the Magi's arrival and coincidentally the ancient Roman feast of the Saturnalia. For one reason or the other, the Carnival season begins about here.

   — **Carnival** is largely ignored in Reformed Geneva but seriously indulged in Catholic Europe. Balls, parades, and parties are held both in adjacent France and in the cantons of Valais and eastern Switzerland on a crescendo of weekends ending with Mardi Gras.

- For 18 days — **Soldes d'Hiver:** The winter clearance sales.

February

- For 10 days. Bienniel, odd years — **Salon du Nautique et Voyages,** the International Boat and Travel Show: Sales exhibit of cruisers, windsurfers, day craft — sail and motor — and nautical accessories combined with stands promoting travel to every vacation land known to hedonism.

- Wednesday, 40 days before Easter — **Cendres,** Ash Wednesday: Day after Mardi Gras, end of Carnival, beginning of Lent. Observed by Geneva's Catholics — more than 50% of population.

- Any day January to May — **L'Eclosion de la Première Feuille,** the Budding of the First Leaf: The opening of the first bud on the Official Chestnut Tree on La Treille (page 99) is ceremoniously observed and recorded.

March

- For 11 days — **Salon de l'Automobile,** International Auto Show: Since 1924, among Europe's biggest and growing each year.

   — **Jet d'Eau** celebrates the Auto Show by starting its annual cycle, afternoons only.

- For 6 days. Bienniel, odd years — **Concours de Saut International Officiel (CSIO) et Le Salon du Cheval**: Since 1927, Coupe du Monde horse jumping competition supplemented by sale of horses and tack.

- Last Saturday in March — **"Mouettes"**, the "Seagulls" passenger boats begin service across the harbor and to the parks. From 07.30 to 19.30, 7 days a week.

- Last Sunday in March — **Heures d'Eté,** Daylight Saving Time starts in Switzerland. Set your timepiece ahead one hour. Remember: Spring, forward; Fall, back. And also,

  a) that some Swiss are much opposed. A referendum (page 23) could end DST here. And, even if DST continues, the starting date may change.

  b) that international coordination is not guaranteed. For years many nations — including USA — have changed their clocks on different dates. Watch international time readings in April and October.

- A weekend, March or April — **Vendredi Saint,** Good Friday: Ends Lent two days before Easter. Public holiday and start of 4-day "pont".

- Sunday — **Pâques,** Easter: The Sunday after the full moon after the first day of spring.

- Monday — **Lundi de Pâques,** Easter Monday: Public holiday and fourth day of the "pont".

April

- 1st — **Poisson d'Avril,** the April Fish or April Fools' Day: Taken very seriously by the Geneva press. Several dailies confect with a straight face outrageous news items ("Sanitation Services Ban All Dogs Within Town Limits"), credible and likely to upset the unwary. Keep your dudgeon in low gear.

- First Sunday in April — **Lake Cruise Boat** service begins on Sundays only. Visit the east end of Lake Geneva, about 6 hours by boat, 2 hours return by train.

- For 10 days — **Salon International des Inventions et des Techniques Nouvelles**: Since 1972, an exposition of international ingenuity with 500 exhibitors from more than 20 nations.

May

- 1st — **Jour du Travail,** Labor Day: European trade union holiday. Some Geneva shops and businesses close for afternoon parade.

- First Sunday in May — **Le Feuillu,** The Full Leafing: A regional rite of spring now growing into an Official Occasion. In the countryside, in a teepee of leafy branches set on a cart, a small boy represents a beast in pursuit of affrighted damsels who are actually hauling his wagon. Onlookers hand out eggs to kids, who finish parade with big brunch. Urban version is more elaborate.

- Last Sunday in May — **Marathon:** Since 1981, the full 43-kilometer (26 miles, 385 yards) run, twice around the town. International-level competition with amateur participation encouraged.

- Last Sunday in May — **Indicateur d'Eté,** Summer timetables: For trains, buses, boats, cablecars, the Summer Edition of the Swiss Official Timetable (page 235), indispensable for the consecrated traveler, takes effect this day.

- A weekend May or June — **Ascension,** Ascension Day: Always a Thursday, 40 days after Easter. Public holiday, start of a 4-day "pont", the opening of the summer weekends-away routine.

  — **Jet d'Eau:** Beginning on Ascension Day Geneva turns on its fountain in mid-morning and keeps it running until 23.00 hours — floodlit after dark.

- The following weekend, May or June — **Pentecôte,** Whitsun: Seventh Sunday after Easter to mark the occasion when the Holy Ghost inspired the Apostles to "speak in tongues". Whit Monday is a public holiday, the third day of a 3-day "pont".

June

- 1st — **Débarquement des Suisses,** The Landing of Swiss Troops: In 1814 Geneva welcomed its Swiss allies — arriving by lake boats to avoid marching across French territory — to defend the still-independent town during its wait to join the Swiss Confederation in 1815 (page 16). Parades and speeches of solidarity.

- Saturday, 2 weeks after Pentecôte — **Bol d'Or,** the Golden Bowl Trophy: Since 1930, the sailing race to the east end of Lake Geneva and return. Over 500 entries crowding the morning starting line is among Geneva's more memorable sights.

- For 4 days — **International des Fournisseurs de l'Industrie du Véhicule,** International Heavy Transport Show: Major sales exhibit of the trucking and road transport industry.

- Friday, end of June — **Concours International de la Rose,** Rose competition: After a week of display in the Parc des Granges, the awarding of dozens of prizes for size, aroma, color, novelty — a rose fancier's orgy.

July

- 4th — **Quatre Juillet,** American Independence Day: Since 1950 in Geneva, sports, country fair, marching bands, acts, and fireworks for tens of thousands in "...the biggest celebration of the Fourth outside the United States..." organized by the American International Club to mark the signing of the United States' Declaration of Independence in 1776.

- For 18 days — **Soldes d'Eté:** The summer clearance sales.

- 14th — **Quatorze Juillet,** Bastille Day: Subdued celebration in Geneva after 300-year ambivalent relationship with France (pages 10, 12, and 16). For parades and dancing in the streets, try nearby French towns: Annecy, Evian, Annemasse, Divonne *et al.* French fête since 1789.

- For 6 days — **Semaine de la Voile,** Sailing Week: Leisurely cruise to series of lake ports for races and regattas. Power craft tolerated.

- Several weeks, July and August — **Vacances d'Eté,** Summer vacation period: Smaller shops, cleaners, hairdressers, repairers, restaurants, etc., take this very seriously and shut down totally. Plan ahead as Geneva's infrastructure evaporates.

August

- 1st — **Fête Nationale Suisse,** Swiss National Holiday: Since 1291, fires on the hilltops to mark alliance of cantons of Uri, Unterwald, and Schwyz into the nucleus of Switzerland at Grütli meadow. Note an increasing trend for shops and businesses to close in afternoon for parade, speeches, carillon concert, and fireworks in the evening.

- For 3 days. First weekend of August — **Fêtes de Genève,** "Geneva's Party": Quayside parade, floats, bands, folklore, thrill rides, fireworks from Friday through Sunday. A highly-organized outbreak of circumspect frivolity.

- For 14 days August into September — **Concours International d'Exécution Musicale,** Competition for Musical Performance: Since 1939 a challenging contest for performers from 15 to 30, en route to professional careers. Three categories of instruments each year plus, in even years, conducting; in odd years, voice.

- For 21 days August into September — **Cirque Knie,** Continental circus: Top-flight, traditional, one-ring show. Unique, totally professional, well-managed by fourth generation of Swiss family Knie.

September

- Weekend after first Sunday in September — **Jeûne Genevois,** the Day of Fasting for Geneva: Always a Thursday, public holiday, start of 4-day "pont", the last of the routine summer weekends-away. In 1572 "le premier refuge" was the arrival of the first wave of Protestants fleeing France after the massacre of St. Bartholomew's Day, 23 August. Originally a day of abstinence, Jeûne Genevois is now a time of plum tarts and thanksgiving feasts. The Swiss day of fasting is ten days later.

- For 16 days — **Festival de la Bâtie:** Since 1977 a youth festival of music, theater, movies, dance, growing bigger each year with happenings in a dozen locales around town.

- For 4 days. Bienniel, even years — **Buroexpo:** Business machine show: More than a 100 exhibitors showing office equipment and electronics.

- For 7 days — **Tournoi de Tennis, Martini Cup:** Tennis tournament, international circuit: Since 1980 Gerulaitis win (Borg in 1981), well-financed tourney attracts top talent and Geneva's smart set.

- For 5 days. Bienniel, odd years — **Rencontres Internationales,** International Round Table Talks: Scholars and intellectuals from several countries discuss philosophical concepts, usually abstract — e.g. "Order versus Disorder".

- For 5 days. Bienniel, even years — **Colloques Wright,** Wright Discussions of Science: Scientists explain their subjects in plain terms for general public. Endowed by Dwight Wright, American industrialist, 1984.

- For 2 days, 3rd Sunday and Monday in September — **Jeûne Fédéral,** National Day of Fasting: Begun in 1832 when the Confederation was still uncoordinated and federal mandate was ignored by several cantons including Geneva. No holiday in Geneva but participation in fund-raising for a different international cause each year — e.g., professional education in Peru.

- Last Sunday in September — **Indicateur d'Hiver,** Winter timetables for trains, buses, ski-lifts takes effect. Get your winter edition of Swiss Official Timetable.

  — **Heures d'Hiver,** Standard Time returns: Set your timepiece back one hour; see "Last Sunday in March" note (page 219).

  — **Jet d'Eau** reverts to afternoons-only performance until shut down for winter in mid-October.

- Weekends, September and October — **Fêtes des Vendanges,** Wine Festivals: Grape harvest celebrations in neighboring towns, dates depending on the ripening of the crop. Amateur pickers welcome in both Swiss and French vineyards. Folkloric parades, dancing, and tasting and testing of the latest pressings.

October

- For 11 days — **L'Arche de Noë,** Noah's Ark: Since 1970, the tasting of dozens of wines at more than 30 stands of international merchants, all for a single fee aboard lake steamers tied up side-by-side for annual sales.

- For 6 days. Quadrenniel, 1987, 1991, et seq. — **Telecom,** International Telecommunications Trade Show: Since 1983, one of the biggest expositions of the latest in electronic transmission, reception, techniques in overflow presentation.
- Middle Sunday in October — **Jet d'Eau** retires until Auto Salon next March.
- 24th — **United Nations Day:** In 1946 the 26th of the 51 Allied Nations originally involved (page 170) ratified the UN charter. Palais des Nations flies flags of all members and offers free tours by way of "Open House" gesture. Geneva symphony orchestra plays a free concert.
- Last Sunday in October — **"Mouettes"** harbor boat service retires to winter quarters.

November

- For 11 days. Bienniel, even years — **Montres et Bijoux,** Watch and Jewelry Show: Since the 1930s some 20 Swiss designers and manufacturers display their latest and finest creations at the Hôtel du Rhône.
- For 12 days — **Salon des Arts Ménagers,** Home Furnishings Show: Since 1953, a sales exhibit to help shoppers see most brands of most household appliances under one roof. Simplifies the selection of washers, irons, toasters, and the latest in gadgets.
- For 2 days — **Salon International du Chat,** International Cat Show: Since 1949 judging and sale of cats and kittens at one of Europe's major shows.
- For 5 days — **Foire Genevoise à la Brocante et de l'Antiquité,** Fair of antiques and odds and ends: Since 1971, Geneva's antique dealers and flea marketers offer a wide selection in an indoor mart.

December

- Weekend before the 11th — **Escalade,** The Scaling of the Walls: Since 1603, celebrated on Saturday by parade of children in costume and on Sunday by torchlight procession through darkened streets to bonfire in Cathedral square to commemorate Geneva victory of 11-12 December 1602 (page 121) over invaders from Savoy. Be prepared to tip kids singing to you "Cé qu'é l'Aîno", Geneva's incomprehensible anthem with far too many verses.

- 11th — **Bal Masqué,** Masked Ball: Since 1972, a costume party on the eve of Escalade with ten bands and groups, bar, grandstands for those who prefer to watch high-spirited carnival. Unique in Geneva because masks may not be worn in streets since 1603 when prankish youths faked a repeat attack on the town and panicked the population.

- Middle Sunday in December — **Coupe de Noël,** Christmas Trophy: Since 1949 a 130-meter swimming race between bridges in the icy Rhone River in a bitter morning frost. Begun as a Christmas treat for a few practicing Scrooges, is now a Sunday attraction for hundreds of entrants, thousands of onlookers.

- 25th — **Noël,** Christmas: Public holiday in Geneva since lifting of Calvin's ban on this and all other holidays. Big moment is the family feast late Christmas Eve — Le Réveillon.

- 26th — **26 Décembre:** Public holiday. "Boxing Day" for the British.

- 30th/31st — **Restauration,** The Reestablishment of Geneva: From 1813 when the French troops left Geneva after 14 years, 8 months, 14 days, 10 hours, and 30 minutes of annexation, celebrated by ceremonies on La Treille. On the 31st the liberating army of Austria arrived and Geneva's provisional government proclaimed independence. Cannon fire at 7.20 a.m. followed by a carillon concert.

- 31st — **Saint Sylvester,** New Year's Eve: The feast of the saint almost no one remembers (he was the Pope, 314-335) except that his name means a New Year's Eve dinner and party also called Le Réveillon.

Geneva In A Nutshell

The Name: "Geneva" may mean any one of three places: the Canton of Geneva — the 22nd canton to join the Confédération Helvétique; the Genève-Ville — one of the 45 communes of the canton; or the metropolis of Geneva as it overflows into adjacent communes.

The name was originally "Genava" from the Celtic roots meaning the "mouth of the waters".

Geneva was for nearly thirteen centuries a city-state like Venice and Hamburg and, from 1536 when the citizens declared this to be the Republic of Geneva, autonomous and "... the oldest on-going republic extant".

Under the Reformation and Calvin's stern regime Geneva picked up such forbidding sobriquets as "The City of God", "The Protestant Rome", "The City of Calvin", and even "The New Jerusalem".

The establishment of the League of Nations in Geneva in 1920 inspired the heady but short-lived title "The Capital of the World". Geneva, now more realistic, has settled into the role of "The International City", a fair description of its present principal but far-from-sole activity.

Coordinates: Geneva is at the southwest extremity of Switzerland where Lake Geneva narrows into the Rhone River on its way to Marseilles.

The town is just north of the 46th parallel of latitude — about on a level with Montreal in Canada, WallaWalla in the State of Washington, and Harbin in China.

Geneva's longitude is 6° East in a vertical line with Bergen, Norway and Ibadan in Nigeria, and, on the other side of the globe, Pago Pago in Samoa.

The time zone is Greenwich Mean Time Plus One; the category is Central European Time. Afternoon in Geneva is morning in America.

The altitude is 375 meters (1,220 feet) above sea level.

Area: The Canton of Geneva covers 280 square kilometers of which some 30 sqkms are lake water. That leaves the land portion equivalent to 100 square miles, say two-thirds the size of the Isle of Wight, the same as the area of Manhattan Island. The town of Geneva occupies one-tenth of the canton.

Population: By the early 1980s the population had reached approximately 350,000, comparable then to Belfast, Tel-Aviv, Quebec, and Buffalo.

Geneva's residents are, however, mobile and mixed — 30 % Genevese, 35 % Swiss from other cantons, 10 % Italians, 5 % French, 5 % Spanish, and 15 % a very wide mixture. The town has issued residence permits to nationals of more than 130 different countries.

Language: The French spoken by the native Genevese is highly grammatical, rather idiomatic and with a slightly sing-song accent. Three-quarters of the population communicate in comprehensible French with catch-as-catch-can accents, few of them classic. Don't hesitate to try your own brand of French, be it ever so rudimentary. If you are not always understood, you may reasonably assume that your auditor's command of the language is even less than yours.

Almost everyone here has another language — German, Spanish, Italian, Turkish, Arabic — and most service personnel in banks, shops, transport, restaurants speak or at least understand rudimentary English.

Climate: Weather along the Lake Geneva is temperate without extremes. In winter, snow coverage is rare and seldom remains for more than a day; in summer, temperatures above 30°C (86°F) are uncommon.

In those seasons when the cool air from the mountains moves across the sun-warmed lake, a mist arises that tends to settle across this valley to give Geneva, on one hand, stretches of grey days but, on the other, the moisture that keeps its parks a verdant green.

Sixteen different winds are identified by name by lake sailors but most residents recognize only three.

The "bise" from the Swiss Alps to the north brings clear skies the year-round and, in winter, a wind-chill factor that is the backbone of local small talk.

The "vent" from the west is warm and often rain-bearing and thus mistaken for the third wind, the "foehn", notorious for spoiling good skiing conditions in winter and for sapping the human spirit at any season.

The winter mists lead pessimists to deplore Geneva as a place of seldom-relenting haze and grey. Optimists, however, recognize that the fog alternates with sun, often in quick succession, encouraging the Scottish point of view, "... if you don't like this weather, just wait a few minutes..."

Health: The temperate climate, healthful and varied food, and extensive sport facilities make Geneva an easy place in which to get healthy and to stay healthy.

Heating by electricity or fuel oil with few fireplaces and little heavy industry keeps Geneva free from smoke and smog. Sanitary services are unsurpassed. Streets and sidewalks are not merely sloshed down but are truly scrubbed by diligent, well-equipped cleaning squads a couple of times each week.

The few insects encountered are apparently defused, as screens are unheard of in Geneva.

Health complaints are not easy to generate here but true valetudorians can lament the sufferings of sinus or rheumatism "from the damp", of hay fever from the profusion of blooms, or of the "ion effect" from a lively imagination.

Medical care is of the highest quality. Facilities include a full range of multilingual specialists, model hospitals, public and private clinics and nursing homes, and equipment so advanced that the taxpayers wonder if their afflictions can keep pace with modern technology.

Geneva's water is drinkable, its air breathable, its views inspiring, the pace unstressed. In the terms of another culture, Geneva is a place to "... enjoy in health". Just be very careful crossing streets.

Formalities: While Geneva has few visa requirements, the police here, as in most countries of the world, may demand the production of identity papers.

For visitors from countries not issuing national identity cards, the passport becomes the essential document.

Anyone staying longer than three months must obtain a local permit defining the status of student, journalist, delegate, resident, etc. This large subject is explained in English in the noncompeting booklet *Living in Geneva*, described below.

For Practical Guidance in Depth: For anyone remaining in Geneva for more than say ten days, the English-language *Living in Geneva* — hereafter abbreviated **LIG** — is indispensable. This highly pragmatic self-help booklet of some 150 pages has evolved over several decades from the experiences of the American Women's Club of Geneva.

Between *All About Geneva* and *Living in Geneva* there is little duplication. **LIG** is a complementary work dealing in depth with permits, housing, schools, personal banking, and other subjects untouched or skimped in this more general approach to Geneva, the common object of our affections.

Short-term visitors and recent arrivals not yet equipped with their **LIG** may find useful a rundown of items encountered day-by-day in Geneva. Among these brief comments the initials **LIG** mean that the matter is covered in greater detail in that volume.

Air-raid shelters: First on this list by alphabet, not apprehension. Shelters are seldom discussed but obviously considered in Geneva where stained glass windows are demountable for safer storage. Recent buildings have deep garages. Other parking facilities under the lake and beneath parks not only clear street space but also — in case no one has thought of it — could serve as shelters for people in the event of threats from meteors, UFOs, or other airborne nuisances.

Automatic Teller Machines (ATMs): Two cash-dispensing bank systems serve all Switzerland, 24 hours a day, 7 days a week. "Bancomat" is a syndicate of commercial banks with machines in selected bank buildings. "Postomat" is run from the popular Swiss postal checking system. The fees are modest, the card and code simple, the daily maximum draw generous, and the locations at postoffices constantly expanding.

Banking: Any bank you identify instantly as a bank will probably welcome your account. Among these, the Swiss Banking Society (SBS) will not only give you a full-scale map on presentation of this book but will also answer all your questions.

The mysterious private banks that you must know about to locate (page 242) will also welcome you if your deposit is large and its origins tidy. Your account will be managed discreetly but perhaps less anonymously than you have heard in the past.

Buses and streetcars (trams): Public transport is clean, efficient, and respectful of schedules. Except for walking, this is the safest, most efficient, and agreeable way to move about this compact metropolis.

The ticket, which you buy with coins from the red box at any stop, is valid for an hour's worth of transport on any and all lines. Transfer at will.

Instructions are on the box in English. For more detail, ask the TPG ticket window in the shopping mall under the railroad station (Gare Cornavin) (page 185) for the booklet in English complete with map, schedules, and rates for an hour's ride, a daily pass, a monthly pass, a student ticket, a "Senior" permit, and other goodies. **LIG** deals with the subject at length.

Bicycles: For the medium distances in not-that-hilly Geneva, bicycles should be the ideal transport. Given the speed and practices of the automobilists here, bikes are not recommended.

In calmer corners of Switzerland you may rent bikes both from shops and from almost any Swiss railroad station. Should you own your own wheels, you will need insurance, registration, and a license plate. See **LIG:** "Transportation".

Cars: As many visitors have observed, driving pace in Geneva is either at a standstill or exceedingly fast. Authorities as well as pedestrians are concerned about the general low regard for speed limits and road courtesies. In any involvement with Geneva traffic be alert for tail-gating, passing on the right, cutting in, horn-blowing, and tire-scorching starts and stops. Such are, alas, the norms and defensive driving is unheard of. Repair shops are understandably numerous, skilled, and not cheap.

Chemist: See "Pharmacies".

Child care: **LIG** lists baby-sitters, day-care centers, nurseries, kindergartens — a wide selection of custodians.

Clothes care: Laundry service is good but expensive everywhere. Laundromats are listed in the telephone book under "Salon-Lavoirs". Dry cleaning is good; pressing of men's clothes erratic. Repairs and alterations are still available in small shops with old-fashioned hand skills.

Clubs: Of interest to some visitors and new residents are the American Women's Club, a very active service organization, and the Professional Women's Club, a luncheon group and international exchange network. Lunch clubs for men include the American International Club and the Club Diplomatique (bi-lingual). The Golf Club of Geneva at La Capite is quite private. The international service clubs — Rotary and Lions — are listed in the telephone book.

Credit cards: Plastic is widely accepted. If the home base for your card is far from Geneva, months may elapse before you face the tab you sign for here. The card companies' exchange rate is usually close to that published in Geneva's papers for the day of the transaction.

Dentists: Although Geneva opened the first dental school in Europe more than a century ago, many of the town's practitioners display with pride their foreign degrees and equipment. Your Consulate keeps a list of dentists here speaking your language.

For emergencies, look in any of the three major newspapers under "Urgences" or "Adresses utiles" for the "Permanence" that is on standby service for 24-hour, round-the-calendar relief.

Doctors: In general, as in "Dentists". For emergencies, use either the "Permanence" or telephone the Geneva Doctors' Association (20 25 11) for urgent advice, ambulances, hospitalization. Americans should realize that their Medicare facilities do not function abroad.

Dogs: Geneva is very considerate of dogs and their friends. Leashed dogs go to movies, some restaurants, shops and department stores, travel on buses and trains, presumably on payment of fare. Curbing and scooping are discussed but seldom practiced. Tread carefully. For the licensing process, see **LIG:** "Potpourri".

Dress: Temperate-zone sartorials — medium weight for most of the year — fit in with Geneva's fairly relaxed, seldom sensational style. In winter a topcoat/raincoat combination is useful, overshoes suffice. Save your snow boots for San Moritz.

Opera first nights, club and charity balls, and other dress-up evenings can be not-overwhelmingly spiffy. Furs, discreet gems, and Paris fashions are popular and don't worry if they are a mite out of date.

Driver's License: Visitors use their home licenses or the "International Driver's License" issued by Automobile Clubs for car borrowings or rentals. Swiss licenses require an eye test, a photo, and sometimes a medical examination. See **LIG**: "Transportation".

Drugs: According to the newspapers a full menu of mind-altering substances is available to the knowledgeable. In this one category of diversion Geneva is not tolerant. The police pursue purveyors closely and handle them unsympathetically.

Gambling: The game in Geneva is "boule" at the Grand Casino with small limits and smaller chances against top-heavy odds. The Geneva lottery is a gift to charity. For the full range of games under professional management, nearby France offers the casinos at Divonne and Evian and Italy's largest is at the far end of the Mont Blanc Highway Tunnel.

Guided Tours: The bus ride around Geneva takes less than two hours and follows a goodly portion of the route traced in *All About Geneva* which can supplement the guide's more compact narrative.

Hotels: If your lodging situation is not in hand by the time you read this, you have several possible solutions.

The Hotel Reservations machines, marked with "**i**" on a green background and equipped with a free telephone, function well at the airport and the railroad station.

The Tourist Office **[64]** is partially subsidized by Geneva's hotels and restaurants. For a small charge they will book you into your preference among some 15,000 beds in more than a hundred Geneva hotels with a full range of prices and comforts.

A third solution is to do your own comparative shopping. The Tourist Office provides a clear, comprehensive brochure, *Liste des Hôtels*, cataloging the established hotels and "pensions", complete with a keyed map of their locations.

Housing: Visitors arriving for a few weeks and new residents needing interim housing may appreciate the independence of a studio with a kitchenette, known here as a "résidence", rented on a weekly or monthly basis. Less expensive lodging could be a furnished room in someone else's apartment — locatable from a list kept in the Tourist Office.

For details on this vast subject and on permanent housing, refer to **LIG**: "Moving to Geneva".

Liquor: Bars, pubs, lounges, terraces, tearooms, and restaurants serve drinks at all hours on all days.

Buy by the bottle from wine shops, most food stores, and department stores. You may even pay with credit cards.

Lost and Found: The record of the Genevese for turning in found objects is above the average. Central depot is in the phone book under "Objets trouvés". Complications arise in that the airport, rail station, and each department store has, in addition, their own service.

Maps: For free copy of map of town of Geneva, show this book at the counter of any branch of the Swiss Banking Society (SBS). Many maps of Geneva and its environs exist. Most are listed on page 249.

Markets: Outdoor markets are an ancient Geneva tradition — the flea market, flower market, clothes market, and the vegetable, fruit, butter/cheese/egg market, etc., are each assigned a precise location one or two days of each week. Most operate all year round. For list and details, see **LIG:** "Potpourri" and "Food".

Money Exchange: To convert banknotes and traveler's checks into any currency you prefer, look for stores and bank counters under the sign "Change". In some banks you may draw cash against your credit card.

Rates of exchanges vary marginally but seldom enough to make shopping around profitable when changing smaller amounts. "Changes" at airport and railroad and bus stations are open seven days a week but not 24 hours a day.

Movies: Geneva's diminishing stock of movie houses often show different features at different hours of the same day, not always alternating. Check carefully the newspaper listings for times which are given in Continental, 24-hour basis. For more on this general subject, see page 204.

Museums: Lists of Geneva's museums by name, address, telephone numbers, with opening hours and days and name of current expositions are available from sources listed on page 217. To pick out the subject matter that interests you and then to learn where it may be seen, turn to page 193.

Newspapers: The larger circulation dailies are the morning *Journal de Genève*, the "newspaper of opinion", and the more popular *La Suisse*. The afternoon *Tribune de Genève* has the highest readership in town. Also published daily is the Catholic *Courrier*.

In English each morning you have today's *International Herald Tribune, The Daily Telegraph, The Wall Street Journal, The Financial Times, The Times,* etc. Magazines in English on local topics include the *Geneva News and International Report, The Courier* of the American Women's Club, the *UN Special* and, from Zurich, *Swiss Scene*.

Opening Times: The pattern is erratic. Some shops open at 8 a.m., others at 10, many close from 12.00 to 14.00, some for just one hour, others not at all.

The post office opens early, closes for lunch, but the telephone office next door is continuous. The Service des Autos opens at 07.00, closes at 15.00. Some libraries keep afternoon-only hours of differing spans. Most museums are closed on Monday. Be prepared for frustrations and a lengthy learning process. **LIG:** "Shopping and Services" makes a great try at keeping up with the changing pattern.

Parking: Paid parking space exists at both municipal and private garages. Many are underground so watch for the sign of a white capital **P** on a blue background.

For street parking, days and times are variable with many areas metered and monitored. Illegal parking ("parking sauvage") blocking sidewalks, driveways, bus lanes, and open malls is common practice and penalties are increasing. The battle for control of sidewalks and crossings is far from over.

Photography and film: Geneva offers a wide range of cameras at reasonable prices and has all sizes and brands of film. One-hour developing/printing service exists at several locations.

If you want to make a professional movie with a Geneva setting, the Tourist Office is experienced and eager to help you with the licensing, police, traffic diversions, and other details.

Postal Service: With on-time daily deliveries, overnight service to any address in Switzerland, courteous multilingual staff, and money orders paid in cash at your door, the system is the world's finest. For many details including the post office open in late evenings and on weekends, consult **LIG:** "Postal Services".

Radio: The quality of signals transmitted and the variety of programming and languages broadcast will feed your portable radio clearly and reward your investment in superior receiving equipment. State radio is non-commercial, supported instead by a monthly tax as explained in **LIG**: "Telephone".

Railroads: The fast, clean, smooth-riding trains are the pride and — with their subsidies — possibly the ruin of Switzerland. Enjoy them now. Schedules are coordinated to provide service at least once each hour between Switzerland's major cities.

Another marvel of the CCF system is its accurate, comprehensive, and logical twice-a-year *Official Timetable*. The schedules of state railroads, private rail lines, lake boats, cable cars, mountain bus service, international connections with fares and supplements and explanations are presented in four languages. Perfection.

Rentals: You can rent in Geneva automobiles, moving vans, airplanes, sailboats, powerboats, furniture, dishware, pianos, formal clothes, typewriters, furs, calculators, TV sets, châteaux, skis, boots, bikes — *alles*. If there is any object you need but not for long, inquire about "Locations", the French word for "rentals".

Restaurants: More than a thousand places to eat in Geneva are listed under "Cafés" in the telephone directory.

Prices and quality cover a wide range and vary with such frequency as to make recommendations highly perishable. For the style of Geneva's restaurants, see page 206.

For specific prices and locations, the Tourist Office brochure, *Restaurants*, is free and lists conveniently several hundred of its cooperating entrepreneurs. Numerous commercial catalogs supplement this basic guide with varying degrees of utility and are on sale at most bookshops.

Shopping: Shopping while traveling falls into two categories: souvenirs for the people back home and bargain-hunting for those items unavailable or more expensive elsewhere.

"Souvenirs" in Geneva still means watches, cuckoo clocks, music boxes, and Swiss Army Knives, regardless of their place of manufacture. These and such items as badges, small toys, film, and postcards are found both in small specialty shops and in Geneva's several department stores where you may wander freely in search of further inspiration.

"Bargains" are few anywhere in the world today with most portable merchandise of recognizable quality available in every major city. For serious spenders Geneva has retailers of the best and best-known jewelry, luggage, and haute couture, at high but competitive prices with no haggling, a wide selection, reliable delivery service, and credit cards accepted.

For shoppers who prefer to winkle out their own specialties, Geneva has its antique shops in the Old Town, its Flea Market, and frequent auctions. Several thrift shops, including that of the American Women's Club, offer the usual temptations but with an added Continental flavor. And for visitors in January and July, Geneva's Soldes (see page 217) are government-controlled clearance sales and genuine reductions. All of these special sources are dealt with in **LIG**: "Potpourri, Antique and second-hand stores, Auctions".

The truly knowledgeable shopper can occasionally turn up interesting values here in rugs, old maps and prints, and modern art.

Sixty-five and over: Men over the age of 65 and women even younger may enjoy some useful entitlements, particularly when holding Genevese residence permits.

— For railroads: Reductions up to 50 % on Swiss, French, Italian and other railroads on purchase of basic "Senior" card and according to routes and time of travel. Available to all. Ask at the railroad station for the latest brochure.

— For air travel: Reductions of 25 % on certain charter flights off-season. Available to all but you have to read the fine print in the brochures and ask for the reduction.

— For Geneva public transport: Reductions of more than 50 % whether with monthly pass or on cut-price, 7-ride punch card. Residence permit needed for initial issue.

— For Geneva movies, museums, galleries, sports events: Reduction of 50 % for movies, variable discounts for other entry fees on presentation of an inexpensive card available on presentation of residence permit. Each Thursday the Cinema Voltaire offers a free matinée for the "over 65s".

— Swiss hotels: Reductions of up to 20 % from published rates, off season, in certain hotels throughout Switzerland on presentation of "Senior" rail pass for Switzerland. Ask for list of participating hotels at rail station "Information".

Smoking: Tobacco in all forms and brands including Havana cigars has long been a Geneva specialty.

Anti-smoking campaigns are afoot and some restaurants have non-smoking sections. Rigid bans exist on trams and buses. On the newest trains the smoking sections in both the carriages and the dining car are half the size of the non-smoking. In congested circumstances, when one shares a café or restaurant table, the form is at least to appear to solicit the assent of neighbors before lighting up.

Social Services: Genevese organizations exist for dealing with problems of drugs, beaten spouses, suicide urges, job training, motherhood, etc.

A remarkable catalog, *La Clé*, The Key— in French only — published by the "Société pour l'Utilité Public", lists nearly 600 helpful groups within the town.

For an emergency or as a first step, dial the "Main Tendue", the Helping Hand — 143.

For a somewhat abbreviated English language summary of such services, refer to **LIG:** "Social Services and Personal Problems".

Taxis: Geneva's cabs are clean and well-maintained. Their drivers are dauntless and, by world-wide standards, honest.

"Official" taxis charge uniform rates, await at the airport, station, and in cab ranks, are identified by an orange roof sign and their license numbers between GE 1 and 400, and are summoned by telephoning 141.

"Private" cabs with blue roof signs and licenses from GE 401 to 800 are run by a dozen companies with varying rates at, above, and below those of the "Officials". They can be had only by telephoning their garage's 6-digit number.

"Taxis d'hôtel" are actually limousines working with hotel doormen. Prices are unmetered and uncontrolled by Geneva's Bureau des Taxis. License plate numbers are in the GE 96000 series. Be wary.

Telephone: Part of the Swiss postal system and with superior equipment and service but few rate concessions. Direct dial both local and international calls. When traveling in Switzerland consider the "Taxcard" — plastic you can insert in specially-equipped phones instead of coins.

International calls are expensive and from hotel rooms may entail heavy premiums. To be sure of paying only basic rates, use the clean, comfortable booths at post office installations including the station and airport. American telephone credit cards may be used by dialing 114. Common practice on international calls is to telephone from here and have the other person call back at rates which may be about 40 % of Swiss charges per minute.

The front of the telephone book (page 251) lists a fascinating variety of services available: wake-up calls, currency quotations, news summaries, snow conditions, etc. For more on telephones, see **LIG**: "Telephone".

Telex: Service through the PTT allows you to cut your own telex tape and to transmit via PTT machine at low time-charge. To receive replies, register with PTT your name and telephone number which PTT will call when they have a message for you to pick up.

Television: Six channels serve Geneva in three languages with a clear picture. Hours of broadcast are limited. Schedules are listed in all newspapers and in specialized TV magazines. Actual timing of programs is loose since commercials come in bunches and the length of any program, particularly newscasts, is set by the importance of the content rather than the clock. For installation fee and monthly tax on your own TV receiver, refer to **LIG**: "Telephone".

Theater tickets: Opera, concert, revue, drama tickets are seldom sold at the box office. For any entertainment you see advertised, look for the name of the agency or department store handling the reservations. Since no cut-price ticket system exists and no returns are accepted, you can sometimes buy a single seat at the door just before curtain time from a ticket holder whose partner dropped out.

Tipping: In 1974 Swiss restaurateurs agreed to combine their complex of arbitrary charges for "couverts" (knife, fork, plate, and napkin), for bread and butter, for taxes, and for "service" (10 % to 15 % to pay the staff) into a single "global" price for a meal. And that is it. The Swiss pay the bottom line, leave nothing over, and admonish unadjusted visitors caught breaking the solid front.

Tipping in Switzerland is thus passé except for taxi drivers (10%) and providers of services far-beyond-the-line-of-duty.

Toilets, public facilities: Geneva may be one of the few urban centers with a citizenry sufficiently cooperative to permit well-built, well-maintained public toilets, discreetly indicated, in a dozen locations. Your hotel or home plumbing is still preferable but these civic facilities are reassuring to the nervous traveler not accustomed to such tolerable conveniences.

Weights and measures and sizes: Although Napoleon I forced the metric system on Geneva in 1800, the town overreacted in 1815 and dropped it. In 1837 they resumed decimalization as the reasonable way to go. Most shops can convert your accustomed sizes in shoes, sweaters, gloves, etc., into metric terms. For an exhaustive tabulation of the differences, see **LIG:** "Equivalents".

Youth: To provide help and accomodation for rambling youth a Swiss coordinating group each summer sets up its office in a van by the Rue du Mont-Blanc mall at the Cornavin railroad station. Eager, multilingual, well-documented, this team has almost all the answers.

Professional Possibilities

To lure reasonable humans out of their home comforts and into the unpredictabilities of travel, some very serious temptations are needed. One of the most potent attractions is the prospect of shopping. Polls of people on the move proclaim that travelers place high among their priorities the fine art of discovering better deals in distant places.

In distant Geneva such shoppers need not consider the quest for the ultimate wrist watch or chocolate bar as the outer limit of interesting opportunities here.

Executives in particular − whether traveling on vacation or for business − may turn up unsuspected riches from among the goods and services available in the Geneva economy. A single nugget panned out of Geneva's diversified resources could convert the casual holiday of an alert entrepreneur into a constructive business trip inspiring a fresh, international approach to the back-home situation.

Geneva's economy

The economies of most metropolitan centers may be classified into their manufacturing and their service sectors.

Geneva numbers among its manufacturing activities the making of its renowned watches, jewelry, and consumer goods but also the less evident and more important fabrication of chemicals, machine tools, fine precision instruments, and an expanding variety of items in the broad realm covered by the term "high technology".

In its service sector Geneva has grown in recent years at a rate that has far outpaced that of the manufacturing side. The majority of workers in Geneva are employed in international organizations, banking, tourism, education and training, insurance, trading, communications in all their aspects, and other white-collar activities that are in themselves viable but also make up the strong infrastructure in support of manufacturing.

Office for the Promotion of Industry: O.P.I.

Geneva takes particular pride in its manufactures and is eager to involve new interests in their development.

For visiting business people concerned with goods – either technical or consumer – the O.P.I. is Geneva's industrial supermarket. Its showroom and offices at 9, rue Boissonnas, just south of the River Arve near the "Jonction" (page 15), cover nearly a quarter of an acre.

In this superior shopping center Geneva displays its manufactured wonders in a "Please Touch" exposition of open and – where feasible – operable exhibits in which visitors can enjoy a close-up, all-at-one-blow inspection of the town's wares.

The multilingual staff of O.P.I. provides guidance to categories of goods of specific interest, excellent documentation in English, the answers to most questions, and, on request, referrals to and meetings with local producers.

Geneva's interest is, of course, in selling its high quality products in untapped markets. Reciprocally, O.P.I. welcomes manufacturers with foreign goods for sale through Geneva's own excellent marketing outlets.

A third area in which the O.P.I. is often useful to larger manufacturers is in the subcontracting with Geneva's technicians of precision items – components, pilot models, samples, or even finished products – particularly in the line of instruments, electronic assemblies, robotronics, and computer software.

In addition to matching up partners for buying, selling and fabricating goods, the O.P.I. can use its network of top-level Genevese and Swiss connections to assist in most aspects of the establishment and development of any new manufacturing enterprise.

Tourist Office

Managers interested in shopping among the services to business offered by Geneva begin at the Tourist Office.

Information in printed form is available in abundance encompassing both a selection for the general public (page 253) and a series of special-purpose brochures such as the presentation of the choice of meeting places designed to aid the administrator and specialist.

The International Conference Center of Geneva

Administrative officers of international companies and organizations recognize Geneva as one of the top cities of the world in terms of number of meetings managed annually.

Geneva offers nearly 200 halls, rooms, and auditoria for all manner of gatherings. The one building, however, specifically designed as a meeting place is the government-sponsored International Conference Center.

This self-contained structure near the Place des Nations [88] can seat 1,800 participants in its main hall with alternative accommodation in smaller areas in combinations down to as few as 16 places. The four largest rooms are equipped with interpretation, audio-visual, recording, and other support facilities while the public space has its own reception rooms, restaurants, bars, radio studios, press rooms, bank, post office, parking, and fully serviced offices.

The Swiss government backed the construction of the Center as an instrument of the Confederation's foreign policy under which the premises are available without charge to intergovernmental agencies based in Geneva.

Corporations, non-governmental organizations, and other private entities from around the world have found it advantageous to rent for their own sessions the facilities of the prestigious International Conference Center.

Geneva's private bankers

The very name "Geneva" arouses in some visitors an interest in the legends of the shadowy high priests of private banking. The fact is that private bankers are quite solid and well within the reach of those able to use their services. Being, however, few in number and with small staffs, these highly specialized establishments cannot afford to use their personnel to respond to every casual inquiry.

The six well-recognized banks, specifically identified by the family names of Bordier & Cie, Darier & Cie, Hentsch & Cie, Lombard, Odier & Cie, Mirabaud & Cie, and Pictet & Cie, were founded by the elite of Geneva. They continue as independent, private partnerships for the custody and management of substantial portfolios.

The latest generations of the old families work alongside a leavening of bright new talent. Today's private bankers continue to be multilingual, well-mannered, and — after years of apprenticeship in prestigious banks in New York, London, and other financial capitals — widely and well connected for investment information. They are practiced in assessing a client's individual circumstances and qualified to tailor investment programs to personal preferences.

The private banks of Geneva provide not only security in Switzerland's stable political climate but also the possibility of diversification of investments through a spread of currencies and foreign holdings not familiar to more parochial bankers.

Anyone seeking to invest funds from impeccable sources and in an amount equivalent to, say, not less than six figures in dollars will find a private banker here happy to discuss the prospect.

The offices of all six banks are clustered whithin a few hundred meters of one another near the Place Neuve, their doors discreetly identified by a brass plaque about the size of a pocket checkbook. Interested inquirers are invited to telephone first to explain the circumstances and to arrange an appointment.

The firms are all listed in the Geneva telephone directory both under their individual names and in a very short grouping headed "Banquiers", a term that distinguishes them from the several hundred establishments identified as "Banques".

To begin with more generalized information in less awesome surroundings one can approach the subject through their "Groupement" — the private bankers' association, listed in the telephone directory at its own separate office.

International Managements Institute: IMI

International businesses operate with techniques unfamiliar to domestic companies. In recognition of this fact the AlCan Company (Aluminium of Canada) established in 1946 its own in-house graduate school to train its executives in international work. This academy of commerce proved its worth within a very few years and broadened into the independent non-profit foundation that is now the International Management Institute.

Over the decades the IMI devised a program of courses, meetings, and seminars to develop in intensive sessions the executive talent on all higher levels of international corporations.

The program is scaled upward through the corporate structure. At the base is a course of a couple of months' duration for middle managers. For managing directors there are month-long sessions, while senior directors may follow compact one-week courses, and, for members of the board, IMI gives even more concentrated programs.

This education-according-to-echelon is supplemented by training-according-to-functions in a choice of two-week courses in specifics such as finance, marketing, personnel, investment, technology, research and development, etc., as approached from the international point of view.

IMI courses are not cheap. Participation fees at the top level can run into four figures in Swiss francs per day and do not include accommodation or meals. The costs are paid by the employers who have been convinced by now that the investment is a sound one.

Participants come from more than a thousand companies in more than a hundred countries to meet with the polyglot faculty and visiting experts. All instruction is in English.

For individuals the IMI has offered since 1979 a 36-week course leading to a degree of Master of Business Administration awarded jointly with the University of Geneva.

The prerequisites of a university degree, at least three years of practical experience, and funds to cover astronomical tuition fees plus living expenses has not discouraged candidates. The number of applicants ranges from six to ten times the number that IMI can accomodate in the classes of fewer than 50 participants.

The International School of Geneva

For many parents of teenage children the exercise of shopping for boarding schools is challenging and all-too-familiar. One possibility occasionally overlooked is that of the International School of Geneva.

The International School was founded in 1924 to educate the families of the diversified staff of the League of Nations. Today it offers qualified students the same broad cultural exposure and international experience with effective language training and excellent preparation for entry into any university.

Within its 13 grades the school enrolls some 2,500 students with a student-to-faculty ratio of not greater that 13 to 1. The three campuses are equipped with modern classrooms, libraries, laboratories, computer rooms, and an extensive sports plant. To house boy boarding students there is a dormitory on campus; girls are lodged in two villas adjacent to the school.

Scholastic emphasis is on language with a variety of classes conducted bilingually. Depending upon the objectives of the individual student for higher education, the school prepares them in either French or English to take the International Baccalaureate — now accepted at universities throughout the world, or for any of the full scale of examinations required for the Swiss Federal system, for the various standards of the United Kingdom, or for the battery of American tests and College Entrance Examinations. In university placements, the school's record is an impressive one.

A unique feature of the International School is its flexibility in the timing of admissions and transfers. To adjust to the professional demands on parents in international work, the school may allow the entry of students at any level at any time within the academic year.

The school consists of a majority of day students starting from the age of 3 plus the group of "5-day" and full-time boarding students from the age of 12. Fees for the latter are competitive with the average of the better schools in the United States, a bit less than those charged by American academies in the highest brackets.

Another of the important attractions of the International School is the reassurance of Geneva's excellent record for political stability and security, the town's first-rate health conditions and care, the presence of national communities within the international complex, and, of course, the quick access by air transport to most cities of the globe.

Geneva's latest commercial hub

Observers of the development of Geneva saw the buildings of the UN and other organizations at Pregny grow into an "International City" (page 164). They now recognize the formation of another configuration — an "International Commercial City" centered in the Cointrin district around the town's airport.

From a dusty runway beside a tumbledown villa in 1948, the airport grew by 1980 to a 5,000,000 passenger-per-year facility with a target for 1990 of 7,000,000 and an ultimate capacity of 15,000,000 passengers annually.

Any such increase in traffic at Cointrin Airport is not expected to come from growth within the canton. Geneva's "conurbanation" extending into the rest of western Switzerland and in surrounding France continues to develop. Geneva is increasing the access of these areas to the airport with constant improvement in its autoroute system and rail trackage to feed both road and rail carriers directly into the air terminal.

The Free Port of Geneva is an important element of the airport. The larger sector of the customs-free area is at the elaborate rail and truck depot at La Praille just south of the Arve River.

International traders use these isolated zones in order to check, sample, sort, finish, and store their goods without advancing cash for customs duties until their items are ready for sale. The extensive Free Port facilities include warehouses, open storage, grain siloes, vehicle parks and garages, a wine cellar for some 6,000,000 liters, and strongrooms for jewels, rugs, art objects, and precious metals.

The Palais des Expositions, the vast Geneva-owned hall designed for trade shows, exhibitions, displays, and meetings is within walking distance of the passenger terminal of Cointrin Airport.

"Palexpo" opened in 1981 with a core building and long-range plans for expansion. Within five years of its first show Palexpo was obliged to start work on the extension of the building to meet the demand for its versatile space.

Of the industrial terrain reserved in various sections of Geneva, the greatest area is in the vicinity of Cointrin. As Swiss law requires each canton to reserve a high proportion of its ground for agriculture, industrial plant space is at a premium. Geneva has already nibbled into the green fields of the countryside to meet its urgent requirements for housing and industry. Allocations of space are possible but are controlled for use by the most desirable occupants.

The Chamber of Commerce and Industry of Geneva services the development of new business operations and answers a variety of inquiries from its branch office in the World Trade Center building at the airport. In downtown Geneva the substantial main headquarters of the CCIG are located just behind the Grand Théâtre [58].

In Geneva's long experience with commerce, the town has been spoiled by the rewards of watchmaking. This trade developer's dream industry is based on the use of minimal raw materials and highly skilled craftsmen working in concentrated space on a non-polluting product with a substantial "value-added" factor.

Some modern counterpart of an industry with these characteristics is as tempting to Geneva as it is to any similarly situated locations.

Geneva, however, points out that few of its competitors can match the town's assets of bedrock stability, unmatched security, banking discretion and flexibility, firm control of local budget and taxes, highly skilled technical craftsmen free from labor dissension, university facilities compatible with industry, increasing availability of venture capital, language versatility, unbeatable communications, a broad and proven infrastructure, central location, and enviable living conditions for family members of all ages.

In counting out these trumps the authorities of Geneva delight in adding even more allurements, in answering all questions and objections, and in listening eagerly to responses and all honorable proposals. Just the attitude that makes shopping in Geneva a joy.

If You Need To Know More...

Maps

The maps on the flyleaves of *All About Geneva* are intended principally to facilitate your walking tour. For more intricate navigation, larger more detailed maps exist in several editions, many derived from General Dufour's splendid Federal topographical surveys. To help you find your way around the area you may want one out of the following selection:

Street maps, fully detailed:

Free: Geneva's official "N.E.T" plan with an "instant street finder" on the reverse side can be had from any branch of the Société des Banques Suisses (SBS) by showing your copy of *All About Geneva* at the reception desk or counter.

— : A less extensive but useful plan is part of the folder "Jeunes Information" distributed from the Tourist Office, the Welcome CAR (Centre d'Accueil et de Renseignements) at the rail station mall, or any youth center.

— : A full-color map is part of the brochure *Excursions Tours* distributed by the Keys Tour Agency.

To buy: Editions Helio "Plan de Genève" is a medium-size, one-piece map in color with street guide — the least expensive.

— : Falk, Orell-Füssli, Bussat, and other printers produce maps of the town and canton, usually of large size in one piece, colored, with street guide, at a wide range of prices.

— : "Plan Officiel" by Chapalay and Mottier is desktop-size, with separate pages for various sections of town, spiral bound, in color, with street guide.

Street maps, less detailed:

Free: In *This Week In Geneva*, from Tourist Office and in hotels, shops, and travel agencies.

— : "Guide Plan, Genève", postcard size, heavy paper map of town center from Tourist Office, Naville, hotels.

— : In *Genève: Hotels et addresses utiles* folder from airport, rail station, Tourist Office, hotels.

— : Main streets and roads on specialized maps from automobile rental agencies: Hertz, Avis, etc.

— : Special purpose maps from Tourist Office showing – according to subject — location of hotels, restaurants, hostels, dormitories, parks, museums, fountains, sculptures. Your choice among a half dozen brochures with "notional maps" showing only main streets to locate points of special interest.

— : *Transport Tickets* leaflet with schematic map of bus and transport system, free from Public Transport sales window in underground mall at rail station.

Regional maps

Free: Well-drawn bird's-eye view of Lake Geneva and peaks to the south in the seasonal timetable of the lake boats, *Horaire, Compagnie Générale de Navigation.*

To buy: Kummerly and Frey, Carte scolaire: Geneva area.

— : Touring Club Suisse/Bussat: Geneva area.

— : Hallwag: Map of Swiss highways.

— : Michelin: Numbers 70 and 74 for area, no town detail.

— : Cartes nationales: Swiss Federal Dufour series. Beautifully engraved with contours and every house, road, path, and feature.

For Geneva:
    — Number 270, scale 1:50,000 covers wider area.
    — Number 1301, scale 1:25,000 provides more detail.

References

Organisations and individuals in information-oriented Geneva record, index, and conserve data about the town's past history and present facilities with great attention to detail.

The following list of publications sets forth considerable information in forms regularly brought up to date by the responsible editors. The list gives the name of the publication, the source, the language of its text, frequency of issue, and a short summary of the contents.

L'Annuaire téléphonique of the Postal, Telephone, and Telegraph Office (PTT) is the Geneva telephone book, in French, issued annually.

The front of the book lists dial-codes for area and international calls and the charges, plus telephone accessories available, postal rates, first-aid instructions, and a choice of 3-digit numbers to dial for messages in clearly-enunciated French on more than 30 subjects such as:

Snow bulletins and avalanche warnings (120)	Correct time (161)
Wake-up service (131 for one-time; 150 daily)	News bulletins (168)
Stock quotations in five markets (166)	TV schedules (165)
Movie programs and times (122 and 123)	Helping Hand (143)
Rates of currency exchanges (160)	Taxi summoning
Lottery and sports results (164)	(141)
Road conditions (163)	

Jeunes Information, Information for the Young, issued by a private group, in English, French, German and Spanish, published each June. The free, multi-panel folder includes a map and lists of:

Inexpensive housing, eating, and camping sites.
Transport, museums, points of interest.
Youth events, sports, marketplaces, rental agencies.
Post and telephone, currency exchange, travelers aid, youth travel services, help on drug problems.

Living in Geneva by the American Women's Club, in English, revised every few years, some 150-pages, and sold at non-profit price. The pooled experience of more than a thousand American women covers:

Permits, living and working	Postage, telephone, radio
Housing and utilities	Schools, religious facilities
Household shopping	Money, banks, taxes
Driving and public transport	Medical and social services
Entertainment and sports	Trips out of Geneva

— and more, more, more — all clear and practical.

La Clé, The Key, issued by Geneva's Société de l'utilité publique, in French, revised every few years, with nearly 200 pages, and sells at non-profit price. This well-organized, carefully cross-indexed book catalogs Geneva's social services, most of them free, dedicated to helping with problems of:

Families and couples	Aged	Young
Handicapped	Foreigners	Ailing
Leisure (vacations and recreation)	Trainees	Consumers
	Workers	

Guide to the English-Speaking Community in Geneva, published by GELCOS (Geneva English Language Coordinating Service) in English, a 16-page pamphlet issued annually and updated by its monthly information sheet *What's On In Geneva* to provide facts concerning:

Information for new arrivals	Useful publications
Public and social services	Adult education
Cultural activities	Social groups
Religious communities	Schools
Sports activities	Children's activities

Les pages jaunes of the PTT, the "Yellow Book", Geneva's classified business telephone book, in French, issued annually. The front of the book repeats the information on services and first aid of *L'Annuaire téléphonique*, then adds useful data on:

Emergency services: Police, general assistance, medical, hospital and sources of help for (in the following order) animals, women, youth, the aged, handicapped, foreigners, etc.

Periodicals: List of some 20 leading Geneva newspapers giving frequency of issue, editorial policy, copies printed, address, and telephone.

For the canton of Geneva and its 45 communes (counties), administrative details including seals, officials, telephone numbers of basic services.

Consulates and major international organizations.

Map of bus and tram routes.

Map of Lake Geneva and ports reached by boat service.

Cointrin airport layout and location of services.

Theaters, concert halls, museums, and libraries.

Schedule of trade shows, conferences, cultural and sporting events for the current year.

Sports associations and facilities.

The Office du Tourisme, the Tourist Office, publishes a series of titles — innovative, often revised, *all of them free.* The Office also is the main distributor of publications issued by the town of Geneva and other sources.

Published by the Tourist Office are:

Hotels, revised and dated each year, listing all accomodation by price category and then alphabetically with locations, capacity, price range, and facilities such as bar, garden, TV, parking, banquets, air conditioning, restaurant, etc., including a colored map showing location of each.

Restaurants, revised and dated each year, listing several hundred by price category and then alphabetically. A series of maps shows location of each. The list details address, telephones, days and hours open, price of "plat du jour", style of cooking, credit cards accepted, access by which public transport, and addenda on view, garden, bar, music, children's menu, air conditioning, non-smoking, banquet facilities, and tolerance of dogs.

Excursions, revised and dated each year, listing in a multi-paneled folder in English suggested trips in, around, and outside Geneva according to means of transport: bus, cable car, lake boat, airplane, walking, and railroad. Subdivided by destinations, dates of the year when excursions available, departure and return times, and fares and prices.

Manifestations, issued and dated bi-monthly, listing events by category — concerts, theater, dance, museums, galleries, sports, conferences, trade shows. Subdivided by date followed by description of the event, time, and location.

Hébergement pour les jeunes, Accomodations for Youth, revised as needed, a multi-paneled folder in French listing inexpensive lodgings with map keyed to locations. Detail is greater than in *Jeunes Information* but may be less up-to-the-minute.

How To Visit Geneva, reissued as needed, a multi-paneled folder in English or in French with colored map. Suggests a short tour of the town, the Rhône, surrounding villages, and lists basic data on museums and international organizations. Map is keyed to location of parks, boat landings, public buildings, churches, museums, theaters, concert halls, open markets, sport facilities, exposition halls.

A Stop in Geneva, reissued as needed, a multi-paneled folder in English, French, or German with colored map resembles *How to Visit...* (above) but without tours. Included is a daring attempt to give range of prices in hotels, restaurants, and for the likes of film, watches, shoes, chocolates, and cheeses. There is also a map of principal autoroutes running out of and around Geneva.

La Semaine à Genève, This Week in Geneva, issued and dated weekly, a brochure of some 50 pages in English, French, German, Spanish, Arabic, and Japanese, with latest information on such entertainment as concerts, opera, theater, ballet, and movies. Suggests a short tour and lists museums and galleries and major events of the month.

Distributed by the Tourist Office are:

Programme de la saison, the official program of the town of Geneva, issued quarterly and dated. A yellow, newspaper-size sheet in French, free, listing major museums, theaters, and concert halls and, for each, the program for three months with dates, starting times, addresses, telephones, and public transport route of access.

Guide pour handicapés, Guide for the Handicapped, published by Pro Infirmis, a Geneva social service, reissued as required. A book of nearly 200 pages in French with a keyed system of symbols explained in English, French, German, and Italian.

Distributed free but donation is requested from those able to pay. Lists establishments by category — hotels, restaurants, shops, banks, theaters, etc. — subdivided by alphabet with address, telephone, degree of difficulty (height of steps, sills, toilets, telephones, access by ramp, etc.) including town map. A major accomplishment.

Monuments et fontaines à Genève, Sculptures and Fountains in Geneva, published by the town, a multi-paneled map with no text but with key showing where to see several hundred samples of three-dimensional art in Geneva's streets and parks.

L'Art dans la rue, Art in the Streets, published by the town, a glossy-paged booklet in French, free, proposing four different walking tours to view sculpture in streets and parks.

Of interest for further reference are:

Coming and Living in Geneva, published by the Chambre de commerce et d'industrie de Genève, reissued as needed. A large, glossy-paper brochure of about 30 pages in English or French or German, giving in condensed form information on the demography, political and economic structure, infrastructure and services, local resources, taxes, corporate laws, and general background of Geneva.

Musées de Genève, Geneva's Museums, published by the town each month. A digest-sized glossy paper magazine with three or four articles in French on museum topics. Free subscription on request to town hall. Lists permanent exhibits and current temporary exhibits in town-owned museums.

Annuaire genevois d'addresses, Geneva's Directory of Addresses, published privately, revised and dated annually. A thick tome, in French, expensive. Lists by computer printout each Geneva resident by name, address, profession, and birthdate. Cross-reference is by street names and the number of each residence and a list of inhabitants of each house or apartment. Consult at Post Office or any Geneva library.

Periodicals related to Geneva include:

The English-language monthlies:

— *The Courier,* published by the American Women's Club to cover matters of interest to English-speaking residents.

— *Geneva News and International Report,* publishes Geneva and Swiss news briefs, articles, reviews, and photographs of the local scene.

— *Swiss Scene,* published in Zurich with some Geneva coverage.

The French-language dailies:

— *Le Journal de Genève,* morning "newspaper of record".

— *La Suisse,* morning including Sunday newspaper for everyone.

— *La Tribune de Genève,* afternoon, largest circulation.

— *Le Courrier,* morning Catholic newspaper.

Index of Names

Index of Events and Places

Composition:
ITP
Informatique Télétraitement Photocomposition
Genève

Impression:
ARTS GRAPHIQUES HÉLIOGRAPHIA SA
Lausanne